CAREER
Mastery

CAREER *Mastery*

KEYS TO TAKING CHARGE OF YOUR CAREER

THROUGHOUT YOUR WORK LIFE

Harry Levinson

Berrett-Koehler Publishers
San Francisco

Berrett-Koehler Publishers, Inc.
155 Montgomery St.
San Francisco, CA 94104-4109

Ordering Information
Orders by individuals and organizations. Berrett-Koehler publications
are available through bookstores or can be ordered direct from the publisher
at the Berrett-Koehler address above or by calling 1 (800) 929-2929.
Quantity sales. Berrett-Koehler publications are available at special quantity
discounts when purchased in bulk by corporations, associations, and others.
For details, write to the "Special Sales Department" at the Berrett-Koehler address
above or call (415) 288-0260.
Orders by U.S. trade bookstores and wholesalers. Please contact
Prima WorldWide, P.O. Box 1260, Rocklin, CA 95677-1260; tel (916) 786-0426;
fax (916) 786-0488.
Orders for college textbook/course adoption use. Please contact
Berrett-Koehler Publishers, 155 Montgomery St., San Francisco, CA 94104-4109;
tel (415) 288-0260; fax (415) 362-2512.

Printed in the United States of America

Printed on acid-free and recycled paper that meets the strictest state
and U.S. guidelines for recycled paper (50 percent recycled waste,
including 10 percent postconsumer waste).

Library of Congress Cataloging-in-Publication Data
Levinson, Harry.
  Career mastery : keys to taking charge of your career throughout
your work life / Harry Levinson.—1st ed.
      p.   cm.
  Includes bibliographical references and index.
  ISBN 1-881052-05-2 (alk. paper)
  1. Career development.   I. Title.
HF5381.L356   1992   92-20192
650.14—dc20   CIP

FIRST EDITION
    First Printing 1992

An *AV Communications* Book
Cazadero, California

Editing	**Alis Valencia**
Composition	**Business-Like Manor**
Proofreading	**Carolyn Uno**
Indexing	**Earline Hefferlin**

Cover Design   **Robb Pawlak**

Contents

Preface   ix

The Author   xv

I. The Personal Dimension of Career Mastery

1. Understanding Yourself   1
   Knowing Your Career Stage • Gaining Self-Knowledge
   • Assessing Your Conceptual Abilities

2. Coping with Change   13
   Coping with Career Upheaval • Coping with Change in
   Your Organization

3. Dealing with the Stresses of Success and Disappointment   25
   Success • Mistakes • Reducing Your Tendencies Toward
   Self-Blame

4. Confronting and Learning from Failure   39
   Facing Reality • Gaining from Defeat • Not Getting
   Promoted • Diagnosing Why You've Failed

II. The Organizational Dimension of Career Mastery

5. Learning the Organization   49
   Recording Your First Impressions • Getting Handles on

the Organization • Gaining Clues to Your Organization's
Culture • Tracing the Organization's History • Identifying
the Movers and Shakers • Preparing a Behavioral Job
Description

6. Improving Skills and Attitudes for Personal Effectiveness   61
On Being Well Read • Improving Language Skills
• Heightening Your Powers of Observation • Using
Aggression to Positive Effect • Being Politically Effective
• Using People to Get What You Want • Succeeding in
Unknown Territory • Learning New Behaviors • How to
Behave Among the Successful and Powerful • Coping
with Problems at Work • Combating Job Stress • Getting
Out of a Slump

7. Keeping Your Work Load Under Control   75
Setting Reasonable Expectations • Refusing Unwanted
Assignments • Avoiding Being Swamped

8. Cultivating Productive Relations with Coworkers   87
Friendships at Work • Making the Most of Being on a
Team • Gaining Cooperation from Peers • Working with
Someone You Can't Stand • Ending Feuds • Dealing with
Backstabbing

9. Speaking Up to the Boss   99
Defining the Appropriate Circumstances for Speaking Up
• Presenting New Ideas • Getting New Ideas Accepted
• Addressing Problems with Your Boss's Behavior • Rais-
ing Problems That Have to Do with the Organization
• Dealing with Conflicts • Negotiating the Psychological
Contract

10. Working Effectively with a Problem Boss   113
The Silent Boss • Unhelpful Boss • Ambiguous Boss
• Meddling Boss • Nice Boss • Abusive Boss • Disapprov-
ing Boss • Weak Boss • Defensive Boss • Exploitative Boss
• The Narcissistic Personality

III. The Transformational Dimension of Career Mastery

11. Preparing for Ongoing Achievement   127
Broadening Your Experience and Perspective • Getting

Contents

the Feedback Needed for Shaping Your Career • Cultivating
Mutually Beneficial Relations with Your Boss • Should
You Follow Your Boss?

12. Mapping Your Managerial Education   139
    A Psychological Foundation • Beyond the Fundamentals
    • Combating Obsolescence • Business in the World
    • Limits to Growth

13. Advancing Without Mishap   149
    Starting Off on the Right Foot • Dealing with Your
    Predecessor's Legacy • Succeeding Where Others Have
    Failed • Leaving a Position

14. Mentoring for Growth   165
    A Mutually Rewarding Relationship • Starting a Mentor-
    ing Relationship • Understanding the Mentoring Relation-
    ship • Ending a Mentoring Relationship • The Growing
    Importance of Mentoring

15. Making Rewarding Job Changes   177
    Adapting to an Era of Career Upheaval • Coping with
    Uncertainty • Recognizing When It's Time for a Job
    Change • Exploring Whether to Change Your Job

16. Handling Job Loss Constructively   191
    Anticipating Job Loss • After Getting Fired

17. Choosing a Second Career   197
    Finding a New Direction • Weighing Options • Succeed-
    ing in a Major Career Change

18. Committing to Continual Change   203
    The New Reality • Maintaining Adaptability and
    Flexibility

Notes   213

Index   217

Preface

For the past 35 years, I have worked with thousands of managers and executives in a wide range of organizations and institutions—businesses, hospitals, schools and colleges, research organizations, and government. My focus, and that of my colleagues in The Levinson Institute, has been significantly on leadership and the management of change.

In our executive seminars, the participants are asked to bring interpersonal cases for discussion. Their cases usually are about relationships with subordinates, peers, and superiors. Inevitably, the participants also discuss the contexts in which they work and therefore their problems in assessing and choosing career directions. Inevitably also, responding to the questions of their seminar peers in such discussions, they reflect on their styles of management and the degree of fit between their preferred styles and the demands of their managerial and executive roles. Reverberations from these discussions then often lead to thoughtful reconsideration of what they are doing and what they might do differently in the future. These options arise when, subsequently, they discuss those issues with the psychiatrist or clinical psychologist who is their discussion group leader.

Many managers and executives have sought individual career counseling at The Levinson Institute. These range from young people about to embark on their managerial journeys to senior executives, including chief executive officers, who look forward to new careers when they retire from their organizations. Many mature managers make midcareer shifts. Some are forced into new roles by downsizing, merger, and radical changes in organizational direction.

Emotionally, their approaches traverse the range of feelings from bright-eyed optimism to gloomy futility. However, one feature characterizes all of them: they don't have enough information. By information I mean not only factual data like wages, hours, and working conditions, and similar objective features of organizations, but, more important, knowledge about themselves. Therefore, a major part of my task and that of my colleagues has been to help people increase their self-understanding.

While clarified introspection is fundamental, it isn't by itself enough. Success in career is not determined solely by the kinds of occupational choices one makes. More important, one's everyday decisions and actions convey a behavioral picture of oneself to others who, often tacitly, then reach conclusions about training, developing, assigning, promoting, and even terminating an individual.

Because these moment-by-moment activities are as important to one's career progress as the broader avenues within which they occur, I have tried to make specific note of such issues as they arose in seminars and consultation in succinct, focused items in my bi-weekly publication, *The Levinson Letter.* In those observations I have included also issues in executive and management development that arose in consultation with corporations about their formal efforts to enhance managerial and executive careers.

These pages contain an integrated distillation of the many items related to careers that have appeared in *The Levinson Letter,* together with my additional observations, conclusions, and recommendations. They are derived from immediate experience and are directed specifically to those day-by-day issues that every professional confronts. Of course, suggestions and recommendations in the abstract can never fully take into account the complexities of any specific situation. Furthermore, different people may recommend other courses of action based on their assumptions about human motivation and their understanding of the complexities. The reader who would use this book wisely should take my comments as points of departure, not recipes.

This book differs from others that discuss careers in that it takes into account unconscious motivation and stages in adult development. These aspects of human development are crucial to understanding oneself and others, although little about them appears in most efforts to guide people in career choices. The title, *Career Mastery,* indicates why knowledge of these dimensions of human behavior is critical: one cannot be a master of oneself and one's career directions without taking these issues into account.

Career Mastery is like a psychological map. The issues it takes into account differ from those of many other career guides the way a topographical map differs from a highway road map. A road map outlines the various routes and junctures that become choice points. Sometimes it touches on notable geographical features. A topographical map describes many aspects of the terrain that may be crucial to making choices, but are not evident on a highway map.

Since the focus of this book is on the more complex psychological aspects of career mastery, I have included topics that ordinarily don't appear in similar volumes. For example, Chapter 2 deals with coping with change, an inevitable concomitant of every career decision. Feelings about change and the manner of dealing with those feelings are crucial to reasonable choices. A particular aspect of change has to do with feelings about achieving success and the disappointment of failure, which I discuss in Chapter 3. Both of these experiences require thoughtful consideration, the first because, perhaps surprisingly, not all of us cope well with our success and some, indeed, stumble as a product of having been successful. On the other hand, many people fail to differentiate between disappointment and defeat and are undermined by experiences of failure. Therefore, it is important, as I have noted in Chapter 4, to try to understand why one has failed and to learn from that experience.

Although anyone who is about to take a long trip would study maps and the geographical environment, all too few who hope to embark on a long vocational journey in an organization take the trouble to learn about that organization. This naivete leads too many people to stumble and fumble and make significant mistakes that interfere with their careers. Therefore, in Chapter 5, I focus on questions you might raise about your current or prospective organization, so that you can make more reasonable psychological choices.

Chapter 6 takes up the continual need for broadening and self-improvement. It recognizes the tendency for all of us to narrow our foci, and therefore the requirement that we combat that tendency.

Having made a choice, one gets caught up in the wish and the need to prove oneself, which frequently means that one overextends oneself and becomes self-harassing and self-critical. Managing the work load is an important aspect of managing one's career, and is covered in Chapter 7.

Often people are preoccupied with their own achievements. That's particularly true of highly conscientious people who are trying to prove themselves. However, when one works in an organization, one necessarily has to work with other people. Many of the managers and executives who are referred to The Levinson Institute are referred because they can't work well with others. Their achievements are often undermined by their inability to manage those relationships, and therefore I give those issues attention in Chapter 8. The primary relationship in all organizations is between an employee and his or her boss. It is fraught with many problems, and in Chapters 9 and 10 specific issues about that relationship are considered.

There is the issue of continued growth. This involves developing breadth, which in turn requires making choices about getting additional knowledge, skill, and perspective. Too many people wait for the organization to make such choices for them, but if one is to be the master of oneself and one's career, it is necessary to take the initiative with respect to these choices, and then be alert to mishaps and missteps that can delay, impede, or even defeat one's efforts. These issues are taken up in Chapters 11, 12, and 13.

The remaining five chapters focus on dealing with the ambiguities of career mastery. Chapter 14 discusses the relevance of mentoring from the perspectives of both mentor and mentee. Chapters 15, 16, and 17 address the radical changes in career status or direction that usually are accompanied by turmoil; and Chapter 18 speaks to managing continual ambiguity.

These various chapters amplify the subtitle of this book: they talk about the keys to taking charge of your career. By implication, they recognize that career mastery is a multifaceted task of dealing with different problems at different times and under different circumstances. These keys lean heavily not only on understanding oneself but also on understanding others with whom one must deal, as well as the complexity of the relationships in which one is necessarily embedded in an organization. One may well navigate with a compass, but one is much better served when one has an understanding of the winds, the currents, the shoals, and the shores.

Another aspect of this book, rarely encountered, is its emphasis on making career choices throughout one's whole career. Even moving into retirement is a career choice point. Regardless of one's professional background or discipline, one necessarily will make career choices over a working lifetime. The same psychological issues are paramount whether one is an astrophysicist or manages a dime store. We are all governed by the same fundamentals of human psychology and human development, by the same complexities of organizational life, and by the same socioeconomic turbulence.

In sum, the primary purpose of *Career Mastery* is to enable people to take more active charge of their careers, particularly by understanding more about themselves and those to whom and with whom they must relate.

Acknowledgments

Much that appears in these pages is a product of extended discussions with my associate editors. In recent years, these have included Janet E. Robinson, John Elder, and Lynne Gaines. Janet Robinson brought both psychological knowledge and a more immediate conversational tone to *The Levinson Letter*. John Elder, possessed of imaginative flights of good humor and a classical education, added depth and perspective, as well as a practical focus. Lynne Gaines's combined experiences in journalism, human resources management, and psychology resulted in increased depth and sharper focus. Their imprints may be invisible to the reader, but they are sharply etched in my own perspectives, for they have enriched and extended my thinking and added flair and polish to our joint product. Marcia Atwood has made certain that our English usage is correct, and both she and Marilyn Farinato diligently and carefully proofread each issue. I am indebted to all of them.

I learned long ago that a firm, perspicacious publisher is a writer's best friend. I am therefore also indebted to Steven Piersanti, who suggested the book, winnowed the items from many years of *The Levinson Letter*, and organized its thrust. The reader who finds this book easy to read should know that Alis Valencia's insightful editing has contributed. She integrated the various bits and pieces from *The Levinson Letter* into a smoothly organized whole from which I hope the reader will profit as he or she returns repeatedly to these pages for reminders, refreshment, and rethinking.

Harry Levinson

Belmont, Massachusetts

June 1, 1992

The Author

Harry **Levinson** is chairman of The Levinson Institute, a consulting firm that specializes in the psychological aspects of leadership and the management of stress and change. He is also clinical professor of psychology emeritus at the Harvard Medical School and head of the Section on Organizational Mental Health at the Massachusetts Mental Health Center.

Levinson received his Ph.D. from the University of Kansas. He created, and for 14 years directed, the Division of Industrial Mental Health at the Menninger Foundation. He has been a visiting professor in the Sloan School of Management at the Massachusetts Institute of Technology, the School of Business at the University of Kansas, and the Harvard Graduate School of Business Administration, among other institutions.

A consultant to and lecturer for many business, academic, and government organizations, Levinson has received several awards, including the Organization Development Professional Practice Award for Excellence from the American Society for Training and Development in 1988 and the American Psychological Association's Award for Distinguished Professional Contributions to Knowledge in 1992.

In addition to numerous articles, Levinson has written many books, including *Organizational Diagnosis, Emotional Health in the World of Work, Executive, Psychological Man, The Great Jackass Fallacy, CEO: Corporate Leadership in Action,* and *Ready, Fire, Aim: Avoiding Management by Impulse.* He is also editor of *Designing and Managing Your Career.*

CHAPTER 1

Understanding Yourself

Philip was age 34 when he asked for consultation about his career. He said he'd grown up in a lower-middle-class neighborhood in a large city where his father had operated a delicatessen. His parents had had limited education, but recognized the need for him to go to college if he were to rise above their modest station. He and they thought of college as an instrument for learning how to earn a better livelihood.

Characteristically, many lower-class men move up through accounting or engineering. Philip chose accounting. He never was very enthusiastic about accounting, but he thought it was better than running a delicatessen.

After he graduated, he got a job in a large accounting firm. He was hired away from the accounting firm by one of the businesses on whose books he worked. However, having seen what accounting and business were like, he now knew about a wide range of work activities, a range that previously he had never grasped, let alone understood. Although he now had a responsible auditing job, he chafed at the limits of his role. He didn't like having to travel, found himself preoccupied with numbers and printouts, and had limited interaction with other people. Fortunately, his boredom was somewhat assuaged when his company sent him to short training programs to increase his range and competence.

Increasingly, Philip began to understand both finance and business. He was not using his broader knowledge in his current role, nor could he see himself doing so as he acquired seniority in his specialty. He wanted to break away from that role and establish himself as a financial planner. But there was a risk in moving from a secure job in a large company to an independent consulting practice. Could he do it? Would he be good at it? And how would he justify himself to his parents, who couldn't begin to understand leaving a secure role for another that had no meaning for them.

As we talked, a number of issues became clear to both of us. Philip's wish to work with people, never fully gratified in his accounting role, reflected the fact that he needed to interact closely with others, to have warm and friendly exchanges, and to have people depend on him for authoritative knowledge and friendship. Until he had developed sufficient experience, he had no perspective on the range of possibilities that might be open to him and how his knowledge and experience compared with that of others.

As his perspective broadened with increasing experience, Philip felt the need for greater stimulation and challenge. He felt constrained in the narrow specialty in which he found himself. He was uncomfortable trading boredom for job security. The longer he stayed in that track, the more impatient with himself he became.

Philip's whole career had been directed to pleasing his parents, to doing what they wanted him to do to meet their own psychological needs and perspectives. He felt it was time to live his own life. He saw the possibilities of being a highly respected consultant and advisor to people whose resources marked them as successful. By serving them as an independent practitioner, he, too, in his own eyes, would be successful.

But how does one break away from an established, secure role? As we talked, Philip reported that some friends and associates were already approaching him for financial advice and recommendations. He could round out his skills by becoming an accredited financial counselor through evening courses. Concomitantly, he could announce his formal availability by distributing his card to friends and acquaintances. He would consult with them after working hours. When that effort became sufficiently stable, he could then leave his company. The directory in the lobby of a major professional office building today includes the name "Philip Fairbanks, Financial Counselor."

This is a typical career problem. It reflects the fact that a career is dynamic. Each of us develops a career trajectory through what becomes a more time-limited future as we age. Our perceptions and perspectives are modified by our experiences, our increasing capacity to understand ourselves and the world in which we find ourselves, and the appropriateness of different kinds of work activities at different points in our lives. We are, therefore, always in the position of having to assess ourselves as we gain more self-knowledge through introspection and experience. Then, we must continually assess the degree to which what we are doing in our careers meets our expectations of ourselves and our personal needs for mastery and relationships with others.

All too often, people make decisions about their careers in terms of external variables: how much they will earn, whether the new opportunity is a promotion, where the job is located, what the perks are, and similar issues. Too few make the same effort to understand themselves so that they can make more accurate and refined judgments about the choices they face. One can't, however, make wise choices without careful calibration of the degree of fit between oneself and prospective career roles. To be in charge of one's career, one must have a solid knowledge of oneself.

Knowing Your Career Stage

Everyone passes through a lifelong sequence of developmental stages. Erik Erikson's conception of the life cycle provides a foundation for defining three major career stages, and the transitional experiences that accompany them.[1]

The Identity Stage

In the identity stage, roughly from ages 21 to 35, people are developing their track records and acquiring skills and the conceptual knowledge to support these skills. The early part of this period, ages 21 to 25, is commonly a time for crystallizing your identity, for deciding who you are and what you should be doing.[2]

The identity stage is the period of greatest energy, spontaneity, and creativity; and thus, in addition to acquiring competence and skills, you should have the opportunity to look critically at the activities of your organization and the chance to undertake experiences that make it possible to test some of the new ideas and practices you originate. This is a time also when work experiences provide you with a way of measuring yourself by the work you've done and assessing your capacities and limits. Rotational assignments and the opportunity to talk freely with a mentor are especially important.

At this stage you are becoming acquainted with the facets and functions of your organization. You may, in fact, become knowledgeable about several organizations, since it is not unusual to make several moves as you refine your career direction. Ideally, in all organizations you should be in close touch with superiors who can stimulate and support fresh, innovative views, as well as provide serious guidance. In the early parts of this period you should have the chance to do some major task alone in order to learn—and show the organization—how you handle your dependency needs and with what range of independence you operate comfortably.

People in the identity stage need the opportunity to act. To support your self-image, you have to establish for yourself and for others your capacity to have an effect, to master your environment. While feeling impelled to act, you nonetheless recognize the considerable risk of making a mistake. This is the point at which having a mentor who gives permission to take risks and make mistakes is particularly important. Coaching is a critical aspect of a person's development in this period.

This is a time when anyone who seeks a managerial role should begin to gain an understanding of the psychology of leadership and supervision. Future managers need to learn about having and wielding power; feelings of guilt and rivalry; problems of managing affection, aggression, dependency, and ego ideal; the experience of loss and change; and being a member of and leading teams.

The Generativity Stage

The generativity stage is the period when people become concerned with establishing the next generation, during roughly ages 35 to 55. In midcareer you have established an occupational reputation and have acquired competence and skills. This period is frequently a time of powerful identification with your profession or the organization in which you work; it's a time in which you act on behalf of the organization and represent it both to subordinates and to its various publics. You are in the mature action phase of your career, one that is closest to the parental role in a family.

During the midlife period you reorganize your thinking about yourself. You assert independence from your mentor, establish yourself as your own person, and engage in a reinvigorated pursuit of your own directions. Taking mortality into account, you restructure your value system, change emphases in life activities, and cope with the loss of your growing family. You come to terms with the limitations on your aspirations prescribed by time, experience, life station, and opportunity. Sometimes these changes make for an emotional experience of crisis proportions. For many this crisis arises at about the fifteenth year of their careers. Sometimes at that point, people feel they have mastered their fields and that there is nothing new or stimulating and that they must do something else to avoid boredom. These are the ones who frequently choose second careers.

Frequently in this stage you have responsibility for starting younger people in career directions. You need support and guidance for doing this. In particular, you need the opportunity to deal with the problems of rivalry that occur any time a younger person threatens the position of an older person, no matter how good the relationship, and you need to learn how to deal with the unconscious guilt that influences your evaluation of another's performance. You also must gain an understanding of your role as mentor and any problems you may have filling this role. One often benefits from particular help in understanding the dependency problems of subordinates, the difference between participation and abdication of leadership, and the need of younger subordinates to have the opportunity to act.

You should have a chance to upgrade your skills by means of refresher courses. At this stage, one learns most easily in groups because the shared experiences help relieve the self-critical pressure that one feels when learning something new. Development activity in midlife should also include the opportunity to talk about the problems of being middle aged—becoming psychologically and physiologically less able to compete in a competitive society, being passed by others who are younger, a growing obsolescence of skills and knowledge, and increasing fear of technical advances and organizational change—and learn to recognize the reality of these events, mourn the losses, and evolve ways to cope with them.

When people suddenly become aware of the limited time now

available to them, they begin to rethink their lives and what they want to do with their remaining years. You thus should take the opportunity to rethink your future, which may mean thinking of a second career. Midcareer counseling at this time can be especially helpful.

The Consolidation Stage

This final stage is a time of consolidation and of coming to terms with how you have used your life. It is also a time when your own dependency is increasing because of declining physical and intellectual resources. People feel less instrumental in the sense of doing what they did in earlier periods, and they must deal with gradual detachment from personal activities or from the organization while still making a useful contribution to both.

Coming to terms with how you have used your life is a painful psychological task. This is complicated by approaching retirement from an organization. The psychological work at this stage requires preparing for a shift from an authoritative or power role to one of consultation, guidance, and wisdom. Ideally, the work you do during this stage should contribute to a sense of wholeness, of career integration, and you should be able to see your integrated life experiences as a platform from which others can start. You should have the opportunity to fill a role that calls for counseling, political understanding, anticipating the future, and long-range thinking.

At this stage you should combat isolation and obsolescence, establish greater equanimity, confirm your own worth, look to the future, and consolidate a lifetime of experience with a sense of having had an effect as an individual. You should pursue continued opportunities for development to gain refreshment and professional updating, and also understanding of the motivations of young people in the organization. Also, it will be beneficial to find opportunities to talk, especially in groups of peers, about the feelings of uselessness, loss of purpose, little or no value to others, betrayal, and so on that you may be experiencing. Only if these issues are discussed, the changes mourned, and new adaptive methods worked out can you learn further.

To avoid experiencing retirement as a crisis, you have to establish yourself in activities outside your historic role. This can be done on a part-time or gradual basis beginning, perhaps, at age 60. Some people do this gradually, spending less time in the organization. Others may well be preoccupied outside the organization but still on behalf of its business. Some represent the organization on boards of nonprofit and community organizations. Some provide leadership to task forces and committees that address community problems. Some get deeply involved as volunteers in the direct work of community service agencies. Still others begin to look at new careers away from the organization.

Gaining Self-Knowledge

At each stage of your career you will make decisions concerning which career directions to take and which risks are worth taking. Self-knowledge is a critical skill in this context. And it is an active skill, not just passive knowledge, because it must overcome such obstacles as denial, pride, and guilt, and because it has to be updated over time. Being the expert on yourself isn't easy, for several reasons:

First, people can get stuck in early, immature perceptions of themselves. This is especially true if the boss reminds you of one of your parents, or a peer's behavior seems to be much like that of a brother or sister. Then, you may unconsciously revert to feeling like a child and seeing yourself as helpless, or to becoming unduly rivalrous.

Second, most of us have been brought up not to praise ourselves—that's considered arrogant or self-centered—and to brush aside compliments.

Third, introspection can be very painful. Some people can't face the angry or ugly feelings they have, especially if they can't imagine that the people they know have similar feelings.

Fourth, many accomplished persons' visions of themselves are clouded by the harsh self-criticism typical of people with strong drives and high standards. They set extremely high goals and feel disappointed when they don't meet them. When they do meet their goals, they rarely congratulate themselves, but immediately set the next goal. Organizations exacerbate this cycle when they give their employees too little specific praise. Some people feel like frauds; they are unable to see their skills and their value, even if they do receive praise and bonuses.

From Someone Who Knows That You Know

One way to start to see yourself is through the eyes of others. Who comes to you for advice? If an expert asks you to double-check her work, she respects you—and she should know. What kinds of advice do people seek from you? If peers ask your opinion of their political and interpersonal skills, they respect your knowledge of people. If people come to you for a variety of advice, they rely on your overall common sense.

Another clue is how often people return for advice. If someone doesn't return, ask how your advice worked out. You may assume that your advice was bad or you would have heard by now. But feedback is the only way to find out for sure how you're doing.

Compliments

We often dismiss compliments we don't want or don't agree with, but they can be very revealing. One manager was complimented for his attention to detail. Since he didn't want to be seen as finicky, he couldn't see that praise as praise. Though you may not like a skill, it's important to recognize that you have it and that others value it.

Your view of yourself may be based on old data. One manager considered herself a pushover. She was pleasantly surprised when a peer came to her for help with a personnel problem because she was known to be tough but fair. She had been seeing herself as she had been when she first started to manage; she hadn't noticed how much she'd improved.

Not By Praise Alone

You won't get an accurate picture of yourself by relying on praise alone. Who criticizes you and under what circumstances? If your boss yells at you during a crisis, he doesn't necessarily think you are unreliable. He might have snapped under too much pressure. The criticism he gives you in your review presents a more accurate picture. Subordinates' criticism should be taken seriously—it's certainly offered at some risk. How often have you heard the same criticism?

Repeated criticism, especially if it comes from different people, means that your behavior is a problem, at least in that particular situation.

Personal Work

There are many ways to see yourself through your own eyes. What works varies from person to person, and from one stage of life to another. Here are some suggestions:

- ☐ Ask yourself what you enjoyed as a child and why. For example, if you loved soccer, you may have enjoyed the team spirit, the competition, or the clear sense of having won or lost. You probably enjoy the same things now, perhaps through working on group projects.
- ☐ Consider the stories you most frequently tell about yourself. Do they reveal you to be pragmatic, a wise mentor, a troubleshooter? Or perhaps a loser, a clown, or an innocent? The stories reveal how you see yourself as well as how you hope to be seen. Some will reveal times when you were close to your ideal best, or ego ideal—that's why they mean so much to you.
- ☐ The way your children talk and play is probably in part an imitation of you. Ask your spouse if one of the children seems to be a smaller version of you. He or she may be able to see things that you can't.
- ☐ Think about how you handle stress. Under stress, deeply ingrained behaviors or attitudes usually predominate. For example, if you tend to accept change at first and then resist it later, you may be able to lessen your resistance to change at work by talking to your boss about the likely effects of the change.
- ☐ Ask yourself what you get out of your hobbies. If some needs aren't fulfilled at work or with your family, hobbies often complete the picture. One manager studies martial arts, in part because he finds the discipline and structure reassuring.
- ☐ Think back over the lucky breaks and the chance events that set you on new paths. What characteristics or drives made you ready to seize those opportunities? What happens to you may be random, but how you react to it is very revealing.
- ☐ What are you inflexible about? Try looking at it this way: "What

is everybody else wrong about, no matter how many times I correct them?" What repeated arguments are you unable to resist, though you know it's no use? There's a lot of self-knowledge there, though it may be unflattering.

☐ What makes you feel good about yourself? Think about specific actions and events: Did you like dealing with that last-minute hassle? Did you feel good about having resolved a crisis? Bad because you had to bring the customer the bad news? Good about leading subordinates through a heavy haul? Bad for pushing subordinates hard? You want to see what experiences make you feel that you're doing what you're good at and that you're valuable to others.

☐ Identify what you hate to do. It's a mistake to incorporate activities you intensely dislike into your striving (provided that you've tried them enough to be sure you really dislike them). Most jobs require doing some things you don't like, but if unwanted duties form much of your job, the work will become burdensome and you won't move toward your ego ideal or think well of yourself. Only if you like what you're doing can you be enthusiastic, spontaneous, and joyful about it.

What if you don't like what you learn about yourself? Recognizing destructive or inappropriate behaviors is the first step toward changing them or learning to avoid situations that exacerbate them. You don't necessarily have to change—we aren't obliged to be perfect. But when you realize what the consequences of some of your behaviors are or have been, you may want to change some of them.

Assessing Your Conceptual Abilities

Joe was getting bored with his present responsibilities, which he had fully mastered. His supervisor felt Joe was ready for promotion, but there wasn't any promotion to give him. So he gave him responsibility for some projects that were based on Joe's own suggestions. The supervisor figured Joe would take a lot of satisfaction in putting his own ideas into action. If nothing else, he'd be too busy to be bored.

And yet, Joe *is* bored. At first he liked the idea, just as expected. He threw himself into the new projects but soon got bogged down.

There was plenty of work to do, but he had a hard time making himself do it. He just wasn't interested. He doesn't understand why he's bored any better than his boss does.

This employee didn't need more work to do; he needed more complex work to do.

To understand why, let's look at some common experiences in a new way. As Saint Paul said in the Bible, "When I was a child, I thought as a child, but when I became a man, I put away childish things." What makes childish things childish and unsatisfying to an adult?

My colleague Elliott Jaques has formulated an interesting answer.[3] He has shown that tasks fall into some eight distinct levels of complexity. Stacking up toy blocks is a pretty concrete task: the blocks are right there and they either stand up or fall down. Learning to multiply and divide requires some conceptualization: the "tens," "hundreds," and "thousands" are not explicitly there, but you have to work with them. Supervising a group of managers involves many nonconcrete factors, such as what the future will bring and how different people will react to what you do.

A person's ability to work in any particular role is a function of several factors, including knowledge, skill, values, temperament, and cognitive power. Cognitive power is the ability to process available information, draw conclusions, and decide on appropriate actions. Jaques has discovered that cognitive power can be measured by how far ahead a person is able to conceptualize and to plan his or her own actions. This is a person's time horizon.

You fit a job that requires the level of cognitive power you possess. If the job requires a lower level, you can do the job but will be bored, as Joe was. If the job requires a higher level, you can't do it and will get more and more lost and behind, not because of the quantity of the work but because of the quality of it.

Jaques has discovered that we each follow a trajectory during our life, which takes us, at certain ages, across the boundaries from one level of conceptual ability to the next. Obviously, this trajectory is different for different people, but the set of possible levels is constant.

Once we cross the boundary into a new level of conceptual ability, tasks at the previous level may still be enjoyable but will no longer be challenging. If your job doesn't include tasks at the new level, you will get bored, although you may not understand why. That's what happened to Joe, and that's why the solution his supervisor tried did not work. The new projects were at the same level of conceptual complexity as the work Joe was already doing. There was some novelty and some satisfaction in having his boss back something he had suggested, but there wasn't the necessary challenge to his new level of conceptual ability.

How can you determine your cognitive level and degree of job fit? Most people will not have the opportunity to undergo an evaluation carried out by a professional. An indirect way to conduct an evaluation is to determine the time frame under which you operate at work (how long your longest assignment is), and then assess whether you feel underused, comfortable, or overstretched in your job.

CHAPTER **2**

Coping with Change

There's much talk about change these days. In fact, in some organizations, people speak of their yearning that the changes will stop. Of course, they won't. There are many aspects of change in one's life: the process of growing up, including physical and mental changes; acquiring skills and competences in school and college; evolving varied relationships with members of one's family; sorting out values as one matures; developing and engaging in multiple relationships, some transient, some enduring; coping with the exigencies of sickness, accidents, and physical and psychological traumas; and living through wars, depressions, and events like marriage and the birth of children.

Certainly one could elaborate many different kinds of changes beyond these, but our focus here will be on changes in career. Generally, these will have two sources, those precipitated by external events like organizational changes or losing one's job, or internal sources like one's decision to take a new job or pursue a second career. Whatever the source of change, one needs to understand the emotional turbulence that characterizes career transitions and, understanding that turbulence, evolve specific steps to cope with it.

When our customary ways of mastering ourselves and our environments are no longer possible for us, we become psychologically uprooted. That touches our deepest fears of helplessness. We experience severe loss of both stability and affectional input. That threat becomes magnified when others, like children, parents, and spouses, are dependent on us. The more helpless we feel, the more angry we get with ourselves and with those persons and circumstances that have precipitated such feelings. Usually, we are also angry with ourselves for being in such a threatened and helpless position, especially if our repeated efforts to cope have not been successful.

As with an airplane being buffeted by high winds, the emotional turbulence of change tends to make it difficult for us to stay on course rather than simply fight the winds head-on. A wise pilot seeks higher or lower altitude or changes course. So it is with respect to our careers. In times of emotional turbulence we need to have ways of deciding about our career course, making appropriate changes, and attenuating the emotional pressures that, unrelieved, may well throw us off course. In keeping with the theme of this book, in this chapter on change, the focus will be on "staying on top," mastering the change process.

Coping with Career Upheaval

Inasmuch as change is pervasive and continual, it is necessary to develop skills to cope with the feelings of helplessness, anger, and distress about your career that can result. To get yourself started:

☐ Rethink old concepts of career progress. That means learning about your ego ideal. Ask yourself questions such as: What are my earliest memories of doing something to please my mother (or father for a woman)? What were my father's (mother's) values? List choices you've made over the course of your life and career, such as choices between one school subject and another or between one job and another. While these may appear to be random, retrospective examination will disclose a pattern to those choices. Also, who were your early models, heroes, and mentors? Think of instances in your life when you felt really terrific about yourself. If you change careers, what kind of ego-ideal fantasies will you have to give up? How would you meet your basic psychological needs for affection and dependency in a new role?

☐ Practice career backtracking. This is an analytic process to identify career options by examining the skills you've used in your career. What were the underlying competences and inclinations that led you to acquire those skills in the first place? Did you become a compensation manager because you're of a

14

particularly analytical and detail-oriented bent, or because you're fascinated by how people meet their needs at work? In what other directions could these underlying competences have led? Can you revisit those "paths not taken" and develop new skills and opportunities?

☐ Try moonlighting. Recently I had my garage framed by an off-duty fireman. Many higher-level people could benefit from building an appropriate second career and exploring other interests.

☐ Train yourself to recognize opportunities to build skills. People are often only a course or two away from a new career. Even if you can't take courses now, do what you can. Read, talk to people, sit in on an occasional lecture, or audit a course. At least you'll be prepared to move forward if you need to later. A single postgraduate programming course at MIT provided the basis for one executive's successful second career. Knowing a marketable foreign language is another valuable skill. Career breaks are a logical time to pick up new skills.

☐ Recognize the new need for individuals to manage their careers more aggressively. You can't count on the company anymore. Seeking young technical talent, Northern Telecom, Ltd., in Toronto announced recently that it will offer a three-year employment guarantee as an extra lure to new young graduates it hopes to hire. The very need to make such an offer shows how much expectations have changed for both sides. It should be some comfort, however, that most people are in the same boat.

☐ Build relationships that will let you externalize your feelings and worries. Many people—especially men—don't build new friendships to replace old boyhood and college relationships. When crises occur, there's no one they trust to talk to. That's dangerous, because fears and anger are more manageable when they're removed from the depths of unconscious fantasy.

Sometimes I call the 1990s the Age of Worry. I've never seen so much profound career upheaval. But, while worry is uncomfortable, it also can be useful. To make it useful, people facing career uncertainty and termination must work extra hard not to succumb to panic or the rage of impotence. By avoiding these pitfalls, most people will harness their aggression and survive. Starting to prepare psychologically now for possible job loss will relieve your sense of help-lessness and help you move quickly in the right direction should the need arise.

Coping with Change in Your Organization

It was clear that the organization had to change, but it wasn't at all clear how. The uncertainty of the planning stages was intense. Rumors and counterrumors were everywhere: they're going to cen-tralize, they're going to decentralize; they're going to drop this line, they're doubling the effort on that; this department will be cut, that one will expand, those two will be combined; he's going, she's stay-ing; he's staying, she's going; on and on, never an end to it. How could you know what to work on and what to wait on? With all the ambiguity and worry, just keeping up with the day-to-day work was exhausting.

Finally, all that is over. The official word has been given, and the long-anticipated change has come to pass. Not all of the pieces have fallen into place, but the general outlines are clear. This is not your ordinary organizational change. It is a dramatic shift in the organization's character. People will have to act differently, even *be* different. The organization has moved from stability to instabil-ity; from now on it will change continually. Instead of leaning heav-ily on their basic learning, as in the past, people will now have to learn continually. Many guidelines will grow out of managers' actions on spontaneous competitive problems, instead of being set in advance.

At times you wish the change would stop and a new equilib-rium would be established. But that's futile. The whole world is chang-ing fast; to keep up and move ahead, the organization must change too. Changing continually will be stressful, but everyone will have to get used to changing and accommodate to the stress. The task now is to recover, refocus, and regenerate.

Regaining Your Psychological Balance

The long period of uncertainty has taken its toll. The first order of business is to recover from it, to regain your psychological balance. And since the level of stress in your work has increased permanently, you need to learn how to recover your balance whenever you need to. That means being able to recognize when the amount of stress in your life is getting beyond tolerable levels, and knowing how to bring it back down to a level where you can handle the situations that are causing the stress, instead of feeling overwhelmed by them. In other words, you need to learn to take care of yourself under these new conditions.

Beyond the feelings of tension and of being overwhelmed, physical symptoms and reactions are one of the major reflections of psychological problems. Up to 80 percent of all the physical problems that a general medical practitioner sees are psychological in origin. Depression, in particular, can be masked by or translated into many different kinds of physical symptoms ranging from headache to backache to upset stomach or worse. And depression often follows uncertainty and change. It is important to know the particular symptoms that appear in you when you are under stress, and the way your behavior under stress differs from your usual behavior. If you are not aware of it, talk to your spouse or a close friend, someone who is able to observe you regularly. He or she can tell you what your pattern of behavior is, and when telltale reactions and symptoms appear. That will help you be alert to the messages your body sends when you are not otherwise aware that stress is affecting you.

One of the most immediately helpful ways of coping with stress is to get out from under it. Other than economic pressures like real or threatened loss of job, poverty, or catastrophic illness, most stress is a product of our own consciences. When we have unrealistic expectations, we place unrealistic demands on ourselves. We can't meet them, so we criticize ourselves harshly. Different people interpret their environments and behavior differently: some are more willing than others to place the responsibility outside instead of within themselves; some are more realistic in their interpretations than others. That's why one person's stress is another person's challenge.

When you withdraw temporarily from the stressful situation, you get out from under your own conscience. You can do that by taking a long weekend, or at least taking the whole weekend *off*; get away from your usual activities and demands, and nurture yourself with good meals, pleasant surroundings, and perhaps some light entertainment. The idea is to free yourself from demands for a time. I recommend doing this every 90 days. And between these breaks, find other ways to get yourself out from under for an evening, an hour, or five minutes when you need to. Any activity that puts your mind in another place—escape reading and light movies, for example—can have this effect. Meditation, biofeedback, and relaxation methods are also good temporary escape mechanisms. They don't solve problems, but, like aspirin, they provide temporary relief—and there's nothing wrong with temporary relief. Temporary escape counteracts the buildup of pressure and supports the process of building up more strength. It also contributes to a sense of being in better control of yourself. Whenever you feel things are getting to be a bit too much for you, find a time and a way to get yourself out from under for a little while. The situation won't be any better when you come back to it, but it may seem better because you are better able to think and do something about it.

Exercise is one of the most helpful ways of discharging the frustration that builds up when you can't act or can't tell if your actions are on target. In addition, exercise can give you a sense of well-being about your own body and your actions. Of course, it doesn't help if you are just as intense about exercise as about everything else, the way some high achievers are. Such people often push themselves to the point of strain. Taking it out on their own hides may relieve their depressive feelings, but it usually creates more problems—toe injuries, for example. That level of intensity makes it difficult to use exercise for its constructive purposes. Exercise that is simple, moderate, repetitive, and noncompetitive can have a meditative quality while relieving that "pent up" feeling. And being in good shape physically tends to make you feel better mentally.

Your family can be a major source of support, or an additional source of isolation and stress. In the face of stress, and threatening changes in particular, the natural reaction of most people is to try to protect their families. They tend not to talk about what is happening or likely to happen to them and their anxieties about it. That is a terrible mistake.

Your anxiety and sense of being threatened will be reflected in your behavior. Some people become less communicative as a way of not leaking information about the possible threats and their feelings about them. Some people become more tense. Whatever the case, your family can easily see that you are not yourself. They are likely to wonder anxiously what they have done to make you angry or to make you withdraw from them. However, if you share with them what happened or what you fear will happen, often they are in a position to help you talk it over, to mobilize around you, and to solidify family ties in the face of potential threat.

One of the ways our children can be helpful to us is by serving as members of a cohesive group where mutual affection and regard help sustain the whole family's ability to adapt. It is unfair and unkind, as well as potentially harmful to them, to deny them that opportunity. You need not fear that they will panic and fall apart. They may worry just as you worry; but shared worry, shared concern, and the solidity of the family group tend to assure them that the whole family will cope with this together. You do better to inform them than to try to hide from them.

Women, who ordinarily carry the larger burden of child care in the family, need to make a special effort to balance their career and family demands. This means a lot of talking together, and setting clear priorities and time boundaries. That is, when time has been allocated for family functions, considerable effort has to be made to keep career pressures from intruding.

Laughter is the best gift you can give yourself. You cannot be depressed and laugh at the same time, so take advantage of every opportunity to laugh. Laughter counteracts negative, hostile, destructive, and depressive feelings. Different aspects of the nervous system are called into play when we are mobilizing anger, fear, and rage than when we are laughing. Laughter helps put things in perspective, particularly when we can laugh at ourselves or things that we were unnecessarily scared about. Laughter induces optimism, which makes us feel better. And our optimism makes the people around us feel less burdened by threat, anxiety, fear, and danger.

Taking Stock of the Situation

Once you have recovered your psychological balance somewhat, it's time to take stock of the overall situation. You need to step back from your immediate concerns to look at the big picture and gain some perspective on how you fit into it. You have heard all the explanations and predictions of your leaders. What do they imply for you? You might take a long weekend or a brief vacation to mull over what has happened and how it has happened, and what the changing nature of the business will be in the future. The reorganization and redirection that have happened so far are only the first major steps in the continuing evolution of the business. How well you survive and how well you do your job will depend somewhat on your thoughtful consideration of your place in that process. In doing so, you establish a new focus for your activity.

As you look at the new ways things are and will be, you will probably feel some sadness and pain mixed with your excitement and anticipation. Many of your connections have been disrupted or severed. Your activities and goals are different; your surroundings and location may have changed; you don't see people you used to see; and you run into new people, activities, ideas, and things all the time. We depend on our established ties to old familiar activities, people, and things for feelings of gratification, affection, and support. In the disruption, much of that affection and support is lost. The days are less satisfying. Even when we face new and exciting challenges, there is still an undertow from the loss of those important ties. Positive and negative feelings can exist simultaneously, but the negative ones tend to give us more trouble. That's because we usually try to suppress them and deny the accompanying depressive feelings. The losses must be identified and mourned. Mourning is a method of detachment; we must let go of the old before we can attach to the new.

As we enter an era of continual change, we enter an era of continual loss and gain. People will need the ability to mourn well in order to repeatedly attach, detach, and reattach. Those who cannot mourn will find themselves gradually isolated; those who can will find their lives immensely enriched.

Talking about what has happened is the way mourning usually takes place. Turning feelings into words helps you detach from old memories. It helps clarify what you are up against, what you miss, what you are angry about, what you are disappointed in, what you fear, and so on. Turning feelings into words also gives you perspective on events. That tends to relieve the usual irrational feelings of guilt about not having done as well as you should have in the past and about imagined inadequacy in the future. Feelings remain part of an undifferentiated mass of emotional turbulence as long as they are contained in our own heads. We need to separate those feelings from each other and from their sources. Most of us can talk to friends, neighbors, and spouses as long as we aren't afraid others will judge us negatively when we say what we feel. We tend to be less comfortable about talking out feelings as we age, but we must do it anyway because for most people it is necessary for successful psychological adaptation.

If you find yourself talking to the same person repeatedly about the same issues, just talking isn't doing the trick. It's time to turn to a professional. This is very difficult for most people. Too many people think they ought to be able to solve their own problems. And too many people think solving problems is merely a matter of being logical and getting on top of whatever issues are bugging them. They act as if self-control were the mechanism of choice. But that's totally wrong. When we try too hard to control our feelings, we push them out of our awareness—we sometimes don't even know we are under stress. Yet our feelings continue to operate, sometimes in turbulent ways that interfere with our thoughts, our behavior, our professional practice, and our relationships with other people. So the idea is not to overcontrol your feelings, but to be able to let them out in such a way that you can recognize them for what they are and deal with them rationally. If you see yourself behaving differently than you ordinarily do, it's a clue that something is going on inside. And just as you would go to a medical professional for a problem inside your body, it is important to go to a mental health professional for a disturbance in your thoughts and feelings.

One thing that makes letting go of old ways so difficult is that we tend to feel we *are* our roles. If you have been in a specific role or function for a long time, it may feel as if you will no longer be yourself when your activities change. But all organizational roles must change, so we are all compelled to accept and adapt to those changes, or we run the risk of being "out on the heap." All of us face the need to compromise at one time or another. Some of us must do so for reasons of health, some for reasons of obsolescence, some to try new experiences and find new challenges. Whatever the case, we cannot hold on to the past.

Still, there are some things that don't change: our basic values. They are like psychological glue, holding us together through changes in roles, directions, and identifications. The better adjusted survivors of prisoner-of-war camps and similar terrible experiences were those who had a set of values, usually religious. Our values give us a way of feeling good about ourselves. In times of change it can be very difficult to know what is right and what is wrong. This is particularly true when you have identified with an established set of organizational values and a given way of doing things, and then they change. Under such circumstances, it's necessary to think through what is important to you, what you believe. These things are often deceptively simple—a belief in being just, or in doing your best no matter what, or in the intrinsic worth of every person, or in learning, for example. When the organization's values change, your own values become the core around which to refocus your efforts and make sense of the change. Then you can find a way to continue to live according to your values.

Rebuilding Your Strength

By this stage of the game, everyone in the organization has been through significant stress. You have expended much energy over the past months in coping with ambiguities, worrying about the future, and anticipating threats, many of which may never have occurred. Worry saps energy and drains both psychological and physiological reserves. The stopgap measures suggested in the recovery stage kept the stress from getting out of hand and made the second stage possible, but did nothing to replace the depleted reserves. Then the psychological work of mourning and refocusing took considerable energy too. Now it is time to rebuild your physical and psychological strength. If at all possible, take a refreshing vacation. Once rested and reinvigorated, you will have a sense of being ready to go again with all of the energy and vitality that you ordinarily bring to your work.

As you get ready to move forward again, you need to mobilize your resources. Working in an organization entails depending on many people in addition to those in the chain of accountability to help you accomplish your tasks. They may, for example, give information, offer support services, or cooperate in joint problem solving. They may provide assistance very specific to your role and organization. But such resources are necessary for all people in all organizations, because they are part of what enables organizations to function. Having mourned the loss of the old connections that have been broken or changed, it's time to reestablish ties with the people who still can help you carry out your work.

Your needs in the current setting may not be the same as those in the earlier setting, but some of the same people may meet some of your new needs. You also will have to seek help from new people and mobilize new resources. You need to define who and what you need, and who can help you get them. You might think of it as drawing a psychological map of your new territory. Then you can begin establishing ties with those people.

It is also important to maintain or rebuild your support system outside work. A study of middle-aged AT&T executives by Douglas Bray and associates revealed that over the years people tend to withdraw from some of their contacts and invest themselves more heavily in their work, thereby narrowing their focus.[1] That is the opposite of what people need. It deprives them of both the affection and the help of others, which all of us need, particularly in times of change.

This Too Shall Pass

We all have experienced many ups and downs, many dangers, many real and anticipated failures—and we have survived those experiences. Even people who have lost their jobs and thought they could not recover have adapted one way or another. The threat—anxiety, danger, whatever—ultimately will pass. One way or another, you will continue to be yourself. If you think of some of the tragic, difficult, painful, and threatening events that you have been through in your life, you will realize that things look differently to you now than they did when you were in the middle of the trauma. If you maintain that perspective, you will understand that what is happening now is only transient. You will ultimately endure.

CHAPTER 3

Dealing with the Stresses of Success and Disappointment

A **central** part of one's psychological makeup is what psychoanalysts refer to as the superego. For most people, this is the same as the conscience, but there is a significant difference between conscience and superego that is important for our understanding. Conscience refers to the rules and moral standards of which we are aware that we develop in the course of growing up. These rules and standards will vary from culture to culture, from family to family, and certainly from person to person.

The superego includes that part of the conscience of which we are aware. It also encompasses the ego ideal, our expectations of ourselves at our future best, and the unconscious aspects of our conscience and ego ideal. These, by definition, are features of our personalities that are beyond our awareness. I discussed aspects of the ego ideal and how to tap into it in the previous chapter. It is important to understand that how we feel about ourselves, our degree of self-esteem, is related to the distance between our ego ideal and our self-image. One might put this into formula form:

$$\text{Self-Esteem} = \frac{1}{\text{Ego Ideal} - \text{Self-Image}}$$

This formulation is especially relevant for the discussion in this chapter of coping with success and failure, because often whether we think we have succeeded or failed is significantly a matter of our own judgment about ourselves. All of us evolve a certain psychological stance toward ourselves, as well as toward others, which causes us to perceive ourselves and the outside world in ways that are consistent with our ego ideals and our self-images. But sometimes either or both may be drastically distorted.

We are our harshest self-critics. That aspect of our personalities, particularly our continual evaluation of ourselves, is fundamental to how well we deal with success and what we define as failure. When we feel we are not moving toward our ego ideals or feel we have increased the gap between the self-image and the ego ideal, we get angry with ourselves. This anger is reflected in the experiences of guilt and shame.

Success

Acknowledging and Enjoying Your Success

It seems as if the capacity to achieve often comes with the incapacity to enjoy having achieved. We strive for weeks or years, dreaming of a cherished goal. Yet when we succeed, the moment seems to pass by without any of the elation we imagined or that we actually felt at key points along the way. There are several reasons why this may happen:

First, what makes you feel good about yourself is moving toward your ego ideal. The moment of success tends to be a static one, not as satisfying as the partial successes along the way, when you were moving toward that moment.

Second, you may be too exhausted emotionally and physically.

Third, the end of a struggle may allow the reemergence of doubts about your worth or ability and of fears that you may not be able to win another struggle. It is the effort to overcome such doubts that often fuels a successful effort in the first place. The struggle is a way of coping with them. The end of the struggle is therefore a sort of cold turkey withdrawal.

Fourth, those women who feel they should not surpass men, especially their husbands, may not welcome their success.

If this sounds familiar to you, build a small reward and celebration of achievement into your plan. Nothing elaborate, maybe just one day off, or a nice dinner out, or tickets to a game or movie you'd like to see. The point is to force yourself to acknowledge your success. If this doesn't come naturally, then it's worth the effort to make a habit of it. Start on a small scale or it'll backfire, being too contrary to your other feelings.

Another suggestion: on that occasion, deliberately seek out the company of someone you know will be impressed with what you've done. If you have a hard time congratulating yourself, bring in someone else to do it for you. That's a fine way of being good to yourself.

Many people who experience success feel like impostors, and as a result can't fully enjoy their own competence and success. They worry that others will discover their faults and expose them as frauds. They know their own limits, and forget that others see only the finished results, not the effort, worry, and mistakes that went into them. So they wonder why peers and superiors are so impressed.

How can you relieve this mental torture?

☐ Trust feedback. Do people who have nothing to gain compliment your work? Does someone you respect have faith in your abilities? Do others depend on your knowledge and skill? Try to understand what they value in your contribution.

☐ Take advantage of opportunities to instruct subordinates and peers, or perhaps teach a class. Teaching can make it clear to you how much you do know compared to others.

☐ Recall the steps by which you learned something, and how proud you were of each small victory. Most people, once they master something, cease to be impressed by their mastery.

☐ Look at the mistakes of a successful peer for proof that the organization doesn't expect perfection.

Feeling like an impostor is more common than most of the "impostors" I meet realize. It takes an effort of will to give yourself the credit you deserve. It may also take a sense of humor. When you take your effort to get somewhere too seriously, you may never see that you've arrived.

Combating the Blues That May Follow Success

Why would you feel the blues as you cross the finish line? Managers are often surprised when, at moments of triumph, they feel sad, anxious, or persnickety. It's common, but people don't talk about it because it doesn't seem to make sense.

Success often means you're leaving something behind. There may even be a sense of loss after shaking a bad habit, if that trait was part

27

of your self-definition. When a habit served to suppress unconscious fear or anger, the conquest of that habit may leave you vulnerable to those feelings.

Often people who have been promoted have feelings of guilt for having passed people they have left behind. This is especially true if they have had close associations in previous roles and feel that they had no special advantage over previous peers. This is also a particular problem for women whose husbands are anchored in trades, or who move more rapidly than their husbands in organizations. In one instance, the secretary who moved into managerial ranks while her husband remained a butcher identified herself to friends as still being in a clerical role. In another, an executive secretary whose husband was a carpenter made sure she never brought him to company affairs. It's not unusual in such cases for the women to turn their paychecks over to their husbands to avoid threatening their husbands' self-images. However, it is far wiser to talk over issues like this with spouses.

Some people feel anxious out of insecurity, fearing they'll blow it. If they typically sabotage themselves, they may already be expecting the blunder they're unconsciously compelled to make. Some people even worry about their ability to pull off what they've already done!

Acknowledge such feelings—say aloud to yourself that you feel sad, frightened, guilty, disappointed, or angry. Then confide to someone who'll understand. You may feel it's wrong to spoil a "perfect moment," but perfect moments are an unrealistic ideal. Brides and grooms are as anxious as they are happy. Mothers often feel depressed after an easy delivery of a healthy child. One mother thought she must be crazy to feel so bad. But when her third child was born, she let herself cry all she wanted, knowing it would pass, and felt much better for it.

Recognizing the Losses That Accompany Promotion

When you get a big promotion, friends congratulate you. But maybe someone should say, "Hey, kid, that's tough." Promotion is a loss, though in our rush for success, we rarely consider how much we're leaving behind: the confidence that comes from having proven skills and competence, the comfort of knowing exactly what's expected and how to behave, and supportive working relationships.

The best way to marshal the inner forces you'll need to tackle your new job is to face your losses and then separate from them. To help yourself along:

☐ Acknowledge how much there is that you'll miss. If you make a list including people, favorite standing jokes, skills that won't be a source of pride anymore, and so on, you'll be surprised at how much you're saying good-bye to.

☐ Talk to the people you trust about how difficult the change is. Talk is our most effective antidote for loss.

☐ Expect to make mistakes on your new job. If you hope to be as competent as before, you'll increase the pain you feel at each misstep.

The goal is to work through your grief so that your unconscious feelings don't stay anchored in the past. Then you can focus your drives on tackling your new job.

Mistakes

Everyone makes mistakes. Everyone violates not only society's but his or her own moral code from time to time. Managers are especially vulnerable because they deal with people, and there's no certainty in decisions about people. Nor are purely business decisions safe from miscalculation and unforeseen disaster, even for the best of managers. And yet managers, by definition, are people who are supposed to be "in control." So the individuals who want to be good managers are often people who have difficulty coping with feelings aroused by mistakes they can't help but make.

Much management education, writing, and shoptalk deals with how to avoid or correct mistakes. Too little attention is paid to the feelings aroused by the mistakes: guilt, embarrassment, and shame. These are very intense feelings, the more so for being little understood and for generally being considered inadmissible or not worth talking about.

Guilt

There are two phenomena to distinguish and cope with—guilt and shame. Guilt is the feeling of having done wrong. We absorb standards of right and wrong behavior—mostly in childhood, but they can be acquired in adulthood too. These internalized standards constitute much of the superego. Guilt is the feeling of having violated the superego.

Guilt can be conscious or unconscious.

Conscious Guilt. Conscious guilt is easier to cope with. You know what you've done wrong; you know that according to your morals it is wrong. Managers may feel conscious guilt for firing an employee, getting someone in trouble, scapegoating, engaging in gossip, gambling or getting drunk, having an affair, or lusting after someone.

In these cases, you know why you're feeling the pain of guilt. What can you do now that you've done the deed and can't go back in time and revise your actions? Three statements provide guidelines for dealing with conscious guilt: I am human—it is inevitable that I will sometimes violate my moral code; I am bigger than my mistakes, so I am not to be written off—by myself or others—for what I have done; and I won't make this particular mistake again if I can help it. With these resolutions in mind, taking the following steps is helpful:

☐ Undo what you have done to the extent possible. Apologize to anyone you've wronged; admit your mistake openly. Make restitution if that's possible. Doing these things allows you to channel your energy into doing better from now on, rather than into defending a shaky position. And precisely because apologies and admissions of wrongdoing are so hard, they offer a special satisfaction that can be very energizing—the satisfaction of having done a difficult thing. Going through with the apology or admission is in itself the first success of the rest of your career.

☐ Do penance—something that provides opportunities to think well of yourself—to counteract the guilt. For some, going to confession serves this function; for others, doing public service work. The penance should coincide with your own ego ideal, so that it increases your self-esteem. Self-punishment for its own sake is simply destructive and wasteful. The penance must also be limited. Some people take their public service too far by letting everyone else dump all their problems on them.

☐ Remember your positive traits. Sit down and make a list of everything you're good at, what you've done well, and what morally good acts you've done at work. It may feel funny, but this can help you keep your perspective and avoid blowing your mistake out of proportion. A manager whose boss had told him off was much relieved when a friend went over all the reasons the boss had to appreciate him. "Sure, you've made a bad mistake," said the friend, "but she's not going to get rid of you—you're too worthy." That gave the manager the self-confidence to face his own mistake and move beyond it.

☐ Consider how the mistake happened. How did you talk yourself into doing something morally wrong? Did you ignore your own misgivings? Is the situation that brought on this mistake likely to recur? Then decide what steps will help you avoid making that mistake again. For example, you may vow never to make a certain excuse for wrong behavior, or not to put yourself in the way of a certain temptation.

Unconscious Guilt. Managerial behavior is hampered the most by unconscious guilt. Unconscious guilt is usually irrational. That's why it can dominate people's lives so powerfully; they can't get a grasp on it because it doesn't make any sense. Unconscious guilt is a response to thinking one has violated one's moral code, but the person feeling it is unaware of the wrong done or the rule broken. He or she may be entirely unaware of the feeling unless someone points out the resulting behavior. Or he or she may feel guilty but not know why, or attribute the feelings to causes that aren't the real cause. For example, one woman suffers guilt about dating men, feeling that if she does, her sick mother might die. This makes no rational sense; the guilt, in fact, stems from something else that she cannot allow into her consciousness.

There are several common causes of unconscious guilt. The Oedipal conflict in early childhood, the earliest experience of rivalry between a child and a parent of the same sex for the attention and affection of the parent of the opposite sex, often leaves a residue of unresolved guilt. The child feels very guilty for wishing to destroy a parent—a wish the child knows is wrong. When the child makes the transition to identification with the same-sex parent, much of the guilt is assuaged and the conflict resolved. If, for complex reasons, the guilt lingers—repressed and unrecognized—it can be a lifelong

burden, an obstacle to achievement, or an impediment to relationships.

Overly critical or controlling parents can leave a child unconsciously convinced that he or she is worthless or bad. This can manifest
itself in a lifelong need to be punished, or in a will to fail. Such people have an uncanny knack for undoing their own achievements,
arranging to be caught doing wrong, dropping out when success gets
too near, or inexplicably squandering their abilities.

Children—and adults too—can be smitten by distortions in their
thinking that leave them feeling guilty. Children may conclude, by
their magical thinking, that their angry thoughts were responsible
for a parent's or sibling's death, or for a divorce. Many adults who
lived through disasters such as the Holocaust or the bombing of Hiro-
shima feel guilt for having lived while others died, as if they had
survived at the others' expense.

Managers often are disinclined to believe in the reality of unconscious guilt. "After all, if I didn't really do anything, why should
I feel guilty?" Yet many people feel nervous when they find a police-
man next to them or have to go through a customs inspection—
even when they have done nothing wrong. When called to see the
boss, most people's first reaction, even if said with a laugh, is "Uh
oh." Why is this? The presence of an authority figure triggers their
unconscious guilt and the resulting self-critical posture.

Unconscious guilt lies behind one of the major chronic problems in management: the inability to criticize, which results in an
incapacity for genuine performance appraisal. This has been the cause
of countless misguided promotions, stalled careers, ill-advised suc-
cessions, and blow-ups in place of discussions. Unconscious guilt is
also a cause of some accidents, which can be a form of self-punishment. And it can motivate scapegoating—an attempt to evade one's
own guilt by transferring it to someone else.

Recognizing Unconscious Guilt. How can you tell when unconscious guilt is at work? The clue is that your behavior follows a pattern of frustration or failure—frequently an inability to do something
you are capable of doing. It often requires an outside perspective to
see this pattern, because you may have perfectly logical excuses or
explanations for each instance. Inasmuch as the cause of the behavior is unconscious and by definition too painful to face, one is unable to see the self-made forest for the trees.

Sometimes awareness of the pattern can help you break it. One manager noticed that every time he did a good piece of work and received praise from his boss, he would follow it with an error—nothing too serious, but disappointing to the boss. When they finally recognized the pattern, they realized that his errors were a protection against his boss's expectations. In effect, he was saying to her, "Yes, I did good work, but just so you don't expect too much of me, here's something dumb I just did." The manager was then able to recognize this kind of situation beforehand, see the behavior coming, and stop it: "Aha, my boss has just complimented me. I'll probably try to talk myself into letting a detail slip by, so watch it." It worked. His impulse to make the mistakes is still there, but he doesn't give in to it.

In more serious cases, where people absolutely cannot stop themselves from making chronic mistakes, psychotherapy is the way to discover the source of the guilt and lessen its control over behavior.

People often mistakenly attribute their unconscious irrational guilt to a visible, rational cause. But if you attend to the alleged cause and the guilt remains, you should suspect unconscious guilt and try to discover its source with professional help. Just knowing that the guilt is irrational can at least take away the pressure of the more "rational" guilt you have assigned yourself.

Shame

Guilt is based on private self-assessment—your accuser is your own superego. Shame is guilt compounded by a public assessment—you feel accused not only by your superego but by the people who know about your wrongdoing. (If you are caught doing something that the group or society sees as wrong but you see as right, you're more likely to feel anger than guilt or shame.) A person who is "shameless" seems utterly unaware of what others think of him or her. Young children are in many ways shameless, by virtue of not knowing what others think. This may seem to be an ideal stage, like that of Adam and Eve going unashamed in the Garden of Eden. But the fact is that no adult, short of being psychotic or a sociopath, can be entirely unconcerned about what others think.

We all transgress the rules we believe in, and from time to time will be caught. Suddenly, our "bad" side is spotlighted and the "good" side seems invalidated or obliterated. One finds oneself hopelessly far from one's ego ideal, and the struggle to gain the respect of others seems lost. Sociologist Edward Gross, examining the embarrass-ment of public figures, explains: "Embarrassment means exposure. You have presented a certain face to the world that you are a par-ticular kind of person, or an organization with a specific capability, and then something happens which shows that face to have been false all along."[1]

There can be no such thing as unconscious shame. Shame burns on the brain like an open flame. Because it's such an intense feeling, and because so many people are not used to coping with strong feel-ings except for anger at work, shame can incite them to rash actions they later regret. Some insist on self-defeating denial, as Nixon did. Some resort to scapegoating or to destructive self-punishment.

Again I recommend beginning with three statements: I am hu-man—it is inevitable that I will make some mistakes and be exposed; I am bigger than my mistakes, so they will not be the end of me; and I won't make this particular mistake again if I can help it. The steps to cope with shame are similar to those described earlier for dealing with guilt. The hardest will be the first: to apologize and ad-mit your mistake openly. But this is a crucial task, a necessary step in order to regain whatever esteem and reputation have been lost. Nixon might well have enjoyed his returning public acceptance much sooner had he admitted and apologized for his wrongdoings.

Shame is harder to shake than guilt. One can assuage one's guilt for a deed by apologizing, doing good works, making restitution, and so on. But we cannot control other people's opinions and memo-ries. Because we cannot read their minds, our unconscious guilt sug-gests to us that others are thinking ill of us, even years later, and the feeling of shame returns.

One way to handle this is to try to become the epitome of what-ever rule you violated. For example, recovered alcoholics and drug abusers often become heavily involved in programs to help others recover. At the organizational level, a company exposed for pollut-ing a local river may become a staunch defender of the local envi-ronment, donate land for a park, sponsor educational programs, and so on. The Union Carbide Corporation said it would sell its last holdings in India to raise as much as $17 million to build and oper-ate a hospital in Bhopal, where a 1984 chemical explosion at its pes-ticide factory created the worst industrial disaster in history.[2]

But in general, only time can diminish shame. That's why it's important to talk your feelings through with a confidant from time to time. An outside perspective can counter your exaggerated negative view of what others think of you. It's also important to formally remind yourself of the good you do by being a good citizen, friend, spouse, parent, or boss. Another helpful method is to try to see the humor in your blunder and exposure. Recount the story as if it had happened to someone else; if you can laugh at the clown you were, you'll do a lot to heal your wound.

Shame on Behalf of Another

Employees may also feel shame on behalf of their boss or their organization. Imagine what it was like to work for Union Carbide after the Bhopal disaster, or Exxon after the Alaskan oil spill—you wouldn't be in a hurry to bring up your employer's name at a cocktail party. Of course an electrical engineer working at some Carbide plant in California wasn't guilty in the slightest. But part of the cost of identifying with an organization is to feel ashamed, irrationally, when it brings public censure upon itself.

This is a problem for many employees, particularly in an era of intense media coverage of business misdeeds and of public mistrust of companies. If you work for a company involved in a scandal, what can you do about a problem you didn't cause and cannot control?

☐ Get together with peers for mutual support. Talking through the feelings and unpleasant incidents doesn't change reality, but it feels better to know you're not alone, your feelings aren't weird, and you're really not guilty. Because managers give so much of themselves to others, I cannot overemphasize the usefulness to them of group support.

☐ Arm yourself with accurate information about what really happened, what didn't, and what's being done. But don't let people draw you into a fight. You don't owe anybody any explanations if their purpose is to attack your company through you.

☐ Learn what conditions created the wrongdoing or allowed it to happen. Find out if these conditions exist or could exist in your unit, and how to eliminate or prevent them. You can bet that's going on in other divisions or plants, and it's a good thing—managers who are taking constructive action against a potential danger are in much better psychological shape.

☐ Make an extra effort to support your subordinates, who are also ashamed and are probably being given a hard time by acquaintances and even family members. Provide them with as much information as you can, create opportunities for them to get together with you and among themselves, and keep them up-to-date on new developments.

Beyond these steps, all you can do is wait for time to heal the indirect shame, and keep an eye on yourself so you don't indulge in sloppy work and bring direct shame down on your own head.

Embarrassment

There are some occasions when you are "exposed" but not guilty. This results in embarrassment. Common embarrassment comes from unintentionally doing something that is disapproved of but not morally wrong, such as making a social faux pas or forgetting someone's name. These are accidents—caused by a moment of physical clumsiness, a lapse of memory, or ignorance of the norms or of a particular person's situation. Grace and good manners will usually get you past such awkward moments.

In other cases, you accidentally appear to have done something seriously wrong. For example, you find yourself extremely frustrated with your desktop computer. Just to let off a little steam and amuse yourself, you pretend as though you're going to smash it—and at that moment, your boss walks in.

Situations like this are often the starting points of comedies, precisely because they create a misunderstanding. The evidence points very clearly to a conclusion that doesn't happen to be true. The instinctive tendency is to feel acutely embarrassed and try to explain as fast as possible. Sometimes that's all you can do, if the other person's suspicion is too serious to leave be. Sometimes it's better to keep doing whatever you were doing and act as if you have every business doing so (which, despite appearances, you do). It all depends on who has "caught" you and the consequences of his or her carrying away a wrong opinion.

In time, your real nature and characteristic behavior should undo the false impression. If the person who caught you repeats the incident to others, they may assure him that you're really not that kind of person. It's impossible not to worry about it, but it's best not to let your actions be distorted by that worry. One helpful thing is to explain to a friend in the organization exactly what happened. This will help you put it in perspective. In addition, you may be compelled to see the humor in it, if only through the other person's eyes.

Reducing Your Tendencies Toward Self-Blame

If your boss criticizes you unfairly, you feel angry. But do you also secretly believe he's right?

Such self-blame likely has roots in early childhood, when we idealize our parents and imitate them. Because our dependence on them is so total, the scariest thing would be to admit they're not perfect. So children often block the perception of parental inadequacy and blame themselves for much of what goes wrong. This can establish a pattern of self-blame that persists into adulthood. Since there are always psychological elements of a parent-child relationship between the boss and his or her subordinates, inappropriate dependency and idealization are sometimes transferred to the boss.

To reduce tendencies you might have toward self-blame after criticism:

- ☐ Evaluate your boss's negative assessments with trusted coworkers. Try to establish what's real.
- ☐ Make a record of what happens when the boss criticizes you. Are you devastated? Usually such a response means that your own self-criticism has been activated.
- ☐ Monitor the extent to which you strive to please your boss. Do you always say yes to extra assignments that don't develop you or teach you anything? Are you apt to forgo a day off that you or your family really need?
- ☐ Lean more on family, friends, and coworkers to reduce overdependence on the all-powerful boss.
- ☐ Develop your skills and knowledge. A sense of mastery counteracts feelings of helplessness and dependence on the boss.

CHAPTER 4

Confronting and Learning from Failure

Not all career failures are self-defined inadequacies. Some are indeed literal failures, as newspaper headlines about the demotions of top executives testify. Sometimes people fail because they don't have the skills or knowledge to do a given job. Sometimes a role outgrows them.

A highly successful scientist who sat across the table from me expressed his anguish at probably having lost the opportunity for a job that would have been a capstone for his career. He spoke quickly, volubly, intensely. He had been so concerned with telling his prospective employer how much he had to offer, what he thought he could do for the new organization, and his ideas for new products that he had overwhelmed that executive and intimidated him with his intensity. By the time he sensed this, it was too late. He was chagrined at his own behavior, and all the more despairing because he had failed to get the promotion in his current company that he thought he deserved. He attributed that failure to political issues, but it was now quite clear to him, as it was to me, that his intensity had frightened his current bosses just as it had the prospective employer.

Now he was concerned with recovering his psychological poise and self-confidence. He also wanted to try to ensure that he didn't make the same mistake again. The first step in that process was to undertake a critical self-examination.

Facing Reality

When you don't get a promotion, it's important to size up the subtleties of how you fit or did not fit a given organizational context. Sometimes, this is a matter of how you presented yourself in the organization, having to do sometimes with dress, sometimes with the use of language, and sometimes with not fitting organizational norms. For example, an executive who was noticeably overweight was the subject of critical comments from his peers in an organization that placed a heavy emphasis on fitness. His upward mobility was likely to be limited in that organization. Similarly, another executive, despite his competence, had a certain lack of polish that made him uncongenial in an otherwise highly sophisticated peer group. While such subtleties should not interfere with one's career, obviously they do, and one must take them seriously.

There are other subtleties for women. Men are often uncomfortable with women who give them direction, and unconsciously may try to undermine them and protect their power from female encroachment. They may reinforce the woman manager's self-doubts in order to perpetuate the assumption "men do it better." At the other extreme, the macho male may well think that his task is to take care of the weaker female.[1]

Likewise, don't get mad at your boss for choosing someone else for a given role instead of you. Try to understand how that other person might be better qualified. Sometimes it's difficult to understand that somebody else can more quickly grasp problems and take more data into account, for example.

Gaining from Defeat

Losing his first two bids for the Republican presidential nomination helped Ronald Reagan win big later.

His former campaign manager explains, "If you lost and it was clear what you'd do had you won, you're in a position to run again. All it takes is a few more people who believe you're right. . . . But if you lost and it's not clear what you stood for, all you proved was that you were the greater of the two evils."[2]

If you've lost out on a promotion or a desired assignment, this is what you can gain from the experience:

Visibility. Trying for a promotion makes higher-ups more aware of who you are and of your availability.

Identity. Make sure the bosses know your positions and the direction you'd take. If you stand for something, they'll be more likely to think of you in the future.

Professional growth. Get a thorough explanation of why you lost out. There may be specifics—you came on too strong or too laid back, you didn't explain yourself well enough—that you can remedy.

Personal growth. Strengthen yourself. Talk about your disappointment with people you trust. Express, confront, and examine your feelings. That's the best way to put the past behind you.

Not Getting Promoted

Are you one of the many people who feel they aren't getting anywhere because their organizations don't appreciate them? You have talents and ambition but are expected to stay where you are and keep doing what you're doing. How come no one wants what you've got?

Unneeded and Unwanted

Probably the most common reason the company doesn't want what you've got is that it doesn't need it. I often receive resumes from people who are justly proud of their achievements and qualifications, but most haven't bothered to find out what The Levinson Institute needs.

In organizations, people may develop a skill past the point which is of use to the company. The headquarters for a chain of hardware stores will need a computer programmer, but not a really innovative and high-level one. The employee who gains such mastery and wants his company to make use of it is wasting his time. I know of a programmer in a small consumer software company who developed an interest in marketing. He did well because, in that company, there was room for him to grow in that direction.

Prematurely Pegged and Plateaued

Sometimes management wrongly concludes that you've reached your limit. This can happen when:

☐ You have performed well in your role for several years but haven't shown any signs of growth. The explanation could be that you are just now moving up to the next higher level of cognitive power (which is the ability to think abstractly, plan ahead, handle complexity, and so on). As I noted in Chapter 1, the development of these capacities takes place in quantum leaps, and those occur at different ages for different people.

☐ Your job provides no opportunities for you to show your potential in other areas. From the outside, it looks like you've reached your limit.

☐ You don't like your job, so you don't put your heart into it. The lackluster performance is taken as a sign that you've plateaued.

More Plusses, but Bigger Negatives

It may be that no one wants what you've got because they're afraid of what else you've got, as in the example at the beginning of this chapter.

If you've been told why you aren't being promoted, then it's time to pay more attention. Many managers expect their technical skill or their bottom-line performance to take them to the top. But past a certain level, behavioral problems such as abrasiveness, overdependence on a boss, or inability to confront others outweigh those plusses. These problems are simply too damaging at high levels. Unfortunately, top managements sometimes hold people back for such reasons without ever making it clear enough, because they're afraid to insult you so deeply or afraid to lose you.

You need more feedback from your boss. Ask why you're not being promoted and what you could do to be considered promotable. Hear your boss out without arguing; regardless of whether you agree, you've got to know his or her point of view.

If your boss continues to be evasive, seek the feedback elsewhere. Can you talk to his or her boss? Is there one of your boss's peers with whom you've worked, who might know what your boss is worried about and would also know about you firsthand? Someone in human resources who would know what others say about you?

Lack of Self-Advertisement

Let's say you've spent three years on staff at a manufacturing company. You've learned a lot about the industry—more, in fact, than your job requires you to know. You know you could be contributing at a higher level. So how come you're not being considered for promotion?

Perhaps no one realizes you've gained this expertise. This can happen when the performance appraisal system is haphazard or nonexistent. As long as you are getting your job done, your boss may not pay much attention to how you get it done or what you learn along the way.

You're in no position to change the organization's performance appraisal policies. So you'll have to take matters into your own hands. This could mean going to your boss and saying, "I think I'm ready for a promotion. The reason is that I've learned a lot about X, Y, and Z during my three years in this position, and now I'd like to move into a position where I can make real use of that knowledge."

Registering Your Potential

Generally, you have four options to register your potential with the organization:

☐ Talk to your boss. If she's written you off as unpromotable, don't wait for her to change her mind. Try to change it for her by telling her how you feel about your current job and what you'd like to accomplish instead. If you can get her to reconsider, that's your best bet.

   Sometimes people whose bosses see no potential in them do much better once they have moved to another area where they aren't saddled with those preconceptions. If you can change her mind about your potential and enlist her help, that's a good solution. You may also need your boss's feedback to become more promotable.

☐ Talk to human resources. If you're stalled and have been stereotyped in one role, you may yet blossom in another. If you can't get your boss on your side, try the human resources department. Find out what positions are available and what's expected of the people who will fill them. Then, if it's acceptable in your company, talk to the managers for whom you would be working. Showing some initiative will make you attractive right from the start. Even if there is no human resources department, you can ask for a chance to talk with some department heads about opportunities. Be sure you can describe clearly and succinctly what you're looking for; rehearse what you'll say.

☐ Talk to others in the company. If you can't get the help and feedback you need from your boss or from human resources, try your boss's peers, his or her boss, and whoever else in the organization either knows you or knows where you might fit.

☐ Take responsibility for your own life. Organizations should be aware of their people's potential. But they often aren't, and if you're the one who's suffering, it's up to you to do something about it.

Diagnosing Why You've Failed

You've gotten the clear message that you have no place to go in your organization, or you've been asked to look for a position elsewhere. Why has this happened? Men and women in higher-level positions fail for many reasons.

Inadequate management of aggression. The people who are able to assume responsibility during a crisis, plunge into their tasks with zest, and accomplish them successfully, become the "comers," the "shining lights" of organizations. They are usually talented, energetic managers who have considerable ability and even more promise. Sometimes they rescue part of the organization from failure or produce outstanding results in resolving difficult problems almost single-handedly. Management encourages them in their wide-ranging pursuit of personal power, but, at a certain point, higher management abruptly changes the signals. From then on, further advancement hinges not on what they can do individually, but on their ability to lead, not drive, others. These highly important, talented managers become problems at this juncture. As "hard drivers," they characteristically dominate their staffs. They concentrate decision making in their own hands, while exerting heavy pressure on subordinates. In short, they are authoritarian. Usually, they are unable to coach and develop subordinates or to work comfortably with other people. They seem to be insensitive to their impact on other people.

Erratic and discourteous behavior. A variant of the foregoing behavior pattern is the hostile manager whose sometimes erratic and discourteous behavior exceeds the bounds of common courtesy. People who are so hostile as to be destructive spew their anger about them—at colleagues, subordinates, and superiors. They are unnecessarily critical. They argue too long and too much. They are crude and rude to others and seem to flay at their working environments. They tend to get away with such behavior for a long time because it is difficult for their superiors to cope with the intensity of their anger, but that intensity tends to increase. Usually, they themselves are oblivious to the pain they cause others, although sometimes, when they are made aware of others' pain, they become contrite.

Self-centeredness. Another common problem is particularly evident in those cases in which self-centeredness is the most conspicuous aspect of the person. The major form this self-centeredness takes is exploitation of or attack on others as part of the manager's efforts to maintain and increase his or her own status. These managers are more manipulative than those who are authoritarian and directive. Self-centered managers are more obviously concerned with their own aggrandizement. Often they seem not to care what they do to others in the process, while authoritarian managers more frequently are paternalistically sympathetic to others. Anger or self-centeredness can be an expression of increased insecurity and anxiety, particularly if job burdens are felt to be onerous, or failure threatens. Sometimes they are exacerbated by rivalry in the organization, frequently stimulated by higher management.

Psychological injuries. Many experiences in life are painful to people. Some, like aging and its accompanying physical infirmities and incapacities, are everyone's lot. Others are specific to a person's work life: failure to obtain an expected promotion, the prospect of retirement. Such painful experiences can be conceived of as psychological injuries. These injuries are inevitable. Those who have been hurt in this manner usually have considerable hostility that is repressed or suppressed.

Those to whom prospective retirement is a psychological injury sometimes stubbornly refuse to train subordinates. They become obstructionists, displacing their repressed or suppressed hostility on both subordinates and the organization. Physical changes, such as hearing loss, also leave residues of resentment as managers attempt to deny their incapacity.

Other major sources of psychological injury include the failure to be promoted to a job one expects, having one's judgment rejected, and having some of one's responsibilities passed to someone else. These events are viewed as a loss: something has been taken away.

Also among the wounded ones are the lonesome people—those who wish they could be gregarious, but simply cannot. They therefore are hypersensitive to rejection by others. Having previously often been wounded, they are ready candidates for psychological wounds and overrespond to new wounds.

Impulsiveness. Impulsive managers act erratically and without adequate thought. Among them are the managers who can do their jobs well "when they want to." They are frequently absent, often embroiled in multiple family difficulties, and sometimes irresponsible with respect to completing their work or doing it thoroughly. Also in this category are the people who, though not alcoholic, drink too much in the presence of their superiors, and others whose worst behavior occurs when they are with the highest-level superiors. The self-defeating aspects of such behavior are obvious.

Inflexibility. Rigidity as a personal characteristic usually is reflected in an inability to plan or accept change. Some people resist change not because they are personally inflexible, but because the organization has prepared them poorly and they are angry. Inflexible people find their self-protection in well-ordered lives. Often they have high standards for themselves. Those who become more rigid under stress, in effect, build a protective shell for themselves.

Inability to assume responsibility. Some managers are simply unable to assume responsibility for others or to act on management problems. Although their behavior might be described as dependent, that rubric does not do justice to the complexity of their problem. A frequent corollary of their inability to perform as expected is the fact that these managers previously have been suppressed in an extremely authoritarian structure for years. Some are able to function reasonably well so long as they have the close support of their superiors. Some cannot make decisions themselves. Undoing dependent behavior is no easy task, particularly if the organization continues to demand conformity. Where conformity is the first rule of survival, no amount of exhortation will produce initiative. Where mistakes are vigorously hunted out and subsequently prejudice a manager's career, few will risk making a mistake.

Different styles. Problems can arise when a person's managerial style differs from organizational norms. For example, women's managerial styles often differ from those of men because of women's greater sensitivity to other people's feelings, a competence which is apparent in early infancy. Women seem to do better at getting their subordinates to share concern for broader goals and to lean more heavily on interpersonal skills and personal contacts, rather than organization position. They tend to encourage participation, share power and information, enhance other people's self-worth, and get others excited about their work.[3] Men more often view job performance as a series of transactions with subordinates, exchanging rewards for services or punishment for inadequate performance. They also are more likely to use the leverage of their formal authority.

Limited ability. Still another problem is limited ability. Much too often managers are placed in the wrong job; half the time, the job is wrong for them because it has outgrown them. There often seems to be almost no anticipation on the part of such people that such an eventuality could come about, let alone the fact that they have reached their limits. Whatever the reason a manager does not grow, often he or she is left to flounder in the job because superiors recognize that the failure is theirs and their guilt precludes their acting quickly.

Of course, usually people who are unable to function adequately when confronted by larger responsibilities often have done well in jobs of lesser responsibility. That they seemed to have promise was the reason they were promoted. Sometimes they are in such positions because they are the best person available. Sometimes they are moved into managerial roles because of their knowledge. Whatever the case, they should come to recognize this fact and seek roles that are consistent with their competence.

Passive aggression. Still another negative characteristic is passive aggression—failure to do what one is capable of doing as a way of defeating the company. Often rigidity and plateaus in performance are products of passive aggression. One way of being covertly aggressive is by not changing, not doing what is expected of one, letting the boss down in one way or another.

The person who would manage his or her own career well has to face the realities of his or her own behavior. This means careful, honest examination of one's job history, one's relationships in previous roles, and consideration of feedback that has been sloughed off previously or even denied outright.

CHAPTER 5

Learning the Organization

Upward of 90 percent of employed people work in organizations these days. That means that anybody who would pursue a career in an organization should understand what that organization is all about. In consultation, my colleagues and I frequently develop an understanding of an organization that seeks our help through a method that I have outlined in *Organizational Diagnosis*.[1] Ordinarily, people have neither the time nor the resources to conduct a full-scale organizational diagnosis. Nevertheless, they can observe many things and integrate their observations to form a comprehensive understanding of the organization.

Recording Your First Impressions

Whenever anybody enters an organization, somebody usually shows him or her around: there is some kind of tour. There is also opportunity in some organizations to visit other parts of the organization, other plants or distribution centers or stores. In doing so, it is helpful to be sensitive to your initial impressions and your subtle feelings as you go along because these reflect the impact of various environmental stimuli on you and, by extension, on others in the organization. Then, it is important to write down what you have seen and how you felt about it.

You can ask these questions: What did I see on tour? What are my first feelings about the organization and the setting? What were people's attitudes toward me? What occurred that made me feel good, bad, indifferent? Even hazy impressions will turn out later to be valuable in understanding the organization. Look at slogans, bulletin boards, display cases, and other forms of communication, all of which indicate what an organization is emphasizing and how it does so. The way the buildings or the offices are kept reflect management's attitude about such things. The presence or absence of places where people may readily eat, take coffee breaks, and gather informally says something about congeniality. Modes for receiving visitors, parking, transportation, kinds of magazines in reception rooms and offices, and similar cues reflect organizational climate and values.

If you are being shown around for the first time, how interested is your guide in showing you? What facets of the setting does he emphasize—people, product, process, services, history? Are people tense or relaxed, hurried or casual? Does your guide seem to see people as resources or as problems? Does he have a differentiated view of them or are they merely masks? How does he approach them and how do they respond to him?

Getting Handles on the Organization

In the course of your work, you will encounter many different people. One way of getting handles on the organization is to ask those people exactly what they do, and, if possible, how they go about doing it. Some people operate machines or equipment that they can demonstrate. Others garner and organize information. Some design products. Some organize services. People usually are pleased to explain in some detail what they do and how their work relates to that of others. Pretty soon, by doing that, you'll develop a network of relationships that will enable you to see the informal modes of communication, which are likely to differ significantly from the formal organization chart.

Sometimes it is helpful to ask people to draw an organization chart and compare it with the formal one. It will be important to know to whom each feels responsible for what, whether on the organization chart or not, and how they are evaluated by whom. This process will reveal a range of settings and reasons for their differences. You will also see boundaries, whether physical or psychological. Often people who work in close proximity can't readily talk to each other because of hierarchical requirements.

Almost all companies make public annual reports and some issue 10K reports to the Securities and Exchange Commission. These are an important source of financial data and say something about the style of management of the organization. For example, an organization that has issued many bonds bearing fixed interest, and has to pay that interest regardless of the economy, is likely to squeeze its employees more than an organization that is significantly financed by stock and has few fixed financial obligations. Wise financial executives will change the financial structure of the organization in keeping with the availability and cost of money. Those who are less knowledgeable are less likely to do so. Those decisions will have a significant effect on anybody's career. If the cost of money is too high, the organization can't readily expand and may not be able to keep up with its competitors. Organizations of similar size and sales may well differ significantly in their profitability just because of how they are financed.

What important information is in financial analysts' reports? Every stock brokerage has such reports, and most are kept up to date for stockholder evaluation. These are important sources of the kind of information that frequently is not passed on to employees. Financial analysts often make judgments about whether to recommend a stock for purchase or sale. Their logic, carefully examined, can be an important guide to career choice. One executive, seeing that his company was failing to develop new products and that financial analysts were becoming cautious about recommending its stock—and that the chief executive was not taking clear steps to remedy these problems—concluded rationally that it was time to go somewhere else.

It will be helpful to get a sense of what is communicated and how. In some organizations, there is a good deal of informal communication by word of mouth. Others depend heavily on written materials, and some people know clearly from the information they get where the organization is going, how it is competing, and what its competitive environment is. All organizations get a lot of information; some don't know what to do with it. Information about marketing trends was readily evident to General Motors long before it experienced a competitive crisis. Nobody there seemed to pay attention to it.

Another way of thinking about the organization is to size up how much attention it pays to its competitive environment. Some companies act as if they had no competitors, and some seem to ignore the fact that the competition is already ahead of them. For example, some medical equipment companies are still trying to sell cumbersome diabetic diagnostic devices for individual testing when competitors have long since marketed simpler devices.

Some organizations pay careful attention to the outside world and their consumers, but give little attention to their employees. Others go to great lengths with surveys, morale studies, group meetings, and so on, in order to listen intently and carefully to what employees are saying—a frontier of new knowledge frequently translated into new products and services. Others seem not to hear about innovations. What does your organization do?

How does the organization talk to its people in employee publications? Are those publications solely concerned with which employee chaired the United Service Campaign, or the local Boy Scout council? Or do they talk seriously about the problems of the industry, of the company, of the economy, and what the organization is doing about them? Do you learn more from the daily newspaper about the organization than you do from company publications?

What is the age distribution in the organization? The U.S. population is getting older as life expectancy increases and the birth rate decreases. An aging population may have implications for a company's competitive position. It will also include more women, and that may well mean a more considerate attitude toward their subordinates, which in turn will affect the organization's climate.

What seems to be the mood of the organization? Is it upbeat, optimistic, enthusiastic, or depressed? Does it differ from one part of the organization to another? How fast and continually does the organization act on its problems? What does it think about its customers and its employees, about regulatory bodies and legislative bodies, about the community, and about its dealers or representatives? Some companies maintain a running battle with regulatory agencies. Others learn to work effectively with them. What happens here?

How do people in the organization feel about themselves and

the company? IBM has been criticized for arrogance toward its customers. Some have complained that the alleged arrogance has reflected itself in poor service and in products that are technically not as good as those of competitors. The way people feel about themselves in their organization will show up in such behavior. Incidentally, of course, reports in the press present a picture of the organization as outsiders see it. What is that picture?

Anybody who works in an organization very long develops a lot of this information. Rarely, however, does one organize it into a better way of understanding what goes on. If you make notes from time to time about these issues, and then integrate them into a general picture of what the organization is all about, particularly delineating who has what power and how that power is used, you can then map the organizational terrain. This will make it easier to make career choices and career decisions. You cannot know too much, nor can you suffer from putting your information together and then stepping back to look at it as objectively as possible before making choices.

Gaining Clues to Your Organization's Culture

Many people fail in organizations because they don't understand the organization's culture or in some cases don't fit it. This can happen at very high levels. For example, several years ago, AT&T—seeking to move more directly into the telecommunications business—hired away an IBM senior officer to take charge of their marketing operation. The IBM culture was predominantly a marketing culture, the AT&T culture at the time predominantly a technical culture. Failing to take that into account, the former IBM executive did not ensure that he would have sufficient support to cope with the fact that the AT&T engineering culture neither adequately understood nor could be sufficiently reoriented to understand the marketing effort. He was soon extruded from the system. The same thing happened when Ross Perot tried to change General Motors. It happens frequently at lower levels in many organizations.

Knowing your organization's culture is essential to your success. Especially as you move up, you need to know what's expected of you in terms of behavior that's not directly performance related. You may even be expected to play (or avoid) certain roles in your community. And at any level, you need to know how to get along and how to avoid faux pas that can mark you unfairly as an inept manager.

There are many clues to organizational culture just waiting to be observed. Most managers try hard to observe the culture when they first come into a company. But they don't always know what to look for, and they're swamped with so much else to learn and absorb. So their impression of the organizational culture can be dangerously incomplete.

That's why you should take some time to think again about culture once you're settled in your job. And you should do so periodically, not only to deepen your understanding but also to be aware of how the culture might be changing. While top managements find it fiendishly hard to change organizational culture the way they'd like to, cultures change naturally over time because of the influx of new people, changing business realities, and the influence of the national culture.

Think seriously about organizational culture every time you are promoted. When you move up, the culture around you changes. You may be expected to behave in a more sophisticated way, to avoid certain expressions, to take certain subtle hints, to get to know certain people. Also, you can now have a different perspective on the culture you're leaving behind. If you will be managing your former peers, that means a valuable perspective on the culture of your new subordinates.

What to Observe

As time passes, you will have ample opportunity to gain clues to your organization's culture. For example, what marginally useful people are allowed to hang on in their positions? Why haven't they been fired or transferred? An organization that lets useless employees hang on is likely to be protectively paternalistic. That's great in some ways, but if you'd like to introduce some innovations and make a splash, you've picked a difficult place to do it. The same culture that protects its dinosaurs cannot be receptive to someone who will make their inefficiency more visible.

You can also learn something about the culture by noticing what tasks are allowed to go undone, or to be done poorly or only sporadically. A restaurant in which the service is speedy but the cook takes liberties with the quality of ingredients has quite a different culture than does a restaurant where service is slow but the cook is perfectionistic about the food. The two places have two different ego ideals: one is to provide convenience and the other is to provide the highest-quality product, whether the customer is still in a mood to appreciate it or not.

Another clue to culture is the organization's stupid practices that are enshrined in tradition. For example, a perfectionistic culture, which reflects the perfectionism of the organization's founder or some other significant leader, often acquires habits that outlast their time. Though they may seem to the incoming manager to be bad habits that need to be shaken out, they might also indicate a dedication and attentiveness that can be put to better use.

On the other hand, what seems to be a very sloppy culture may be the remnant of a period in which the organization was smaller but growing quickly. Success convinced people that they didn't need forms and protocols. The sensitive boss will not attack the laid-back culture without acknowledging it and trying to tap the drive and pride that spawned it.

Friendships to some extent reflect the organization's culture. Therefore, observe them if you hope to make a career in the organization. Humor, for example, is usually a revealing aspect of group camaraderie and organizational culture.

An atmosphere in which people feel abused by higher management may produce camaraderie among people who otherwise wouldn't like each other much. Close as they feel to each other at work, they don't socialize with each other outside of work. Or, take a company where the conversations are almost always about work, even when people go out to lunch together. At one company, even major news events such as assassinations simply weren't discussed at work. That's probably a fairly uptight organizational culture.

Mapping Cultural Differences

You will find it useful to map the cultural differences of different units in the organization. For example, the values and orientation of a research department will differ significantly from those of a sales organization. The time orientations and specific behaviors will vary as well. To describe these differences is like taking depth soundings of the sea and laying them out on a naval chart. In order to navigate an organization successfully, you should have some accurate sense of what these cultural differences are and what difference they make when you have to deal with people having those differences.

Summing the Parts

As with significant incidents of an individual's behavior, a single observation of organizational culture doesn't tell you anything for sure. The perfectionistic culture described earlier might also have resulted from an overcontrolling power elite that forced subordinates to watch their every step. The sloppy culture might simply have grown out of a period of weak leadership or demoralization due to a business slump. You need to take many readings, many soundings, and over time see what they have in common.

With that warning in mind, here are some other observations you can make:

- ☐ Do people in your organization or department gossip? About what? How well do they know their bosses? Do they swear? How do they dress?
- ☐ What kind of furniture does the company provide? What perks?
- ☐ What and who are considered funny? Do people laugh during meetings? What and who are considered sleazy?
- ☐ What is the rhythm of the work day, week, and month? Are there regular breaks, parties, celebrations? Do they take place at work or after hours?
- ☐ Do people talk to each other in the halls? Are important decisions ever made at lunch, in the bathroom, or in the hall? What kind of language does the organization use in official communications: formal, bureaucratic, slang, macho, military, or athletic?
- ☐ How are new people helped to fit in? Are some left to fend for themselves?
- ☐ What gets you in the most trouble? Do people hold grudges? Do others try to mediate conflicts or are two people left to fight it out themselves?
- ☐ How do you know when you're in higher management's good graces? Who gets promoted—and what do they have in common?

Tracing the Organization's History

You will find it helpful to have a history of the organization. Many companies already have established histories, but other critical historical events are transmitted orally. Most people in most organizations don't know their organizational history. As a result, they don't know what the continuing and dominant themes in the organization have been, how the organization has developed, and why it's going in the direction that it is currently following. Sometimes, aspects of history like natural catastrophes, major fires, or financial emergencies have had a significant effect, or changes in management have turned the organization in new and different directions. All these events usually are accompanied by organizational folklore, reports and stories of key achievements or heroics that are passed from person to person, sometimes elaborated to make a better story.

It will be important to assess the major failures of the founders. What direction or directions did the organization take early on that have not been fruitful? What major investment was made early on that the organization finds necessary to continue even though it depletes resources and perhaps never will be fully successful?

What was pursued because of a founder's whim? What folly has entered the organizational lore? As a result, what directions did the organization take, or is it still taking, and what are the implications for you and the organization? I think, for example, of a decision made by an early petroleum pioneer not to go outside the boundaries of the United States. That decision prevented his company from developing sources of petroleum overseas when domestic sources began to dry up, and it was difficult for the company to compete with other companies that had such sources. Also, in recent years, Lee Iacocca admitted he made a big mistake funneling some of Chrysler's resources into activities other than those that would improve the competitive position of Chrysler automobiles. If he had invested that money in boosting his own organization's competitive position, presumably Chrysler would have been better able to compete against the Japanese.

Identifying the Movers and Shakers

If you're trying to map out the influentials in your organization, ask who are the people who get things done, regardless of their titles.

There are such people in every organization, and they are the motive power behind organizational accomplishments. If you ask that question of a range of people in the organization, you'll soon have a map of the movers and shakers and the people, therefore, that you should be involved with if at all possible.

Preparing a Behavioral Job Description

A way to become sensitive to your relationships with others in the organization is to prepare a behavioral job description. To do that, on a blank sheet of paper make three columns, headed "Who," "Expectations," and "Attitude." Then list under "Who" all of the people you are in touch with in the course of your job. These would include your boss and perhaps a range of others above your boss; people who may monitor your work—for example, safety experts; those whose task is to inform you, such as people in communications; those who exert some control over you, as, for example, auditors; those whose role is to advise you, such as lawyers; those whose task is to know what you're doing and inform you about your progress; and so on. Beside each name, indicate what that person's role is with respect to you, whether managerial, monitoring, informing, controlling, advising, or something else. Then, under "Expectations," list what this particular person expects of you. In the third column, describe the attitude each person has toward your role and your work.

For example, your boss may have given you specific assignments having specified time limits and resource use. You may have agreed with her on budgets, projections, profitability, and volume. Those are specific expectations. Your boss may take a relatively casual attitude about your responsibilities, leaving you free to do them and to report when they're accomplished. Another boss might be looking much more closely over your shoulder.

You may be required to respond to an auditor's request for information, or request to justify your expense account or limit the money you spend if there is a downturn in the economy. An auditor who is closely in touch with your boss, and who is meticulously detailed and rigid, may reinforce your boss's demands on you. Similarly, if you are in marketing, you may be advised by the company's legal counsel about the wording on a package, though you may not necessarily have to take that advice. You may have to inform the public relations department of a manufacturing blunder that necessitates a recall, so that they can represent the company adequately. If, however, there is a major tragedy, as in the case of the Tylenol scare and the Bhopal catastrophe, you might have to be directed by the legal and public relations people to reduce negative consequences.

Once you've laid out what the expectations of each of these persons are with respect to your own role, you can specify what kind of attitude you have to maintain toward them in order to meet their requirements and needs, and also to enlist their help as you may need it. If you want to extend the behavioral job description further, add additional columns to define *your* expectations of and attitudes toward these same people.

Drawing this kind of a map will make it possible to be more sensitive to the nuances and differences of behavior in these relationships. Also, doing so will give you a basis for negotiating differences between yourself and others when their concerns and yours are in conflict. And you will know what the possibilities are for you in that organization.

CHAPTER 6

Improving Skills and Attitudes for Personal Effectiveness

According to James Bowditch, associate dean of the Boston College Business School, an increasing number of undergraduate business majors have been adding second majors in the College of Arts and Sciences. The trend is increasing because wise employers seek well-rounded people with intellectual interests, not just entry-level skills. Business school administrators are avidly encouraging this trend because of the changing needs of the management profession, the job market, and the desire of the management students for a more broad-based, competitively advantageous education.[1]

In another, yet related, context GE chairman John F. Welch, Jr., has told his managers, "We cannot afford management styles that suppress and intimidate." Instead, he called on his managers to adopt a set of "soft concepts," including having "the self-confidence to empower others and behave in a boundaryless fashion." Trust and respect between workers and managers is essential, he has said. Managers must be "open to ideas from anywhere."[2]

In his view, the sort of manager who meets the miracle goals but has old-fashioned attitudes is the major obstacle to carrying out these concepts. "This is the individual who typically forces performance out of people rather than inspires it: the autocrat, the big shot, the tyrant."

This demand by their chief executive will require many GE managers to change their behaviors because GE has been managed relatively autocratically for many years. Indeed, Welch himself has been criticized for his autocratic management style. His change of managerial tune will become a model for other executives, for many companies emulate GE. That means more and more people will have to learn new behaviors. For most, that will be difficult; for some, impossible. Nevertheless, each must try to do so.

These trends will likely spread. The reasons are fairly self-evident: As the world becomes more complex, those who would succeed in it must have an increasingly broad frame of reference. They need to be able to grasp and understand the many complex forces that have an effect on society at large, as well as specific organizations and particularly organizational and occupational roles. They need to be able to anticipate some of the significant changes that are occurring, to observe trends, to infer likely consequences, and to develop modes of coping effectively with them.

Those who have gotten training in a given discipline, often sacrificing their undergraduate opportunity for education to training, frequently find themselves at an advantage when it comes to entry-level jobs. However, the higher they rise in an organization, or even in a given profession, the greater their need to think conceptually, to anticipate events, and to choose optimal courses of action. Also, the higher they rise in an organization, or even in their given profession, the more important their interpersonal relationships become. That means they have to understand themselves and understand other people as individuals, and also—in a diverse world where there is great ethnic mobility—understand cultural differences, historical antecedents, entrenched values, and even tribal animosities. All these become the social crosscurrents of the workplace and, increasingly, of the marketplace as well.

A good manager these days must be a sociologist, psychologist, economist, linguist, and anthropologist. Every manager who goes to a country other than her own or has foreign suppliers or customers necessarily must develop these kinds of knowledge. Even tourists who are only temporarily in a distant land usually need guidebooks to understand what they are seeing and hearing.

The fundamental requirement for continued career progress is, therefore, both breadth and depth of understanding. Each of us must fight the propensity to be content with learning more and more about less and less, to become more specialized at the expense of perspective. In recent years, we have seen the failure of large American business organizations to compete effectively because their leadership, too technically narrow, could not adequately perceive trends and directions, or, despite much marketing research, sense quickly enough what customers wanted. Only the threatening competition of the Japanese finally awakened much American business leadership to the need to serve the customer and to begin to understand the motivation of employees.

As components of organizations become smaller and more nimble in their flexible response to both customer needs and employee motivations, people who would build careers in such organizations have to develop for themselves a solid base of understanding from which they might pursue different career paths as compelling change requires. Most people do not practice the discipline in which they majored in college. Many shift focus and role again and again in large organizations. Of course, people who become proficient specialists are always in demand. But if they cannot become generalists, then, whether curators in museums, engineers in corporations, or nurses in hospitals, their advance to higher managerial responsibilities is inhibited. A solid educational base, therefore, is the foundation of flexibility. It will not replace wisdom or intuition, but both derive significantly from that fountainhead.

On Being Well Read

Monsanto's CEO, Richard Mahoney, a devoted reader, regards reading skill as essential for success: "People who read more seem to have that marvelous ability to see linkages between unrelated events. That's the most important quality an executive can have."[3] Research backs up Mahoney's point. In general, the higher a person's reading skills, the higher his professional achievement.

Improving Language Skills

One is always presenting oneself, and as managers move up, they do so increasingly through language: reports, letters, presentations, and interviews. Participants in our officer seminars generally have better language skills than those in our general manager seminars. So it's clear that language plays a part in promotion, whether or not it's a stated criterion.

To improve your vocabulary and grammar:

☐ Read well-written periodicals such as *The Economist,* the *New York Times,* the *Wall Street Journal, Time,* and the *Christian Science Monitor.*

☐ As you read, look up words you don't know in the dictionary. Write them down with brief definitions to help fix them in your memory.

☐ For spelling, use the "bet your life" test. If you won't bet your life on a spelling, look it up. Use this rule for grammar and meaning, too. Not having had Latin is no excuse for misusing "data," "media," "criteria," and their singulars—it's a reason for extra care.

☐ Keep a list of grammar rules you never get straight, such as when to use "that" or "which," how to form possessives of plurals and names, or when to double the final consonant before adding "ing."

You'll still make mistakes. A reasonable goal is not to make the same mistake twice.

Heightening Your Powers of Observation

Do you feel that you don't notice enough about other people? Is your career in danger of stalling because you keep missing clues that they're angry, bored, or offended?

Writer and radio commentator Daniel Pinkwater began his career as an artist, and he, too, felt he wasn't seeing enough. He trained himself by watching the sun set every day for a year—just watching, carefully, from start to finish. Decades later, he was still able to remember some individual sunsets.[4] In the same vein, I used to stop to watch the surface of the Charles River between Cambridge and Boston each morning on my way to teach at the Harvard Business School. Wind, rain, and sun changed the river surface daily, and it came to have its own personality in my mind.

You might try a similar exercise by sitting in a restaurant alone for a half hour and doing nothing but watch other people. Don't read the paper, don't think about anything. Just watch. Observe how many different expressions a person makes, even during a simple conversation about the weather. After you've done this a number of times, see if it helps you notice people's faces at work. Are you seeing their nonverbal messages?

Our brains are usually so busy that we screen out much of our sensory input. That's why artists and writers go to great efforts to teach themselves to see. Managers might benefit from some of the same discipline.

Using Aggression to Positive Effect

What does it take to get ahead in organizations? It may or may not require you to compete and get into conflict with your coworkers. It will certainly require you to take action about problems and to require that others take action.

Taking action—causing something to change the way you want it to—is a form of attack. Its energy derives from what psychoanalytic psychologists assume to be a biological drive that we refer to as aggression. Aggression may or may not be "against" other people, but it is always against what the individual feels is a problem to be mastered. So when we ask in our *Levinson Letter*, "How does the person handle aggression?" we're asking how he or she tries to solve problems, master new skills, make sense of confusing information, or improve the grammar and style of a report, as well as how this individual manages anger or conflict.

What's Appreciated? What Works? What's Possible?

As Elliott Jaques has pointed out, work in an organization can be defined as the application of aggressive effort to an organizational goal.[5] But since aggression includes so many kinds of behavior, you need to know what kind of aggression is appropriate for you in your position in your organization. Think of three overlapping circles:

What the organization values. Who is looked up to in your unit or in your organization? How do those people use aggression? Were they the fiercest competitors, the ablest politicians, the people who made the fewest enemies, the people most likely to get results?

What actually works. This, of course, may be quite different from what the organization values. When a culture of in-house competition pervades a retail chain, it is eventually reflected in poor service and a sinking reputation. Sometimes an organization values forms of aggression that once worked well, even later on when new forms of aggression are needed. For example, blatant forms of financial manipulation were encouraged in some major Wall Street firms. Some prominent banks compensated their officers for making large loans, even when they were unlikely to be repaid. Later, under the threat of government action, the focus of aggression shifted from manipulation to self-control in the form of greater internal enforcement of rules and regulations. Indeed, some brokerage firms began to sell their ethical positions by advertising the integrity of their relationships with their customers.

What you can do. You may enjoy fighting a mechanical problem to the death, but hate hassling with people. You may be decisive in firing a subordinate who performed poorly, but wobbly in negotiating a contract.

In a given situation, if your choice of action (or inaction) lies in the intersection of what the organization values and what you can do, but not what really works, you will be valued but ultimately ineffective. An example is the abrasively tough manager working for an abrasively tough boss. He will thrive, but will also be contributing to the company's future troubles with its employees.

If your actions lie in the intersection of what works and what you can do, but not what the organization values, you will be unappreciated and frustrated. If you can learn some of the behavior that is valued, you may be able to gain enough credibility over time to take a stand and change what the organization values.

If you try to do what the organization values or what you know will really work, but this just isn't what you are able to do, you will be seen as ineffective, a loser. You need help from your boss, and perhaps from a mentor or additional training, to learn these behaviors that don't come naturally to you. In some cases, you will have to go back to school for further education.

If all is well and your actions lie in the intersection of all three categories, you are in tune with your organization. This is not a rare celestial event; it happens all the time.

Shopping for an Aggressive Style

To gauge where and how well you can fit in your organization, begin by examining the organization's preferred style of aggression:

First, do your own organizational diagnosis as suggested in Chapter 5. How are problems identified and attacked? By cooperative groups? By lone gunmen? By appealing to someone higher up? Is there a lot of wheel spinning? Is there a tendency toward precipitate or impulsive actions? How are decisions made? Is there debate? Is the debate well managed and productive, or angry and divisive? Does the organization see itself as having enemies? Do parts of the organization see each other as enemies? Are these enmities acted on?

Second, learn as much as you can about the history of the organization, especially the characters of its founders.

Third, pay attention to key people's verbal styles and slang. Are insults an accepted form? Does management favor military or sports-inspired terminology? Is there much humor? Humor is often an expression of criticism or disapproval; it's healthy humor when it serves to sharpen perceptions rather than being a tool to hurt other people's feelings.

Now, examine your own preferred style of aggression:

Take the questions about the organization listed above and ask them about yourself. How do you make decisions? Do you see yourself as having enemies? How do you solve problems? What do you do when someone makes you mad?

Review the feedback you've gotten from bosses and others over the years. What were they telling you about your style of expressing aggression?

You may come to the conclusion that you haven't got what the organization wants. If you'd like to have what you currently lack—say, you'd like to be a lot more assertive in meetings, or more decisive, or less impulsive—select someone on whom you can model yourself. If possible, find a mentor and make it clear that this is what you want to learn.

If you can't get anywhere by your own efforts, try some professional help. You may be asking the impossible of yourself, but it may be that you can change with some assistance. It's also a good idea to have friends who know what you are trying to do and who will give you psychological support by listening while you talk and giving you honest feedback.

Being Politically Effective

You can't duck politics. In fact, the most frequently promoted managers seem to be the ones who spend the most time making contacts.[6] While these fast-track managers need other strengths, too, they take responsibility for letting people know what they can do. They don't kid themselves that their work will speak for itself.

For shy people, politics can be agony. How can they glad-hand when their severely self-critical superegos make them expect others to be as critical of them as they are of themselves? Ironically, it's this same sense of not being good enough that often pushes shy people to work hard and to produce so well.

If you (or a subordinate) are having trouble being politically effective, your career growth depends on addressing the problem. Begin by recognizing that good politicking is a skill, not a vice. Respect it. Figure out who the masters are in your organization and study them.

Next, mobilize your powerful superego to develop some political skills. Monitor your progress, preferably in writing. How frequent are your interactions with higher-ups? How often do you ask for help? (Shy people avoid asking for help, but without teachers and mentors, their career growth will be stymied.) When you do a good job, who finds out? How? How do you spend your lunch hours?

It helps to find a confidant to support and evaluate your efforts. Politics isn't inherently slimy. You don't have to become a smoothie or a backbiter. But you do have to blow your own horn a little or risk having your hard work overlooked and undervalued.

Using People to Get What You Want

When is it okay to use people to get what you want?

Take the case of Gene Roberts, former executive editor of *The Philadelphia Inquirer.* Roberts's 18 years at the paper had brought an astonishing 17 Pulitzer Prizes and put the local competition out of business.

Roberts manipulated and exploited his people without demoralizing them.[7] He could do this because:

☐ The manipulation wasn't destructive. Roberts didn't work against subordinates' self-interest but instead helped them move toward their ego ideals.

☐ He knew when to stop. Even Roberts's critics don't tell horror stories about his behavior or methods.

☐ The manipulation was perceived as being in the service of an organizational purpose (to be a great and successful newspaper) rather than in service of Roberts's personal needs. Everyone knew that the *Inquirer* was trying "to assess and report the news, and to write, edit, display, and deliver it so artfully as to virtually guarantee readership."[8]

- ☐ Roberts encouraged people to speak out. He valued the messenger. So people didn't feel helpless or powerless.
- ☐ He hired strong subordinate managers, not the yes-men and yes-women an extreme narcissist attracts.

Succeeding in Unknown Territory

We love it when a novice walks in and does what the experts said couldn't be done. If you are thrust into such a role—"I don't know what I'm doing, but I'm trying to do it"—here are the elements of success:

- ☐ Know your goal. You may not know how you're going to achieve it, but know clearly what you're after. Your goal may change along the way, but it should never be vague.
- ☐ Gain relevant experience. What's relevant is not always obvious. One manager of a technology division found himself drawing heavily on his earlier experience as a medical student, because that's when he'd learned to absorb huge amounts of information under pressure. Some skills, like managing change effectively, are always relevant. Look for opportunities to manage change. Few do it well.
- ☐ Consult others for advice and reality checking. Build a network you can count on for information, support, and validating (or debunking) your judgments.
- ☐ Enjoy the process of learning. You'll give yourself a big boost in self-esteem. I think of a professional musician who told a friend about to start piano lessons, "Be sure to pay attention to how your fingers learn. It's amazing."

In short, use what you know how to do to do what you don't know how to do.

Learning New Behaviors

When you start a new managerial job, you tend to do what you did before until you find out the hard way that new behaviors are required. You may have to run into a few walls before the lesson sinks in, and both you and your boss will wonder why. Often, it's because of your unconscious fear of losing your identity if you cease doing what you did well. Bruce Springsteen spoke of having to leave behind the blue-collar world which was the root of his musical success. "You can't say, 'Well, I'm the same old guy I used to be.' You have to go ahead and meet that person who you're becoming and accept whatever that's about."[9]

How do you do that? Make a differential diagnosis: precisely how is this job different from the last one? Focus on required behavior, because that's what's most frightening to alter. If you had a behavioral job description—a set of specific, concrete answers to the question "How are you expected to perform the various aspects of this job?"—before, go over it sentence by sentence and compare. Say you were expected to keep your boss on top of fast-changing situations, for which she was grateful. Will that be true now? Your new boss might see that as an intrusion or as a misuse of your time. If you didn't have a behavioral job description and don't have one for your new job, then write them yourself and make the comparison.

How to Behave Among the Successful and Powerful

Executives who grew up poor may carry their poverty, emotionally, for life. Despite even spectacular achievements, they often report feeling like frauds once they've passed their father's (or for women, their mother's) level of success (see Chapter 3). And they really are at a professional disadvantage if they never learned (as richer children often did) from a successful father/mother/identification figure how to behave in the milieu of the successful and powerful. If you're an executive in this fix, help yourself by doing the following:

- ☐ Finding a mentor who has overcome similar difficulties.
- ☐ Talking about anxieties with a friend you trust or a professional counselor.
- ☐ Learning the social skills. Superficial polish is a first step for which training programs are available.
- ☐ Learning language skills. When someone confuses "anecdote" for "antidote," or says "axed" for "asked," or speaks of "data" as singular and "phenomenon" as plural, that says he or she

simply hasn't learned English adequately or correctly. When one is sensitive to such issues, one can correct oneself.

☐ Not apologizing or seeking reassurance except from people you know you can trust. Calling attention to your minor mistakes or encouraging others to collude with you in your self-criticism can hurt your career. It also tips off exploitative people about your vulnerabilities.

☐ Channeling some of your anger about what you missed into being an identification figure for your own children.

☐ Celebrating your achievements. Find someone—a family member or friend—who'll help you focus on what you've achieved. Reward yourself when things go well. Buy something you've always wanted, take a day off, go out to dinner. The treat will serve to remind you that your success is something to be proud of.

Coping with Problems at Work

If you never have problems at work, we'll gladly refund the price of this book. Otherwise, let's look at how to cope.

Try listing all the problems you deal with, both current (you're already unhappy with a new hire) and chronic (your boss is always dumping last-minute rush jobs on you). Then write down a few sentences about how you cope. For example, you may cope with your new hire by complaining to others, by trying your best to teach him, or by preparing to fire him.

Examine your ways of coping, using these criteria:

☐ Are they effective in the long term or only in the short term? Complaining to your boss is fine if your boss acts. If he or she won't, complaining may still serve if it makes you feel better and your boss doesn't mind. But it isn't making the problem go away.

☐ Are you replacing one problem with another?

☐ Are you learning anything through the way you cope? Coping with his fear of a coming appraisal by talking to friends, a manager picked up some helpful tips about how to act during the appraisal and how to interpret it.

☐ Do you cope at someone else's expense by taking out your

anger on others or by avoiding problems that then land on someone else's lap?

☐ Are you flexible in the way you cope? Do you cope with most problems the same way, be it "damn the torpedoes" or evasive maneuvers? It's not even wise to cope with the same problem the same way, because circumstances change and because you don't learn anything new.

☐ Do you fawn upward and dump downward? Some people go to great lengths to please their bosses while being hostile, critical, and unsupportive of their subordinates. Sometimes they exploit their subordinates in the interest of pleasing their bosses. That mode of coping makes it impossible to develop constituencies of subordinates who become one's most ardent supporters and collaborators. When the need to please power figures is so important, one has little time or energy for anyone else.

If you're not satisfied with your coping style, perform the same analysis on some other people and see what you can learn from their styles.

Combating Job Stress

Research indicates that stress is a function of lack of control (real or perceived) over the threats and tasks one faces. That being so, what can you do about job stress besides quit? You can exert control over two important factors: your own actions and expectations.

☐ Control your actions. In *Controlling Work Stress,* Michael Matteson and John Ivancevich pinpoint time management, problem solving, and assertiveness as areas where controlling oneself translates into more control over the environment and therefore less stress.[10] Do you work on one task when you know a more important one is waiting? Do you do things the hard way on your computer because you've got a mental block about reading the manual? Do you get sidetracked because you can't tell people you're busy?

☐ Control your expectations. This can mean admitting how much you can do during a day versus how much you feel you ought to be able to do. It can also mean taking the philosophical view that some delay, confusion, and failure are inevitable, so one shouldn't be upset by them. Those with

72

family responsibilities will have to make specific plans to budget and control their time for their families. Despite all the talk about men sharing family burdens, most don't. Those may have to discuss these issues with their husbands or partners.

The dangerous—even fatal—effects of a lifetime of stress are increasingly well documented. Much of your work environment is outside your control, so these two constructive approaches make more and more sense.

When you do experience stress, what can you do to improve how you handle it? One thing, as suggested in Chapter 2, is to establish a good support system that can provide both emotional and practical support. All of us should have at least one confidant to whom we can tell our troubles and joys with something approaching their true intensity. Usually this would be a family member, but if you don't have—and can't establish—such a relationship with a family member, try to do so with a close friend. In addition to a confidant, it's important to maintain family ties, or to develop some kind of substitute for family if you don't have one, and to continue building friendships throughout your life. In essence, we need relationships that provide affection, love, care, concern—the things that enable us to know that we are valued and esteemed by one or more other people. We also need people who can mobilize resources— monetary, technical, educational—to help us solve problems. Friends, doctor, therapist, business partner, auto mechanic, lawyer, pastor— all are part of a person's support system.

A second thing you can do is learn to recognize when your thinking capacities are being affected by stress, and then initiate contacts with appropriate members of your support system. Asking for help is not a trait for which managers are widely known, but it's an important one to develop. The manager who keeps going in spite of everything looks like a real hero—until he or she makes a disastrous mistake while not thinking clearly due to stress, or is clearly disabled either psychologically or physically, leaving the unit leaderless.

Getting Out of a Slump

You're in a slump. But hold on before you switch jobs, take up skydiving to energize yourself, or buckle down to work twice as hard. Are you really in a slump, or just feeling insecure? If your boss's criticism has become vague or infrequent, he or she probably notices a drop in performance but doesn't want to confront you. If subordinates no longer seek your advice, you may be slipping. But if people rate your performance as highly as ever, you may be overly self-critical.

If your slump is real, pinpoint what work is stalled and whom it involves. For example, if work with a specific peer is suffering, you may be angry with him and be taking it out on the work. Discuss with him what's angering you, but don't accuse him of causing your problem. That will make him defensive and make you look like a whiner. Be prepared to hear some criticism from him.

What was happening when you started to slip? Managers often go into slumps after reorganizations because they didn't get the position or the resources they wanted. Often that slump is a product of their rage—their intense anger not only with higher management, but also with themselves for being in that vulnerable position. In such a case, you need to complete your grieving process. You may also be genuinely overloaded and need time to master new responsibilities or to train subordinates so you can delegate more to them.

If a specific kind of event, be it your annual appraisal or your family get-together at Christmas, always brings on a slump, talk to a therapist to find out why you are so vulnerable to that particular stimulus. This may only require some counseling, not full-scale psychotherapy. But if your slumps occur cyclically, without any particular provocation, I suggest psychotherapy. The sooner you begin it, the sooner you have a chance to get this monkey off your back.

In whatever case, talk to your boss if he or she is someone in whom you can confide. Your boss probably already knows you're having troubles, and it's better if you mention it first and show that you want to do better.

CHAPTER 7

Keeping Your Work Load Under Control

It is no longer possible, if even it ever was, to put yourself in the hands of an organization and count on that organization to look out for your personal career interests. You have to take active charge of your career and not let yourself be buffeted about by fate. This includes taking steps to ensure that your work load does not become an unmanageable burden.

Setting Reasonable Expectations

"Success," says Wendy Reid Crisp, director of the National Association for Female Executives, "is what happens while you are trying very hard to be as good as you think everyone else is."[1] It's natural to compare yourself with others, but it can become self-defeating. As children, we internalize our parents' expectations of us. Those expectations become a part of our ego ideal—our image of ourselves at our future best. Throughout our lives we compare our actual progress with our ego ideal, and judge ourselves harshly when we don't live up to that ideal. Yet we don't always judge others as harshly, so they may seem to be doing much better.

One reason I encourage peer support groups is so managers can see just how hard they are on themselves. You will find your peers judge themselves as harshly as you judge yourself, and may be as intimidated by you as you are by them. If you feel you can't talk to them, try writing down your work goals and asking your boss how realistic they are. In my organizational diagnosis course, I taught students to formulate a prognosis: What can I reasonably expect of myself and of this management—given our skills, limits, and resources—and in what period of time? That sets reasonable boundaries. We tend to expand our expectations with our achievements, and forget how far we have exceeded our original goals. By writing them down you have undeniable proof of your success.

Refusing Unwanted Assignments

Are you the one they always ask to organize the company picnic or chair the annual exhibit for customers? Put together a few numbers after hours? Adopt someone else's problem employee into your department for some remedial development?

If you're often stuck with unwanted assignments:

- ☐ Ask yourself why you always say yes. Do you have an excessive need to please, to buy love? True, your boss has the power to recommend raises, promotions, and transfers, and it's wise to keep him or her happy, but if you're swamped with busywork, you're probably neglecting more important aspects of your job and your own development. You're almost guaranteed to lose in the long run.
- ☐ Evaluate your boss's next request. Before you say yes, ask yourself if the assignment will teach you anything. Will it bring you into contact with new people or someone you might learn from? Is it of vital importance to the company? How much time will it take?
- ☐ Learn to say no. If that's a new skill for you, talk it over with a friend first to get comfortable with the idea. It becomes easier with practice.

Avoiding Being Swamped

"After single-handedly defeating Nazi Germany and Imperial Japan, . . . I decided to devote myself to finding a cure for all diseases known to Man. . . . However, before I was able to do this, I found that my country still needed me to serve as President of the United States."[2] That's the way it goes. Just when you're already swamped with work, somebody hands you another job and it can't wait.

Being swamped is a universal experience of managers. It affects both the quality of their work and the quality of their lives and the lives of their families. The manager who comes home too tired to talk or even stay awake is a frustration to his or her spouse and children. The manager who never has time to talk or help subordinates deprives them of the support and development they expect and need. And the subordinate who is always carrying the world on his or her shoulders is an obstacle to the boss—who may feel guilty about assigning more work—and an irritant to coworkers.

Reasons for Overloading Yourself with Work

Many managers swamp themselves by getting in their own way. What ought to be a manageable work load becomes an ever-growing pile on the desk and a pain in the neck. For them, being swamped is characterological—that is, part of their unconsciously motivated pattern of behavior. This pattern is the individual's preferred means of handling unconscious motivations and adapting them to the outside world. But sometimes this behavior interferes with work and relationships. Examples of unconscious motivations and resulting characterological behaviors that cause managers to overload themselves with work include:

Unconscious guilt. Some people carry a great load of unconscious guilt, which begins in early childhood (see Chapter 3). The causes are various, and, whatever the cause, certain people unconsciously consider themselves bad people who deserve to be punished. If the world doesn't oblige by punishing them, they punish themselves. This may take the form of self-inflicted failure—botching up work, forgetting details, procrastination, or taking on so many tasks that they cannot possibly finish them. All these behaviors swamp the manager and ensure the anger of both boss and coworkers; thus the "guilty" person is punished. In most cases, professional help is needed to get at the unconscious sources of chronic self-destructive behavior. But many managers would rather keep squeaking by, perpetually swamped, than attempt psychotherapy. And our culture favors the notion that people—especially men—should pull themselves up by their own bootstraps.

Fear of success. Some managers are unconsciously afraid to succeed because it would represent the defeat of a parent—which to their unconscious mind may be equivalent to destroying the parent. These are among the people who never live up to their potential. One of the classic symptoms is chronic procrastination; another is almost but never quite finishing tasks. Both behaviors cause work to pile up unnecessarily.

When the behavior is not characterological, some people have been able to conquer procrastination by sheer willpower, telling themselves to "do it now!" One technique that can help is to make a catalogue of the evasive maneuvers you usually employ, such as getting up from your desk, reading, eating, talking to people, and so on. That makes it easier to catch yourself and tell yourself, "We know what you're up to, you're not fooling anybody." But if the behavior is too deeply rooted, professional help may be necessary.

Noncompulsiveness. "Compulsive" is a derogatory label now, but it takes a certain amount of compulsion, or single-mindedness, to focus one's efforts effectively. People who can't be single-minded have trouble organizing tasks, establishing priorities, and finishing work. They may be capable, but they're all over the place. They may work hard, but it never seems to add up.

Need to be loved. Anyone who can't turn others down soon finds himself or herself swamped. Others learn where they can dump unwanted tasks. A major psychological source of this behavior is a need to be loved. This results from the unconscious fear that one will be unloved and abandoned should one fail to please others, so the person cannot make appropriate use of aggression. He or she cannot say no, and allows subordinates to pass the buck for making decisions and taking risks. People who feel that others' affection for them must be earned over and over cannot distinguish between a request and a demand, so they feel put upon even by suggestions that have no real force. The irony is that such "people-pleasing" often backfires. At first such a person is very popular, but coworkers come to have contempt for a sucker, however charming and useful. Besides, the person often can't keep all the promises he or she has made.

Perfectionism. Much behavior consists of people's attempts to achieve their ego ideals—their images of themselves as the best they could be. Extremely high ego ideals drive some managers to work as much as humanly possible in order to achieve perfection, so they are often swamped. These managers need their bosses to define explicit boundaries—what the manager is responsible for and what he or she is not responsible for. Unless the latter is spelled out and enforced, perfectionistic managers keep taking on more tasks.

Self-image. Some people deliberately take on the overworked role because it makes them heroic in their own eyes and, they hope, in others'. They are like the character in Arthur Miller's play *The Crucible* who exhorted his executioners to pile on "more weight." Unfortunately, most people who do this come off looking like fools, not heroes. Some managers have ego ideals that demand that they constantly bear great responsibility. They can make sure to do so by letting work pile up so that they constantly have a great load on their shoulders. Others respond to their own sense of inadequacy by reaction formation—that is, acting out just the opposite of what they feel. So this kind of manager acts as if it's the subordinates who are inadequate and only he or she is competent to do the work. Oddly enough, some managers use procrastination or failure to finish as ways to enhance their self-images. They may be able to build up high expectations and make themselves feel in demand. The fame of novelists J. D. Salinger and Thomas Pynchon rests as much on how few and far between their works have been as on their quality.

Lack of self-confidence. One finds managers who really aren't swamped and are doing fine, but feel swamped. These people are likely to have low self-images; they aren't convinced of their own abilities. They learn and improve, but have a hard time recognizing and believing in the improvement. Sometimes they need a dramatic round of applause—such as winning an award—before they can believe in their own accomplishments. This tends to be more often true of women, who characteristically tend not to have spoken up as often in school as men. Historically, teachers seem to have preferred boys' responses in class to girls'. In business meetings, it's an old story that the male participants pay less attention to the females and that females get less floor time. Women, therefore, need more encouragement and support in such activities.

In some cases, when people learn a new skill, they're afraid they won't be able to assimilate the new information, so they get all flustered even though they're catching on. A math teacher described a student who finally learned to solve quadratic equations, but then reverted to her previous confusion. The student needed to be walked through many more examples before she would believe she could do it.

Overstimulation. People with a constant flow of ideas get into trouble when they can't manage them all. (That may have been what spurred Thomas Edison to invent the modern research laboratory, with teams of people working on his ideas.) Creative people often need someone they trust, either a boss or subordinate, to help them judge ideas and set priorities. Otherwise, they expand out of control. IBM's Thomas J. Watson, Jr., expected his executives to have the courage to tell him when one of his ideas was no good, so that he didn't waste time and resources on it.[3]

Failure to delegate. Delegation is one of the major activities a manager has to master—not only for the obvious purpose of getting all the work done, but also for the purpose of developing subordinates. What makes managers hold on unnecessarily to more than they can do? Some have so great a need to be in control that they can't bear to give the work away to anyone else. In other words, "This is my job and I'll do it." They don't want to be dependent on a subordinate. Some act this way out of narcissism, structuring the unit or organization to maximize their sense of being indispensable. In other cases, the manager fears competition with subordinates, insisting, "This is my job and no one but I can do it right." Such managers experience the competence of their people as a threat to their own. Some bosses are known to do all their subordinates' work over.

Unconscious guilt also makes it difficult for some managers to delegate. Those who unconsciously feel they are unworthy will behave as though they have no right to control others, even when their position gives them that right. So they find it very difficult to assign work, give direction, and set boundaries—and end up swamped.

The Organization as Culprit

Being swamped isn't always a result of characterological behavior. Organizational structure itself is frequently the culprit. Most organizations have too many levels. One result is that managers spend too much time in meetings and other activities just keeping up communication with other managers. Theoretically, downsizing and contraction ought to alleviate this problem. But often they have the opposite effect. That's because they aren't done logically, with attention to people's capacity for abstract thinking. Some managers will get stuck doing work that should be done by someone with a lower capacity for abstraction. They tend to put off this work because it bores them, and end up swamped. Others will be asked to do things at a higher level of abstraction than they can manage, and will be overwhelmed.

Furthermore, most organizations don't define functions well enough. Elliott Jaques defines work as the exercise of judgment within prescribed time limits.[4] If there's no time limit, the task hasn't been defined. This is often the case, with a predicable result: tasks pile up—especially the most difficult or emotionally uncomfortable ones.

One of the chief causes of managers being swamped is the lack of adequate performance appraisal and behavioral job descriptions. Without these, there cannot be a logical system for filling positions as they open. When a manager is simply moved up the ladder for good performance in his present role, there's a good chance he won't fit the new role, however much he might "deserve" it. In particular, the manager might lack the necessary capacity for abstract thinking, for handling complexity and ambiguity—in which case he will find himself in over his head. I have met many managers, even CEOs, who worked their way up and now have responsibilities they simply aren't intellectually equipped to handle. There they are—successful, swamped, and unhappy.

In many other ways, a poorly managed organization breeds swamped managers. Sometimes departments are understaffed, either to keep costs down or because higher management hasn't given attention to the department's growing work load. Not only are people overworked, but also they often have tasks pushed down to them that they aren't qualified to carry out. Usually they know it, but have no choice but to try.

Many managers endure repetitive periods of overwhelming work because the organization lets itself get into crises. This is usually the result of top management's failure to look ahead. Sometimes higher management tries to build morale by creating a pressure-cooker atmosphere. This can work for a while, but it's a quick fix with long-term costs.

In other cases, top management doesn't really know what it wants. Managers get swamped trying to keep up with changes in direction, or trying to cover all the bases when the direction is unclear. Higher management can't always help it. For example, companies that build or operate nuclear power plants are subject to the Nuclear Regulatory Commission's changing rulings, as well as to unpredictable legal outcomes. As more organizations try intrapreneurship (allowing certain employees to act as individual entrepreneurs within the company), more managers will be operating with less guidance—and a greater danger of being swamped.

We often see women and minority managers doing more work than they need to because they feel very insecure and need to have every base covered. They have good reason to feel that they're always being watched, that they have to do twice as much as white males, and that they have no leeway to make mistakes.

When a manager has just been hired or promoted, he or she frequently feels overwhelmed, especially when coming to a powerful position from the outside. He or she doesn't yet know which issues are most important, who is to be trusted for impartial judgment, who has more power than his or her title indicates, who's playing what games, and so on. Yet he or she must take charge and make decisions. One new manager insisted on seeing all subordinates' correspondence that left the office. It was an unpopular move, but it gave her an intensive education in what business was most important and how well individual subordinate managers handled things. Of course, she kept this up only for a while. Otherwise she would have become buried in everyone else's work.

Unless a person has been promoted past his or her level of competence, the experience of being swamped in a new role is usually temporary. What a manager needs under these circumstances are confidence in his or her own ability to catch up, support and guidance from his or her supervisor, and support from family and other trusted outsiders.

When Your Boss Is the Problem

Sometimes the problem is not the organization as a whole but the employee's boss in particular. For a variety of reasons, the boss may load too much work onto subordinates. He or she may be driven and perfectionistic and expect others to be the same, or may feel swamped and try to unload the work onto subordinates.

Some bosses simply don't know what they're supposed to be doing because they can't get clear direction from top management. So they pass the responsibility for setting direction (and the risks involved) on to their middle managers. That happened in one major company after deregulation turned everything upside down: many middle managers felt swamped trying to reinvent their jobs and do them at the same time. In other cases the boss may be inadequate, so subordinates end up picking up the slack. Either of these two situations can occur when people who were successful in one activity are put in charge of another about which they know little or nothing. If the person is a clever manipulator, subordinates may not realize they are being unfairly overburdened and instead will feel inadequate.

A boss may deliberately swamp subordinates as a demonstration of power. This can be the result of sheer narcissism, need to compensate for feelings of inadequacy, or a paranoid need to control others, who are seen as hostile and potentially dangerous if not tightly controlled. In some cases, the underlying issue is rivalry: the boss needs to sabotage subordinates to feel assured of his or her own superiority. This is a common behavior, though often rationalized or unrecognized, even by the victims.

So-called "tough bosses" are notorious for keeping subordinates swamped. Managers never know what will be demanded of them and have to be prepared for everything all the time. John Teets, CEO of Greyhound, once asked a manager the exact price of certain condiments in Belgium, then stopped the whole meeting while the man ran back to his office for the figures.[5] Another CEO gets up at 5 A.M. and immediately starts telephoning subordinate executives.

Swamp Reclamation

The first step in getting out of the swamp is to find out exactly why you are there. This requires outside perspective from such people as your boss, his or her boss, your peers, or a company human resources person. Get some feedback on whether your work load really is too much, or whether you're not going about it efficiently. It will also help to talk to your spouse or a trusted friend, and to consider whether you are chronically swamped in your private life as well. That's an indication that characterological behavior is at work. All these perspectives taken together will help you triangulate your problem and decide how much of it you should blame on yourself. Outside perspective is necessary to compensate for how hypercritical most of us are toward ourselves. Our feelings of unconscious guilt and our ego ideals tend to act as a kangaroo court—other people are more likely to give us a fair trial.

On the other hand, most people think they're going about things rationally even when they're not. They can't see the illogic in what they do, even when the results repeatedly disappoint them. Besides, self-detrimental behaviors are usually the products of strong psychological needs, so when people are first presented with an outside critique they often reject it, saying the observer "doesn't understand." As the person seeking help, you must prepare yourself to hear things you won't like to hear and to have your cherished ways challenged. Remember that something must be wrong—or you wouldn't have a problem—and be willing to consider that you may be part of that something.

The next step is to get a fix on your boss. Use the method we use in our case studies: ask how he or she handles affection, aggression, dependency, and ego ideal. What does it take to make your boss pleased with himself? What does she do to be liked? How does he react to frustration? What gets on her nerves?

If your boss is the problem, or part of the problem, you will need to speak to him or her. Explain that you're having trouble getting everything done and would like some clarification about the priorities. Sometimes the boss may not realize you are overworked, or thinks you already know which tasks could be put off. But if your boss is trying to exploit you or is on a power trip or says things that only make you feel more inadequate without offering any help, you may have to say no to some assignments or try talking to his or her superior. But before you do that, get a good reading on your boss's standing in the organization. If he or she is highly valued for years of success, or has powerful political connections to top management, there's little use in trying to fight. You'll be better off leaving and making a new start elsewhere.

Unless your boss is bent on mistreating you, you will have a much better chance of improving if he or she is aware of your effort and is actively on your side. He or she might decrease your work load or might assist you in planning your time, choosing priorities, and resisting inappropriate requests. It also helps if the boss includes this problem and your efforts to solve it in performance appraisal. When people view this kind of effort to improve as part of their job, it means that working toward their ego ideal is part of their job. And striving for the ego ideal is the most powerful motivation there is.

If the situation calls for a major change, such as getting professional help, quitting, or relocating, it is essential to talk things over with your spouse or partner to enlist his or her support.

Above all, it is essential that you do not deny reality. Time after time, I meet managers who know what's wrong but are still hoping someone (such as myself) can show them which magic button to push in order to change their bosses, their subordinates, or themselves. There are no such magic buttons. To believe in them results in the inexcusable squandering of one's own and other people's time and opportunities.

Being swamped is a terrible feeling. It hangs over you and spoils everything. It may be worth the trouble for a specified period in order to learn a subject or to accomplish a specific task. But as a way of life, it's masochistic—whether you're taking the beating from your organization, your boss, or yourself.

CHAPTER 8

Cultivating Productive Relations with Coworkers

There is an increasing trend in business organizations to turn to teams, to draw people together from various disciplines at the earliest stages of product development rather than follow a linear sequence of design, production engineering, manufacturing, marketing, and sales. As more people operate in groups, obviously their ability to get along with each other becomes increasingly important. Team leaders need to understand the individuals in their groups and resolve differences between them. People from different disciplines and orientations must go to some length to understand each other's contribution to the total task or product. Each must also represent his or her own discipline vigorously but considerately.

At different times in the development of a product or a service, or even a marketing campaign, different people may take the leadership of a group as their own specialty becomes the valued knowledge necessary at any given point. People who can't work in teams will be extruded from them, or, if they are too disruptive, may find themselves no longer employed. Even at higher management levels, teams of people from different disciplines must be brought together to create and implement strategy. Higher-level managers are aware of the need to be in touch with what happens on the plant floor, and to enable people to solve as many of their problems as close to the point of contact with the product or customer as is possible.

This orientation is not limited to business organizations. The same issues prevail, for example, in multipastor churches, school-based management, and the growing number of small musical ensem-bles. In health care organizations, as more specialists demand their independent place in the sun, cooperation among them becomes increasingly important. And we have learned that if communities are to be resuscitated, the rescue effort must arise out of neighborhood organizations.

In sum, then, being able to work with others has become an increasingly critical aspect of your skill and competence. It will become even more important for your career in the future. Women generally have an advantage because their managerial style leans more heavily on skill in interpersonal relationships. Men may well learn from observing women in managerial roles.

Friendships at Work

When people speak of camaraderie, they mean the friendship formed between people doing a job together, whether they be soldiers in action, students studying for an exam, or you and your coworkers.

Such friendships occur naturally, unless company culture or policy inhibits it (for example, bureaucratic rules that require people to get in each other's way) or the larger, external culture inhibits it (for example, racism). The spontaneous development of camaraderie is a common theme of movies, from the unlikely band of loners in *The Wild Bunch* to the two ill-matched women (played by Bette Midler and Shelley Long) hunting down the same two-timing boyfriend in *Outrageous Fortune*. Over and over, we see characters who would normally ignore or despise each other, but who can't help getting to like each other under shared adverse circumstances. This happens for several reasons:

First, the scope of the relationship is limited. You're not married to your coworkers and you're not always exposed to the full range of their behaviors.

Second, aggression can be channeled into the work, or against some mutual enemy (be it the competition, or a deadline, or a flaw in the product). With no shared target, some of that aggression easily can be turned on each other.

Third, it's natural to seek friends at work because you're surrounded by people, so if you're not friendly with them, it can feel pretty lonely—like eating all your meals at a restaurant, but alone.

Fourth, people want pals at work to relieve the tension that work causes. A friendly face and a friendly chat are important antidotes to the worries, self-doubts, and aggravations that occur every day.

Limits on Camaraderie

The conditions that make for camaraderie also impose some limits on it. Basically, the friendship should not interfere with the group's ability to accomplish its goals. (Or, one might say the friendship should not burn its own house down.) That's what happens when psychological distance—the balance of affection, control, and privacy—is upset.

For one thing, friendship between a boss and a subordinate should not interfere with the boss's role as a boss. I don't say this because I worship hierarchy, but because the managerial role, when properly carried out, is essential for the group to accomplish its goals. It is also important for the individual subordinate; good supervision is a cornerstone of advancement.

When a subordinate says admiringly, "I don't think of her as a boss; she's a friend," that's a warning sign that important needs may not be met. People need behavior from their boss that doesn't belong in a friendship. They need someone who can insist on settlement of a conflict. They need someone whom they can see as having more power, both political and conceptual, than they, as long as that power is used to advance and protect their interests within the organization. They need someone who will give critical feedback and insist that it be heeded; a friend can give critical feedback, but usually doesn't demand change. In short, the boss can't do what he should do for subordinates if he feels limited to behavior appropriate to a friend.

Meanwhile, the organization needs a boss to promote only those people most qualified to do the job, a decision that can easily conflict with friendship. The organization may also need the boss to implement unpopular changes; these too will conflict with the promptings of friendship.

Also, the organization needs the boss to be an identification figure for subordinates. That becomes difficult or impossible for many subordinates when one or a few are perceived as favorites. You'd be surprised how often bosses are unaware that their behavior toward one person or group is seen as favoritism, when the boss didn't mean it that way. One boss often went to lunch with a particular group; the reason was simply that they all liked the same kind of food. But since a boss has equal responsibility to all subordinates, he must be equally accessible to them. Because accessibility is significantly in the mind of the subordinate, appearances are important.

Dealing with Sexual Attraction

Sexual attraction has even greater capacity to disrupt a supervisory relationship. The feelings are stronger and more private, and the degree to which others feel shut out is much greater.

If you are determined to get into such a relationship, it would be best if either you or your partner found a different role in the company. (But be wary of accomplishing this by promoting the person; that's likely to be perceived as favoritism.) Trying to stay where you are and get romantically and sexually involved is a case of trying to have it all at other people's expense—namely, the boss's other subordinates.

The Effects of Promotion

Many people are frustrated by the way promotion casts a shadow over friendship with former peers, even when the promotion is to a different unit. It is part of a boss's job not to become friendly with subordinates to the extent that he or she can't act against their wishes or even against their interests. If a new boss already has such friendships, it is an unspoken and painful part of the job to renegotiate those friendships. This is something that business schools and organizations don't teach you.

The best way to do it, in most cases, is to have a private talk with each person. Face the coming changes up front: you're going to miss sharing certain kinds of gossip, hanging out freely in each other's office, and so on. Too often, what happens is that there's a sort of silent confrontation over one of these issues, and both parties go away with hard feelings without ever having tried to settle it.

Making the Most of Being on a Team

Ask not what your team can do for you—but let's do ask what being on a team can do for your career development. The current vogue for operating in teams provides a greater opportunity to learn what others do in their work and also to build networks and constituencies. Other team members will want to know about what you do and also how they can call on you and your skills to help them in their efforts. One of the significant elements in choosing executives for given roles is who will likely follow them voluntarily, who are their constituents, and, therefore, who thinks well of them.

Your assignment to a special team or task group gives you opportunities to take certain kinds of risk with less actual risk, develop bonds of affection and camaraderie, and observe and understand group process, including your own characteristic behavior in groups.

Taking Risks

It's not that teams are risk-free environments. But if they are well run, they can provide a safe haven for brainstorming and creativity because team members are working largely with their peers and because they don't have to make final decisions alone.

An assignment to a team that includes people you don't normally work with is also an opportunity to try out different behaviors. We often see this when a teenager goes away to college: behaviors that seem to have been etched in stone suddenly vanish because the teenager is finally free of the context that stimulated those behaviors. In the same way, you might try out a less aggressive style of confrontation—or a more aggressive one—without the risk of having it flop with your everyday coworkers.

Whenever you try out a new idea or a new behavior, take notes:

- ☐ What did you do?
- ☐ How did you react to what you did? Were you scared—before, after, or both? Exhilarated? No big deal?
- ☐ How did people react? Describe this only in terms of what they did and said, not in your interpretation of same. That is, don't assume that you correctly read their minds.
- ☐ How did you react to their reactions? Were you embarrassed, pleased, angry, indifferent?

Developing Camaraderie and Affection

There's a special camaraderie and affection that can develop among people brought together for a limited time and a specific purpose, whether it be kids at summer camp, travelers on a tour bus, people stuck in an elevator, or members of a team assigned to evaluate expansion sites.

The intensity of the affection is due to a built-in safety factor: you know you won't be stuck with these people forever. But that's no reason to undervalue such affection and such relationships.

First of all, affectionate relations are generally good for mental health. Like proper food and exercise, they contribute to your wellness. While there are some people who find it upsetting to be liked because it implies dependency obligations or because they feel they don't deserve it, most people feel closer to their ego ideals when others like them.

Second, affection is a great motivating and lubricating agent. It can make people glad to do their jobs. The group leader must make sure, however, that the group's tasks aren't sacrificed to their affection for each other, as can happen when, say, the group makes a poor decision in order to avoid a conflict or debate that would pit members against each other.

With these points in mind, make sure to have fun together. Combine your meetings with a meal on occasion. Give the funnier members of the group leeway to entertain you; don't take yourselves so seriously that humor is self-censored.

Studying Group Behavior

Because there's a lessening of managerial responsibility for team members (except for the leader, of course), teams provide a good opportunity to study group behavior, including your own behavior in a group. Here are three suggestions:

First, get out a tape recorder and dictate your initial impressions of your teammates—what you think about how these people handle aggression, affection, dependency, and ego ideal. Explain why you think what you think, even if your evidence seems rather flimsy. (I suggest a tape recorder only because writing this up would seem too much of a chore for many people.) A few weeks later, do the same thing; you should have a lot more to say this time. Then listen to your first tape. How right and wrong were you? What can you learn about your unconscious reactions to other people? This is useful information to you as a boss who must select and train new subordinates.

Second, when the team has been working together for a while, try describing it as a family. Assign roles to the members, such as mommy, daddy, big sister, spoiled child, creepy uncle, or whoever. Describe your own position and how others treat you. You shouldn't take such a description entirely seriously, but it's a good way to articulate the group dynamics. I describe a similar exercise—describing your organization as a person—in *Organizational Diagnosis*.[1]

Third, use part of the team's last official meeting to talk over your feelings about "the breaking of the fellowship" (as J.R.R. Tolkien put it). Loss occurs throughout a career; it's part of the emotional impact of every promotion and every significant organizational change. Here's a chance to examine the experience without the heavy overtones present in other loss experiences, such as layoffs or reorganizations. The team members should get together again a few weeks later for another talk on what it's been like without each other. This needn't be all that weepy, and people don't need to pretend that they miss the teamwork if they don't.

One Last Lesson

My colleague Ronald Ebert suggests an easy experiment for those of you who can't get enough of charts and tables. After the second or third meeting of a long-running team, draw up a seating chart showing where each team member (and you) usually sits. You'll find that almost everyone assigns himself or herself a seat. Watch what happens when someone arrives late to find "their" seat taken. If you are of an experimental bent, get in early enough to sit in a new space. Note the reactions.

Now, see if you can explain people's reactions as aggression, affection, dependency, and ego ideal. Which people sat closest to the team leader? Why? Which members were angry to find their seat taken?

As you can see, even the most innocuous behavior can hold

meaning about ourselves and our personalities. Challenge our expectations or assumptions (like which seat is "ours"), and our underlying feelings will rise to the surface.

Gaining Cooperation from Peers

Teams aren't built in a day. When higher management forms a team to create a new plant, for example, engineers, technicians, lawyers, and finance people don't even seem to speak the same language. How can they achieve high levels of interdependence overnight?

Managers in teams complain to me that sometimes they can't reach their objectives because they can't get peers over whom they have no control to give them what they need. When you're stymied by an uncooperative peer:

☐ Take time getting to know the other person. Go to lunch together. It takes time even to glimpse how another person ticks, but without that knowledge you're helpless.

☐ Establish a quid pro quo. Use your understanding of his or her ego ideal and characteristic handling of aggression, affection, and dependency to help spell out what you want or need from each other.

☐ Look to others in the group for support. Every team soon evolves an informal power structure. Seek out the leaders and explain how their success, too, depends on your getting what you need.

☐ If all else fails, try leverage. A technician who could never get the numbers she needed from a finance officer knew that the finance officer was ambitious and up for promotion. The technician said, "Let's work out our differences so it doesn't have to go any higher," and achieved her objectives that way.

Working with Someone You Can't Stand

"I was looking at my boss, but I was seeing Aunt Marcia," said one young manager. "And I couldn't stand Aunt Marcia!"

"When someone at work resembles someone we've known in the past—say, a parent, an ex-husband, or a childhood friend—it arouses unresolved feelings from the first relationship," says my colleague David Adler. So, if you're still angry at Aunt Marcia, it's hard not to displace those feelings onto your (perhaps) innocent coworker. Sometimes, when people speak of bad chemistry, it's attributions based on resemblance to others that's behind their dislike.

To avoid this discomfort, Adler suggests two actions: First, become aware. Get in the habit of asking yourself, when you don't like a person, if he or she reminds you of anyone. If one character from your past keeps surfacing, that's a clue that you're still troubled about that relationship. Second, talk to a friend or coworker about the disturbing resemblance. It's a relief to take these feelings from the private realm of worry and fantasy out into the open where they can be discussed. "Usually," says Adler, "it doesn't take long to identify ways in which the new person is different and to ease your discomfort with the resemblance."

Under some circumstances you may not be able to trace dislike of a coworker to past associations. What happens when you're stuck with intense dislike of a coworker?

Hatred can operate like a telescope: you see a small portion of what you're looking at, but you see it highly magnified. Hatred is an expression of rage. We are enraged by physical or emotional harm— the boss who insults us or the subordinate whose incompetence makes us feel ineffective. But anger and fear introduce distortion. Then we exaggerate some details and ignore others. That was a valid survival mechanism when life-or-death decisions had to be simple and fast. But it won't do in complex organizations where the goal is maximization of group effort, not individual survival.

So when you have to work with someone you can't stand, watch for these distorting mental behaviors:

Assigning one (hostile) motive to many different actions. Once you get a bee in your bonnet about your boss being, say, secretive, you might accuse him of being secretive for telling your peer something he didn't tell you, even though there was no reason on earth to tell you. You can fight this tendency by talking with someone you trust, whose judgment in this person's case is not clouded with strong dislike. Take notes as you talk and write down anything positive about your enemy. Writing gives you a better chance of absorbing it—a useful learning technique.

Repetitive mental harangues. You're mad and you keep going over and over it in your mind. This is a common ritual: one way of coping with fear (often hidden beneath anger) is to keep rehearsing the known facts. But it tends to exaggerate the offense and reduce the flexibility (and therefore accuracy) of your thinking. One antidote is to catch yourself and force yourself to think about something else—even counting sheep will do.

One-sided conversations with friends who agree with you. Again, this hardens your mental arteries. Catch yourself and make an excuse to get out of such conversations or change the subject. (If you're brave, you can tell people the real reason.)

You can't be a manager without meeting some people you dislike. But you can manage that feeling so that it doesn't impair your judgment and your perception of reality. Those are a manager's most important tools.

Ending Feuds

A manager who's stuck in a feud with a coworker or a boss knows how much energy she's wasting. But a feud can be hard to end. Just when one of you wants a truce, the other puts up his or her dukes. To promote peace:

- ☐ Do some homework. Write down how you and your adversary characteristically handle aggression, affection, dependency, and ego ideal. That exercise will give you some perspective. Ask why the feud has continued so long. Are you, for example, using the feud as an outlet for painful aggression that emanates in part from something else, say, troubles at home? Are you using it to prove to yourself that you're a man, not a mouse (and thereby moving closer to your ego ideal)? Is there a less costly way than feuding to accomplish these psychological objectives?
- ☐ Talk to the person. Use the knowledge gained in the previous exercise to avoid pushing her buttons. If you know she feels threatened by your friendly relations with the executive vice president, don't mention the executive vice president. Encourage her to talk about your specific behaviors that trouble her (use the significant incident method) and to tell you what she wants changed. Listen. Establish a precedent for future talks. This direct approach works best when neither of you has invested so much in the feud that your psychological equilibrium is somehow protected by continuing it.
- ☐ If talk fails, consider using an outsider, possibly someone from

human resources or a therapist, to mediate. He or she should be someone who's trained to determine more precisely what the behavior patterns are and which behaviors are amenable to change. When this works, results can be dramatic. I was called in to mediate a dispute between the manager in charge of siting plants and his new boss. The manager got excellent performance evaluations. But his new boss felt he relied too heavily on real estate consultants. The boss felt the subordinate was cavalier, while the subordinate felt his competence was being attacked. The manager now gives his boss hard data justifying his choices, and the two men are getting along just fine.

Know when you're licked. Some feuds can't be resolved in a realistic time frame. If, for example, your adversary has characterological behavior patterns that can change only in long-term therapy, you'll have to make a hard decision about whether you can succeed in an organization with such an obstacle in your path for the foreseeable future.

Dealing with Backstabbing

"How come every time I get stabbed in the back my fingerprints are on the knife?" asks Jerry Harvey, a social psychologist.[2]

The cure for backstabbing is talk. When deceit and duplicity aimed at you comes to your attention, your silence is really collusion with your attacker. Speak up. Let him or her know you're aware of the behavior, how you experience it (as an attack, for example), how you feel ("I don't like it"), and what you want to happen ("I want you to stop misquoting me to the boss").

By definition, backstabbing can only exist so long as it's not exposed to the light of day. Once exposed, the backstabber is forced to either leave you alone or attack you directly, in which case you'll at least have a chance to defend yourself.

CHAPTER 9

Speaking Up to the Boss

The head of a major company had sponsored a training program for his upper middle managers. He hadn't been sure how they would feel about it. But in talking with the consultant who had led the training experience, he learned that they thought it was highly useful. So he was pleased with himself. "How," he asked, "can the knowledge these men and women now have be applied to the way the organization is organized and how it functions? What should be done differently? How might it be done better?"

The consultant reported this conversation to the managerial group. A few said, "Let him take the course." The consultant pointed out that the executive had given permission for the managers to formulate ideas and suggestions and was seriously interested in furthering their efforts to make the company better. The managers made a few suggestions, but couldn't seem to take advantage of the opportunity that was being presented to them. The boss had invited them to speak. They were silent.

How to speak up to the boss becomes increasingly important as more leaders seek to involve their followers. Few people are comfortable speaking up to superiors, even when invited. This problem is even more complicated when the boss is a woman or a member of a minority group. If a subordinate has significant feelings about such differences, often there are good reasons. And in most organizations the boss has the power to hire and fire, or at least to recommend these alternatives. The boss appraises performance and makes recommendations about compensation, promotion, and transfer. Bosses are individuals, too. What will be acceptable to one may not be to another. An offer of cooperation and support from a subordinate might be interpreted by some bosses as arrogance. To some, raising questions is tantamount to being disloyal. Discretion is certainly the better part of valor here. How, then, does a subordinate speak up to the boss?

Defining the Appropriate Circumstances for Speaking Up

First, one must answer two questions: What is the organizational climate? What is the political structure above the boss?

Any subordinate's action, as well as that of any boss, occurs in an organizational context. In many organizations, the unwritten motto is "Don't make waves." These organizations are usually highly structured companies where superiors reward passive acquiescence. In such an organization, any approach to the boss will have to be tactfully indirect.

It is important for the subordinate to know the political structure in which the boss works and, as much as possible, what forces are operating on him or her. To illustrate: a group of managers in a company for which I was a consultant, discontented with their boss's inability to act on a series of problems, wanted to go to his superiors. Before they did, one of them called me. I asked them to wait until I could check out what was going on above their boss. I discovered there was so much conflict in higher-management ranks that their boss could not be heard, nor could he get decisions from his own superiors. Going over his head not only would have done the subordinates no good, it would have harmed them and their boss.

Having considered the organizational climate and the political structure, you should now think of the kind of person the boss is and under what circumstances you might wish to speak up.

The basic question to ask when trying to understand the boss (or anyone else) is, "What is the boss's ego ideal?" What is he or she striving toward? What does it take for the boss to like himself or herself? People may not be able to put their ego ideals into words, but we usually can infer from their behavior how they are trying to look to others and where they are aiming. Since we are always striving toward our ego ideals, we tend to see others in terms of whether they help us in our striving or whether they make us feel disappointed in ourselves—either by blocking our efforts or by criticism. The successful subordinate must be allied with the boss in that direction or he or she cannot be a good subordinate.

Consider the boss's characteristic way of handling aggression. What does he or she do when angry? Does he or she take out anger at one person on another? Does the boss absorb the hostility and anger of others? Does he or she have prejudices about women and members of minority groups? Does he or she take an active part in deliberations and discussions or wait until others have thrashed things out? What kind of reaction can you expect when you do speak up, and how would you deal with that?

How does the boss handle affection? Does he or she need lots of approving people around or does the boss prefer to work in a more isolated fashion? Does the boss find satisfaction without notice or need to be applauded frequently? Is the boss self-centered or can he or she give approval to others? How is the boss apt to interpret what you have to say?

Finally, how does the boss handle dependency? Does he or she prefer to stand alone or does the boss need other people around on whom to lean? Does the boss lean heavily on organizational structure or rely on flexibility? Can the boss take what you have to say in stride?

Having sized up the boss and the boss's environment, you are now in a position to take up specific issues with him or her.

Presenting New Ideas

It's important not to overload the boss with information. One boss, asking for what the subordinate thought needed to be done, began to become glassy-eyed at about the third topic. He was simply not the kind of person who could handle many items at once and felt overwhelmed. A smart subordinate will assess how much information his or her boss can absorb at a given time.

Be careful with surprises; they can turn both ways. A manager wanted to impress his boss, so he worked out a whole new accounting system on his own. But when he pulled the rabbit out of the hat, his boss wasn't applauding. The new system had problems that the more experienced boss perceived. Furthermore, the boss was angry at what he took to be his subordinate's one-upmanship.

If you have a pet project, explain to your boss what you intend to accomplish and what the possible benefits will be to him or her. For example, if you devise a training program that eliminates some chronic personnel problems, your boss will be seen as a skillful manager for developing your talents and supporting you. Including your boss may take some of the spotlight off you. But without his or her support, you might not make it into the spotlight at all.

Your boss will rightly be concerned that you don't neglect your regular work. Talk is cheap, so don't just reassure him or her that you won't. Tell your boss how much time you plan to spend on the project, which part of the day, and when you'll be doing your other tasks. Perhaps he or she will approve delegating some work to subordinates, if they are competent and ready. Be sure to set a deadline for finishing a certain amount of the project and reporting back.

Keep your boss posted. If you need more time, expertise, or resources than you expected, your chances are better if the boss isn't taken by surprise.

Be receptive to his or her suggestions and criticism. It's glorious to do something entirely on your own, but the most valuable people in organizations are those who can mobilize and include others.

Getting New Ideas Accepted

"Top management wants new ideas, but when I bring a new idea to my boss, he treats me like a cat with a dead mouse. Then every so often he likes one. So I keep trying, but the uncertainty drives me crazy."

Sometimes the boss can't help rejecting an idea the first time, because he may never have thought that way, so it seems unreasonable at first; he feels helpless to use the idea because he's too busy, has no idea how to implement it, or foresees trouble; or he is a rigid or very conventional person, to whom creative people seem a little out of control.

Pay attention to the objections he makes. If they seem irrelevant, they can at least show what buttons of his not to push. If he won't explain, try again later. Experiment with how to approach him; don't keep trying something that doesn't work. But if you're angering him, let it drop.

Assuming the boss is fussy but not impossible, try coming back with any idea that was rejected but is particularly important to you. The boss may agree after he's had time to consider. But if you had never brought it up again, he would have let it drop. Also, you may have improved on the idea since you first suggested it. And sometimes it's only a matter of catching the boss at the right time.

If you have a rigid boss, minimize the "exciting new idea" angle and emphasize the concrete benefits, the method of implementation, and how the change fits in with the existing structure (that is, the extent to which it isn't a change). Specify the boss's role in carrying it out, so he is drawn into the idea rather than kept at arm's length from it.

Addressing Problems with Your Boss's Behavior

Fairness

Your boss may be critical of you because his or her personality and yours are so different that what seems right to you is wrong to him or her. He or she may be scapegoating you or may not have adequate information about you. If you are being criticized unfairly because the boss doesn't have enough information (or the information is incorrect), you have to take into account the climate of the organization and the forces operating on the boss. You may have to say, "I didn't do what you say I did, but let's look at the situation and see how I can keep you more accurately informed so this won't happen another time." In this way you direct your efforts toward preventing the recurrence of the problem and ally yourself with the boss against the problem.

If the criticism consistently points to differences in personality, you may have to tell the boss that this is the case and ask for a transfer. This kind of problem usually cannot be resolved without intervention or support from a higher-level third party.

Some bosses continually attack their subordinates. They are usually responding to their own low self-images and perfectionistic aspirations. If such a bully-boss attacks you, you should say very clearly that the behavior is offensive, that you will not put up with it, and that further recurrence will be discussed with higher management. However, it might be wise to talk this over first with a human resources representative or someone else you trust. This stance involves some risk. Most people are not prepared to take the risk. But the bully-boss will usually back off and be more circumspect in his or her behavior if the subordinate takes a courteous but firm stand and refuses to be victimized.

Sometimes bosses turn on their subordinates for reasons that are unclear to either of them. Such was the case with one woman who appointed her subordinate to a managerial role and then turned on her. The subordinate didn't understand why this had happened. Essentially, the "queen bee" had created a rival for herself quite unconsciously and was dealing with that rival by attacking her. In that particular situation, there was no point in going to the boss's boss, who held the senior manager in high esteem and couldn't begin to understand the unconscious dynamics in play. The only alternative was for the subordinate to find a new job.

Some bosses call late meetings, demand overtime, or otherwise preempt subordinates' personal time. A similar courteous, but firm, response is appropriate. If the boss's bosses are doing the same things, then you have organizational pathology. You might want to take another job rather than take a stand with a superior who can't do much anyway.

Sometimes the boss is critical of a subordinate in public. The problem may not be that the criticism is wrong, but that he has chosen the wrong place to be critical. If this happens, request a private meeting and indicate that, while you welcome criticism, particularly if it will help you improve your work, you do not want to accept public humiliation or be scapegoated. You might point out that perhaps the boss didn't realize he was doing that and say you feel that, knowing the impact of this behavior on you, he will probably want to approach you differently.

A critical issue you may have to face is the request from the boss to do something you view as unethical, irresponsible, or dishonest. In these circumstances, you may point out your own values and why you are reluctant to do what is asked. Ask the boss to review with you how he or she sees the same issue. Perhaps once you see it through the superior's eyes, it may seem different to you. By approaching the problem this way, you are not accusing the superior. If, after discussion with your boss, it becomes clear you are being asked to violate your conscience, you probably should take whatever stand is required for you to live with yourself. Your job may be at stake, but you should not raise such issues unless you are prepared for that risk. There is, of course, the possibility of recourse to your boss's superiors, but only if the organizational climate is conducive to that kind of an appeal.

A variant of this problem is sexual harassment. Although many organizations have now established policies for dealing with this problem, and a good deal of managerial education has tempered various forms of harassment, nevertheless a woman may have to take a firm stand. The general tendency for women to be more sensitive to other people's feelings may bring them closer to others. It is therefore important that they maintain an appropriate psychological distance from their male peers and superiors. It is important to know what a given company's policies are with regard to sexual harassment, and to whom a woman may turn in the organization to support her stance.

Direction

One of the problems of being a self-starter is that one often doesn't get specific directions on projects. As a result, you may simply pick up the ball and get going only to find out that you have exceeded the boundaries of the ill-defined task. It is important to try to get from your boss as explicitly as possible what he or she wants and how much time you have to accomplish that task, with what quality levels, and with what resources. Even when the charge is vague, it is important to push for as much information as you can get.

Accountability

One vice president, faced with an absenteeism problem in a plant, called the human resources director and the plant manager (who didn't get along) into her office. "You guys solve this problem," she said. "I'm holding both of you responsible for the results. You'll sink or swim together."

This was an abdication of management. The vice president was avoiding the difficult tasks of evaluating each man's contribution separately, resolving their differences, and choosing between their proposals. She didn't care that human resources didn't run the plant and couldn't control the outcome.

If the boss charges you with a task whose outcome you don't feel you can influence, protest. For example, try to get the boss to increase your authority to get the task done; divide the assignment so that your accountability reflects your authority; or agree in advance that your contribution won't be measured by results but by fairer indices, such as the quality of your diagnosis of the problem, and the number and quality of suggestions made.

Performance Appraisal

Performance appraisal is the most difficult of all managerial tasks. Most managers fudge on this effort because it arouses their feelings of guilt. You can help your boss appraise you adequately by telling him that you want honest, direct feedback about how you do your work. Invite the boss to tell you more frequently, more directly, and in a timely way when your behavior does not meet organizational expectations so you can try to correct yourself. You will have to encourage the boss repeatedly, even expressing appreciation for those comments which may seem somewhat harsh and unfair. By asking questions, you will be defining and describing what the boss does or doesn't like, enabling the boss to spell out what you need to know.

What should you do if you think you've received an unfair performance review? Unfortunately, many people in such circumstances deny the boss's judgments or make excuses. But those responses can fuel the boss's anger and stifle future communications. Another common reaction is to write the boss off as impossible to please.

All these reactions leave you stuck with a bad review and no understanding of why you got it or how to remedy the situation. Often a poor review is the result of misunderstood directions. Ask your boss what exactly you did or didn't do and what he or she wanted you to do. This shows the boss that you want to do well and won't hold a grudge. It also gives you a goal and a way to achieve it, so you aren't stuck wallowing in disappointment or resentment.

Take time to think about what your boss has said, then meet again to present your side. Don't dwell on your innocence, just state the facts and let them speak for themselves. Your boss may understand what you are up against but still be appropriately angry that you didn't bring up problems earlier. Ask for more frequent appraisals until you are sure that you are doing what the boss wants.

I don't advise you to lie down and be abused. I do advise you to learn as much as you can from a bad review. But if the bad reviews continue despite your attempts to do what is asked, the job may not be for you or your boss may have it in for you. Rather than let your self-esteem and reputation take a beating, look for another position.

Promotion

If the issue is promotion, it will be particularly important to be sensitive to the boss's defensiveness and feelings of guilt. You might say, "I see that others around me have moved up, but I haven't. Can you tell me how I have to prepare myself to qualify for consideration?"

People often fail to get promotions because they do not manage their relationships with other people well. In my experience, most people who have such a problem don't recognize it. Frequently they resist all efforts to help them see how their own behavior gets in their way. If your boss points out such a problem, take him or her seriously. If the boss doesn't mention your behavior, ask him whether the way you behave is getting in your own way. You must then accept that feedback without hostility. If you don't believe the boss, check it out with someone else.

Career Guidance

Ideally, everyone should discuss career options with his or her boss-once-removed because that person usually has greater knowledge of higher levels in the organization and the range of possibilities than does one's immediate boss. However, this is not yet customary procedure in most organizations, so you probably will have to discuss career options with your boss.

Many organizations encourage the boss to offer career guidance. While the intensity of competition sometimes keeps a boss from spontaneously helping subordinates, most will respond to a reasonable request for guidance. If you have been intensely rivalrous with your boss, if you have rejected, competed with, or been contemptuous of your boss, you cannot expect the boss to help you. Also, there are bosses who are too envious of their subordinates or too insecure about their own positions to help others. You will have to evaluate the climate of the organization and the boss's position within it along with your own boss-subordinate relationship.

Support

Bosses must support their people, represent them to higher management, protect them, and mobilize resources to help them do their work. Not all bosses do all these things equally well, though many assume they do. You can point out those areas in which you feel your boss is falling short. If, for example, adequate information, supplies, materials, personnel, or budget are not being provided, the boss ought to know that and what the work consequences are. Your boss needs to know, too, if other levels of management are interfering with subordinates' work. If you feel your boss is not representing you well at higher levels, he or she ought to know that. Raising such issues gives the boss the opportunity to explain both the problems he or she faces and what is being done.

If you have raised an issue two or three times and nothing happens, then it is clear that the boss can't or won't do anything about it. You will have to determine whether the problem is a personal one between you and your boss or a problem of organizational mechanisms. It will be particularly important for you to assess whether the boss needs to please his or her own boss by not making waves, by showing greater profitability, or by being a "good boy" or "good girl."

If you are having problems relating to cost or profitability, it is usually better to ask the boss to discuss them with you and your peers. Together you can work out a way of attaining the necessary goals. Most subordinates make the mistake of presenting a problem to the boss without offering to solve it, assuming that the boss knows how to deal with all kinds of issues. The truth is that the boss is human too, and needs more than just another red flag. You have to point out an issue, offer examples of its occurrence and their costs, and offer some possible solutions. Unless you do all three of these things, you may merely increase the boss's helplessness. You also increase the possibility that the problem will become worse.

Idiosyncrasies

Often the boss's personal manner or idiosyncrasies get in the way of a good relationship. Some can't stop talking. Some lose control in a crisis. Some want to control their territory and their people very rigidly. Some have to do it all themselves; they cannot delegate. Some scapegoat and manipulate others. Each will have to be approached differently.

Of all these behaviors, overcontrolling is the hardest to deal with because the boss can offer standards, goals, targets, and other objective reasons for his or her behavior. Nevertheless, in most organizations there is increasing concern among higher-level management about overcontrolling bosses because they cannot adequately develop younger people. The earlier quotation from John F. Welch, Jr., chairman of GE, in Chapter 6 is an example.

It is a psychological axiom that the more a person must repress feelings, the less that person is able to be sensitive to someone else and to the nuances of interpersonal behavior. If you are going to speak up to such a boss, it will be important for you to cite chapter and verse—to refer to specific behavior and the impact of that behavior on your work, your feelings, your experiences, and the work of others. Such bosses will usually want to debate the issues. Don't enter the debate. Reiterate the circumstances. If the boss starts becoming defensive or tries to debate again, point out that this is exactly the behavior to which you are referring, if such is the case.

Sometimes bosses, especially those with a heavy financial or engineering orientation, have difficulty understanding the impact of their decisions or their behavior on subordinates. They don't appreciate shifts in the experiences or training of people who report to them. For example, sometimes younger people coming into an organization have learned to work more comfortably in teams or to be more sensitive to the feelings of other people and, in communicating that to their bosses, they run into a blank wall. The bosses simply don't understand. In one organization about to undergo significant change, for example, the executives who were trying to make use of an internal organization development consultant told that person that they didn't want to hear about any of this "soft stuff"— namely, the importance of people's feelings and how one should deal with those issues. In such circumstances, people like that have to be told quite frankly that there's no way of dealing with the impact of change without being sensitive to how people feel and managing those feelings.

Some managers can take advantage of feedback about their own idiosyncrasies and will work hard to improve. When they do, it is important for subordinates to recognize their effort and to offer encouragement and support. For those whose bosses cannot or will not change, it may be helpful to go to the next higher superior or to the human resources department or, in the last extreme, to seek another job.

Raising Problems That Have to Do with the Organization

Almost everybody in a large organization can see problems in somebody else's operation, sometimes problems that are amenable to solution if only somebody else knew they existed. It is often difficult to point out such problems because others feel that their territory is being invaded. Sometimes it is even difficult to raise the problem within your own territory because of fear of your own boss. However, when you see an organizational problem, whether it is wasted money, wasted human resources, exploitation, or illegal activities, it is important to inform your boss. It is his or her responsibility to carry it to higher-level management.

There is great social pressure in our culture against squealing. This allows problems to continue for long periods of time without people higher in the organization becoming aware of them. Subordinates who are caught up in such a problem assume that higher management wants things that way, since it wouldn't tolerate—let alone promote—bosses who, for example, have orgies at sales meetings, manipulate accounts, bribe public officials, or indulge in other detrimental behaviors.

People frequently feel they are putting themselves in jeopardy by reporting such matters and, indeed, they are. There are highly publicized examples of whistle blowers who have been fired for their efforts. Others have resigned from their positions because the problems they pointed out were not dealt with. There are also examples of people who have spoken out against abuse or exploitation of themselves, of the organization, and of their fellow employees where top management, previously unaware of the problems, immediately took corrective action. You serve your organization (and yourself) best by reporting what you see and allowing the matter to proceed through proper channels.

Dealing with Conflicts

There are frequently conflicts with others when functions or competitive positions overlap. Sometimes these problems result from conflicts among superiors, or from inadequate leverage on the other person or other area, or because one function thinks it is being exploited so that another can look good. In any event, when you find yourself in such a conflict it is important to take it up with your boss at an early stage.

Explain the nature of the problem and its consequences without attributing blame. Otherwise, you place your boss in a position of having to choose between warring factions. You can then ask your boss to help you explore what is happening and to suggest ways of coping. This places your boss in a position to act constructively, to use his or her good offices to arrange opportunities to talk over problems with the other parties, and to support appropriate solutions.

Of course, there are bosses who want to avoid any possible conflict. Sometimes they don't want to act like bosses. Sometimes they themselves precipitate the conflict. By using the criteria I advanced earlier, you can decide which of these, if any, is the case.

Negotiating the Psychological Contract

The critical issues of speaking up to one's boss are how you do it and with what intentions. A wise old editor once told me, "Never underestimate the intelligence of your audience or overestimate the amount of information they have." The same applies to the boss. You should always seek to inform.

In speaking up to the boss it is important to maintain your own personal dignity. Maintain appropriate psychological distance; don't try to be too friendly or too distant and aloof. You are there to accomplish a job. You are not there to be buddies or to treat each other as enemies.

There are times when it is appropriate to be angry. When you repeatedly have been attacked unfairly, when you have been manipulated, it is entirely appropriate to speak your anger. To fail to do so—to smile when you are really enraged—is to send two messages to your boss that contradict each other and result in no communication at all.

In my experience, most people do not tell the other person clearly how they feel. As a result, they end up talking past each other, increasing friction, hostility, distance, and anger. We can't assume that another person knows or even should know how we feel. People in our society have to stand up and speak for themselves. Nobody else can do it for them or do it as well.

It is always important to have examples when talking with your boss, particularly when you want him to behave differently because he's getting in your way, or when you're doing an upward performance appraisal. Vague statements like, "You need to improve your communication," don't really say very much. A specific incident, including the behavior, the time, the effect on others, will be more relevant.

Working with a boss is similar to a marriage. Each person has expectations of the other that are not clearly specified. I call these the psychological contract. You need to let the boss know how you think and feel—not in a hostile, argumentative way, but in an informal way. Then you can continually renegotiate the psychological contract, redefining mutual expectations as time passes. This continual renegotiation is the basis for effective superior-subordinate relationships.

CHAPTER **10**

Working Effectively with a Problem Boss

Employees with boss trouble ask if they should go to their boss's boss for help. The answer is no, unless:

☐ You have a close working relationship with your boss-once-removed and are sure of her trustworthiness. One sales manager, alarmed at the way his abrasive boss alienated customers, and unable to get through to the boss on his own, went to the boss's boss, who subsequently repeated the entire conversation to the sales manager's boss. The sales manager is now job hunting; he feels his position is untenable.

Ideally, you should have had lots of past contact with your boss-once-removed for your training and development. She's better positioned than your immediate boss to recognize the traits needed for higher management and less apt to feel threatened by your success or to feel guilty about criticizing you. But beware: in most organizations, hierarchies prevail, and going to your boss's boss can seal your doom.

☐ You're willing to accept the risks. You're sticking your neck out and burning your bridges. The boss's boss may get angry. He may resent your asking him to do something unpleasant, or he may feel that, indirectly, you're criticizing him.

☐ You can live with the costs. Even if you win changes, you'll have to deal with the guilt of squealing and possible damage to your reputation. Fellow employees who grouse with you at

113

lunch may not support you at all when you go to higher management. And when your boss finds out, you'll pay a price.

If you decide not to go to higher authority, you'll either have to change jobs or stay and grin and bear it. That means accepting the limits a bad boss puts on what you can accomplish. Managing a bad boss can have its rewards. Higher-ups might give you credit for doing it well. And one famous executive told me that, having survived a particularly bad boss, he learned he could survive any boss.

It's also possible to benefit in another way from having a difficult boss: the most difficult boss I ever had was a man from whom I learned a tremendous amount. Sometimes subordinates don't realize that even an intolerable boss has inherent strengths. Preoccupied with a boss's abrasiveness, overcontrolling behavior, or failure to give adequate direction, they miss the opportunity to learn from his or her skills.

To discover the boss's intrinsic strengths, ask yourself how such a person made it despite his or her faults. If you resent his authoritarian style, consider the strength it takes not to be intimidated. Did he need to be overcontrolling to get the department back on its feet? What good things have come from his control—increased productivity, higher quality work, the notice and praise of upper management? Or imagine you are your boss's boss: why might you have promoted her? What successes has she had since then?

Showing your desire to learn from these strengths may lead the boss to ease up on some of the unacceptable behavior. But even if that doesn't happen, future bosses will appreciate your ability to learn from a difficult person and your capacity to see the good side of a bad experience.

There is a good chance that you will encounter one or more problem bosses during your work life. Here are some of the most common types and ways of making the best of a difficult situation.

The Silent Boss

Does your boss hold you at arm's length? Some bosses are afraid to show any warmth at all toward subordinates. Perhaps they fear the dependency obligations such feelings might entail, or perhaps they've overreacted to legitimate concerns about becoming too friendly with subordinates. These bosses often avoid giving criticism, compliments, and guidance. This means that you're out of touch with appraisal of your performance, and you will have no opportunity to improve. Decisions about operations, compensation, promotion, and transfer are being made without you.

How do you please this boss? You want to do well, but his silence allows too much internal paranoid fantasy. You wonder if he's unhappy or disappointed. On the other hand, what if you want to pick up the ball and run with it? Would that make him angry? Would you be usurping his role?

To figure out why this situation exists, ask yourself the following questions:

Is your boss "too busy" for good communication, or is he a poor communicator? Does he avoid all his subordinates?

How much of the problem is yours? Why haven't you initiated more frequent communication? Are you intimidated by authority figures? Was your father a formidable or arbitrary power figure, of whom you're unconsciously still afraid?

Whether it's he or you, I'm all for taking the initiative with a silent boss. You can't expect to change the boss, but you might be able to get him to accede to three requests:

First, frequent feedback, based on significant incidents that illustrate your performance, whenever you do things that he either likes or dislikes.

Second, establishing deadlines for your tasks. That will relieve you of the boundless anxiety of feeling that you'll never know what progress you've made and whether you're meeting quantitative and qualitative expectations.

Third, a behavioral job description that explains what you're supposed to do and how you're supposed to do it, not just the desired outcomes, but also how, in terms of attitude, manner, and behavior toward significant others in the organization, he expects you to achieve those outcomes.

The Unhelpful Boss

Managers often complain that their bosses aren't of any use to them. "She doesn't know what's going on any more than I do." "He waits for me to decide what to do, but I still have to get his okay."

Sometimes the problem is that your boss is at the same cognitive level that you are. His or her ability to handle complexity, to plan and predict, and to coordinate simultaneous activities is no greater than yours. So what stumps you stumps your boss too.

My colleague Elliott Jaques has discovered the long-term solution to this problem: structure organizations so that each level of management is exactly one cognitive level above the one below it and below the one above it.[1] But all that won't help you right now. Here's what you can do:

☐ Use your tenure in your position to learn what you can from this boss. Even if he's no smarter than you, he may have more knowledge and experience.

☐ Expect to feel some guilt. Because unconsciously the boss is equated with a parent, it seems wrong if he's not someone to look up to.

☐ Set your own priorities (that is, identify what you think would be best for the unit and organization) and present them to the boss for approval. He probably feels as uncomfortable as you do when you keep asking him questions he can't answer. He'll appreciate being let off that hook, as long as you don't make him lose face. Keep him informed. This is a test of your political skills.

☐ Don't make him angry. He still has the upper hand politically. Make it your goal to get into another position with his blessing and his high recommendation.

☐ Look out for mentors and others in the organization who can give you the broader view. Don't put them in the position of replacing your boss for you; many will be unwilling to insult their peer.

The Ambiguous Boss

If your boss doesn't give you clear directions, he is keeping you from doing your job. If he then berates you for not doing your job, he's abusing you. What can you do about it?

☐ Ask him to be more specific. Request specific deadlines and quantities and check on which people to involve. Cover whatever has come up in his previous criticisms. If he says, "Do I have to tell you everything?" or, "I pay you to think, not ask foolish questions," most likely he has an unconscious need to use subordinates as whipping boys. He will not allow you to do the job right no matter how rationally you approach him.

☐ Defend yourself. When your boss starts in on you, tell him not to berate you. His directions were unclear. If you stand up for yourself, he may stop using you to vent his unconscious anger, at least for a while. In any event, such a stand is important for your own self-esteem.

If your boss's boss conducts an upward appraisal, or just asks you what you need to do your job better, say that your boss's directions are unclear. You may want to keep quiet because you don't want to come off as overly dependent or slow. But your boss's boss can't pressure your boss to change unless he or she knows exactly what is going on and how it is affecting your work.

The Meddling Boss

A hands-on boss may be telling you "Hands off." Usually a hands-on manager is considered a blessing because she teaches subordinates. But if she meddles in tasks that you can do, she stifles your development.

Sometimes the cause is external: your boss may be worried about an important project. Tell her you appreciate her concern but her supervision is distracting. Offer regular briefings. If she doesn't back off even when you have things under control, console yourself that things will return to normal when the project ends.

If your boss always looks over everyone's shoulder, telling her to back off won't work—at least not for long. Her constant intervention is characterological. But don't give up. Ask her exactly how she wants a task done. You may not be meeting her perfectionistic standards. If you prove you can, she may leave you alone. However, once you slip below perfection, she'll be back. Even if she doesn't back off, you will feel better for having stood up for yourself.

Don't accuse her of treating you like a dummy or of always having to have it her way. Both may be true, but such a comment may also end the discussion. Focus on your ability to learn and to satisfy her standards. Show that you still need and want her supervision.

This is important because a meddling boss is anxious about her own standing, so she may see your bid for independence as a threat.

In the end, all you may be able to do is learn what you can from her and move on when you can. Because she gets your back up, you may resist learning from her. But then you are stifling your own development.

The Nice Boss

A nice boss can ruin your career.

Some people are "nice" in order to keep other people from behaving aggressively toward them, or to keep a lid on their own aggression. Bosses who are nice tend also to be paternalistic. They are so kind and helpful that they don't give you the criticism you need to grow.

And because the boss is so nice, you feel guilty about complaining, let alone being angry at her (her strategy has worked). If you try to speak up, she says that you're doing fine. But if you don't let guilt paralyze you, you can help the boss help you by:

☐ Talking to her about your need for frequent feedback, with specific examples.

☐ Reminding her before each session that you're very interested in hearing the critical part of her assessment. It is possible, though, that her guilt or fear about criticizing you will be impossible to overcome.

☐ Considering the possibility of discussing your performance with the boss-once-removed.

☐ Finding mentors elsewhere in the organization. This boss can't teach you about your own weaknesses, nor can she educate you in the realities of business life, which are often far from nice.

The Abusive Boss

You can't wish away an abusive boss. "Why can't he be reasonable?" you wonder. But reasonableness isn't what got him where he is. Many a manager gets to the top because of an intense need for power over others. He craves this power in order to convince himself that he's not as weak and helpless as he feels underneath. A boss with this pattern has low self-esteem and a high ego ideal, so he's always dissatisfied and angry with himself. His anger comes out when he attacks, overcontrols, and abuses subordinates.

In *Psychological Man,*[2] I recounted how Winston Churchill, who was an unhappy, unloved child, screamed at school yard bullies, "One day I shall be a great man and you will be nobodies, then I will stamp and crush you." Years later, as a leader, he showed the traits you'd expect: overweening pride, a tyrannical nature, a lack of concern for subordinates, and an insensate drive for power.

What should you do about an abusive boss?

- ☐ Ask yourself how deeply your boss disrupts your work and peace of mind. Does he explode once a year or once a week? While many bosses are power driven, there is a wide range of resulting behavior.
- ☐ Evaluate how much you're suffering. Do you often feel helpless, hopeless, or trapped? Do you have stress symptoms, such as sleep interruptions or irritability? Friends, family, or an experienced therapist can help you determine if the situation is too much for you.
- ☐ If your boss has periods of reasonableness, talk to him. You're not qualified to psychoanalyze him or to attempt to change his behavior, except as it relates directly to you, but you can tell him what he does that bothers you. Use significant incidents to help him understand. Say how you'd prefer him to have acted.

Many abusive bosses eventually gather round them a group of subordinate managers who have some immunity to their bullying. If you aren't immune, and your boss won't modify his behavior, going elsewhere may be your best bet.

The Disapproving Boss

"The boss just doesn't seem to like me, and I don't know why." Your belief that someone doesn't like you can influence his or her opinion, because you may act in a cautious manner that is interpreted as being unfriendly. Employees can be hard on themselves and think the boss doesn't like them when he or she is just disappointed. A defensive employee may then avoid the boss; an aggressive one may get into conflicts. Either behavior may bring about the very dislike that supposedly caused it.

If you think your boss doesn't like you:

☐ Pinpoint when the feelings began. Was it after a failed project, either yours or the boss's? When do they recur? In private or public? When things are hectic or slow?

☐ Prepare for your encounters with your boss, so you don't repeat slipups or forget to say things. Write a script of what to say and how to say it.

☐ Ask the boss if you're doing something to displease him or her. If you already have an idea what it is, offer possible solutions. That relieves the boss of some of the guilt of negative appraisal, and shows you're interested in solving your own problems. If you don't know what's wrong, describe specifically how and when you feel his or her disapproval. Avoid accusing the boss of having it in for you.

☐ Talk to an experienced peer. He or she knows the boss's idiosyncrasies and can point out when you are reading too much into the situation.

It's hard to nip problems in the bud; you don't want to be a nitpicker or troublemaker. But I can tell you from experience: the water's cold, so jump in and get it over with.

The Weak Boss

The boss knew he had to do something about an abrasive subordinate, so he asked another subordinate to talk to him. She was flattered that the boss thought she could handle a sticky situation. But when the man put up a fight, she realized that she had no way to control him and that her boss had put her in a no-win situation.

If your boss asks you to handle one of his problems, say no. Explain that you lack the authority or experience and that taking on that role could alienate you from your peers. If your boss doesn't usually push things off on subordinates, chances are he just felt stymied by this one problem. He will probably accept your reasoning.

However, if he regularly avoids difficult personnel problems, it's probably because he doesn't want to be seen as mean. Essentially, he is asking you to be the heavy. He may present the problem as a chance to develop your managerial skills, but he is exploiting, not developing, you.

In this case, there may be little that you can do. If you continue to refuse your boss's requests, you may become the "difficult subordinate" in his eyes. If your job isn't worth occasionally doing the boss's dirty work, look for a boss who can take care of his or her own problems.

The Defensive Boss

If your boss says, "It'll never work here," or "I don't buy that psychology junk," his defensiveness isn't unusual. Due to recent rapid change in technology and business, a younger employee often finds herself in conflict with a boss who "worked his way up" in a different era, succeeding more by perseverance, discipline, or toughness than by knowledge or tangible contributions.

Such a boss may feel threatened by the newcomer's credentials and ability. He secretly wonders if he's outdated and ready for the scrap heap. The boss may become even more inflexible and authoritarian in order to maintain his self-esteem and to convince himself he's still in charge.

To grow under such a boss:

☐ Find other mentors and managers for role models to meet affection and dependency needs, to validate your perceptions, and to help you become visible to higher-ups.

☐ Accept the challenge the boss presents. Figure out when he's most approachable. Be sensitive to his need for self-approval. Do you talk down to him? Do you threaten him with didactic "shoulds" and "oughts"? (The many "shoulds" in this book are suggested behaviors that you can take or leave. Face-to-face "shoulds" exacerbate a sense of inadequacy.) Do you attack his ways, prompting him to defend them? Are you reenacting unconscious old rivalries with parental figures?

☐ Try putting some of your suggestions to him in writing. Your own machinations will be more apparent to you as you review what you've written. He'll be less likely to be defensive when he's not pressured to answer right away.

☐ If all else fails, the high-risk strategy is to work around him.

Should you do so, consider minimizing the risk by not going behind his back. What would happen, for example, if you saved new ideas to bring up informally when your boss's boss was present?

If you're being badly stifled, the temptation to bad-mouth the boss may be nearly irresistible. Try to resist. If he hears that you're grousing, it will only convince him that he was right about you all along. Any hope of winning him over will be gone. When it comes to a difficult boss, an obstacle is better than an enemy.

The Exploitative Boss

If your boss is taking credit for your work, what can you do without jeopardizing your career?

- ☐ Master parts of the job that your boss doesn't like or can't do, so you aren't fighting for the same turf. And if others know your boss isn't good with numbers, it will be more difficult for him to take credit for your accounting.
- ☐ Build up a network in the organization. Go out of your way to meet people from other departments and ask what they do; then discuss how it relates to your work. This gives you a chance to show what you know.
- ☐ Volunteer to help other managers with short-term projects. Of course, you need your boss's permission. And you must keep up with your own work.
- ☐ Take advantage of opportunities to demonstrate your expertise publicly. But don't show up your boss. He may retaliate by further limiting your visibility.
- ☐ Write articles for trade journals.

If your boss thwarts these efforts, you may have to transfer or leave the organization to get a boss who will develop you, not exploit you.

If you decide to sweat it out until you're assigned elsewhere, try to learn what you can from this boss. When the French writer Colette was young, her husband made her write novels that he published under his own name. She got out of that situation, but also admitted that she'd learned much from him about how to write.[3]

The Narcissistic Personality

All of us need to like ourselves well enough to have a healthy self-respect. Without plenty of self-confidence, a manager couldn't assert himself or herself, take charge in a crisis, learn new skills, and teach subordinates. But for some people, their narcissism spills over onto their subordinates and others, usually at the cost of the work. Sooner or later everyone will encounter such a boss, sometimes because the boss is under increased stress, as a result of which his or her controls slip somewhat, but more painfully when such behavior is characterological.

Whatever the variety of narcissism, those who choose to live with intimidation are likely to see it intensify over time. They often pay a heavy psychological—and sometimes physical—price. They may even start to pick on their subordinates too.

Generally speaking, one has to confront such behavior, but it's necessary to do so respectfully; the boss still has the power. When it seems timely and reasonable to do so, tell the boss specifically what behavior of hers you can't tolerate. Specify how a given kind of behavior offends you, intimidates you, interferes with getting your work done, or may be offensive to your subordinates, and therefore how ideally you would like her to behave. Don't get sucked into a fight or debate. Excuse yourself if you have to. Open hostilities with self-centered people often mean a fight to the bitter end. Also, they are typically adept at putting others in the wrong.

Narcissistic bosses take many forms. Perhaps the most common is the *abrasive personality,* the boss who is rigidly right, who engages in sometimes vitriolic debate with peers and often with subordinates, who is inconsiderate and insensitive, who in effect wears his hostility on his sleeve. The late Admiral Hyman Rickover was notorious for such behavior. As with many abrasive bosses, he could get away with it, because he turned out to be right in his emphasis on nuclear submarines and became highly important to congressional committees. Not much can be done with a man who has that kind of power, but, if such a person doesn't crush those who express their pain, sometimes in a quiet moment they can hear and try to do something about their behavior.

The *disdainful boss* is usually quite bright and therefore often has difficulty understanding why subordinates can't master a certain skill or can't get along without more direction or feedback. Such people are quietly contemptuous of those who are not as bright as they are. For example, one manager was an engineering expert. When subordinates came to him with questions, he answered impatiently, using technical jargon. They stopped asking for help and muddled through on their own, knowing he would correct their work and congratulate himself.

Usually, the abrasive personality and the disdainful personality have severe superegos. Their consciences drive them to perfectionistic achievement, and their criticism of themselves is what spills over onto other people. However, being aware of this, one can appeal to that same punitive conscience, because usually such people don't want to hurt others. When their attention is called to the pain they cause others, usually they try to make amends.

Most of the other forms of narcissistic behavior reflect inadequate or erratically functioning superegos. Chief among these is the *exploitative boss,* who was considered earlier in this chapter.

The *dependent narcissist* is the person who needs constant and continual applause. He or she wants others to recognize his or her every achievement, however minor, and is hypersensitive to the least show of criticism or disapproval from subordinates. Usually with such a person it is helpful to give appropriate recognition and applause, but not to overdo it so that one feels like a hypocrite. Confrontation is not going to help; indeed it may make you an enemy.

The *grandiose boss* has ideas far beyond the possibility of their realization. The late British publisher Robert Maxwell is a case in point. His empire collapsed because he had overextended it by making poor deals that less narcissistic executives would have avoided. Sometimes a trusted subordinate can help such a person review the downside risks of what he proposes to do or clarify the steps necessary to get to the ultimate point he seeks. Introducing reality that way may have a sobering effect without undermining the self-image of such an irrational boss. Of course, one has to be careful about such people, for sometimes their imagination and farsightedness do seem to make the impossible come true. A recent example occurs in the movie *Bugsy*: Bugsy Siegel's financial backers couldn't envision turning the desert into Las Vegas.

The *sadistic boss,* the one who says, "I don't get ulcers, I give them," psychologically flails subordinates. He is the boss who, no matter where in the world he is traveling, calls at an hour that disrupts the sleep of his subordinates. He tells them publicly about their failings, as Harold Geneen, former CEO of ITT, used to do. He has little concern or care for his employees, subordinates, or family responsibilities. His behavior tends to be crude and cool, and he feels he has every right to behave that way. Sometimes, in angry desperation, subordinates finally tell such a boss off, but rarely does that have any effect. The very fact that one works for such a person makes him so ignominious in the boss's eyes that his angry criticism doesn't matter.

The *fawning boss* tends to be a combination of the sadistic boss and the dependent narcissist. It is he who is notoriously sensitive to how his superiors feel but hostile to his subordinates. He cannot stand up for his people, present a point of view that represents them, or otherwise incur possible negative feelings on the part of his boss. When things go wrong, he will blame those who report to him, assuming no responsibility for whatever has happened. Apart from pointing out the behavior, which usually does no good, not much can be done with this kind of a boss.

The *charming boss* is frequently but not always narcissistic. Some preen themselves, dress to perfection, and in other ways indicate that they give themselves too much attention. The truly charming person is thoughtful, considerate, and genuinely interested in other people. The narcissistically charming person is usually putting on some kind of show at the expense of sensitivity to others' feelings. To confront or criticize such a person is to deflate him or her. Any feedback, therefore, would have to be gentle and specifically recognize that the person was unaware of the impact of his or her behavior on others. Subordinates have to be careful in dealing with charming personalities because, as a result of their charm, they usually have friends in high places who are unable to see the negative aspect of their behavior and, even if they do, are unwilling to act against such a charming person.

Finally, there is the manipulative personality, the *con artist*. Con artists pride themselves on their ability to manipulate other people. Frequently, they have little or no conscience, in which case they usually become criminals. But those who are manipulative bosses tend to be contemptuously dismissive of rules and of other people's interests. Sometimes they manipulate people against each other so that their own positions will not be threatened by rivalry. Sometimes they assiduously develop friendships all over the organization so that they are invulnerable to dismissal. Sometimes even their bosses are prisoner to the network of relationships they have established. Such people certainly can't be trusted and never will develop their subordinates.

It is important not to spend valuable energy trying to make a boss like this like you. That makes him feel he has succeeded in his ruse and increases his unconscious contempt for you. Don't antagonize him, but you are within your rights to make him aware of the behavior you won't put up with. Steer clear of labeling—calling him a liar, for instance. Stick to describing episodes of behavior and their cost to you and the organization. Above all, hold on to your sense of self-worth. Fight the tendency to accept his contemptuous view of you. Do not be fooled into thinking you can change him. Better to keep your distance and focus your efforts on developing yourself, since your boss won't be doing it.

In general, if a narcissistic person can hear it at all, give him or her behavioral feedback, both positive and negative. And do so continually. If you stop, she will return to her old ways. Sometimes, too, it helps to explain the benefits of controlling her behavior. If a narcissistic person can get ahead faster by being sensitive and developing subordinates, she may try it, at least under certain circumstances and for a while. Remember that she has a fragile sense of herself. Expect resistance, hostility, and outright rejection if you don't carefully circle her psychologically.

CHAPTER 11

Preparing for Ongoing Achievement

Although the downsizing of organizations and the propensity for reducing levels and becoming as managerially lean as possible are likely to reduce the opportunities for advancement in any given organization, that doesn't necessarily mean that there are or will be fewer opportunities for achievement. You may have to move more frequently from one organization to another as you choose new options in response to the demands of your ego ideal or your exploration and inquiry, as opportunities open up spontaneously, or as your focus changes with your development. No doubt you will evolve new interests and skills that also may make for greater mobility. To sustain motivation of people who can't move as rapidly hierarchically, many organizations are giving added emphasis to lateral moves that will help people continue their development and give them new stimulation.

Whatever the case, you need to focus on how to best use your current experience to understand yourself, to hone your skills, to gain and solidify knowledge about the workings of this and, by extension, other organizations. It is particularly important to gain information about yourself, the impact of your behavior on others, and aspects of your latent talents that come to the fore. Information about oneself is hard to come by in all organizations, particularly in the early stages of one's career. The unfortunate consequence is that too many people learn too late about negative aspects of their behavior. Early, specific feedback that enables you to hone your behavior and try to remedy your faults is crucial.

A second crucial factor in continued achievement is the nature of your relationship with your boss—and subsequent bosses. Too few people recognize that the reporting relationship is a fundamental device for acquiring knowledge, skills, and guidance. It is potentially a seedbed that, nurtured and cultivated, can yield a rich harvest of nuggets of know-how that in turn become the necessary components of achievement.

Broadening Your Experience and Perspective

The late Isaac Asimov once said of a fellow writer who had gone right to the top: "I wonder if he has any sensation of having passed through."[1] People in a rush to move up often forget that passing through is more than paying dues; it's preparation. Those who rise quickly in organizations usually master each level along the way, including areas not directly related to their work. That's one reason they are so promotable.

If you're waiting for a promotion, look around for what more you could learn where you are. Once you've learned it, make sure your boss, or higher managers, know about it. Make suggestions, ask to be put on a task force, or just ask managers in other areas if you can talk about their work with them. If you're hell-bent on a certain goal, this may seem like a waste of time. But broadening yourself never is.

To advance, you also need to appreciate the careers you didn't choose. As you move up, you are more and more responsible for activities entirely outside your area of expertise. You must trust others to do what's needed. You can't trust them, though, unless you genuinely value what they're doing, even if it doesn't interest you much. To prepare yourself:

- ☐ Learn as much as you can about what others do. Ask them to tell you about it. Ask your boss for assignments that will put you in contact with people outside your own unit.
- ☐ Go out of your way to make contacts with people in other areas. If there's no compelling work-related reason, simply invite them to lunch and explain that you're interested in what they're doing.

☐ Show appreciation for what others achieve. When you hear that another department scored a sales success, write a note to the sales rep who pulled it off.

☐ Develop the "dream team" you would assemble if you were in charge. Think what skills are likely to grow in importance in the future—perhaps negotiation, perhaps advertising, perhaps computer programming—and who has them or would be the right person to learn them.

Leadership requires you to get inside the heads of people who do well what you can't and wouldn't want to do.

Preparing for advancement means making certain that you do not become a prisoner of your role. For example, it's easy for a person to be so identified with a financial or management information system role that he or she can't shift. If you are going to move up in an organizational hierarchy, it is important to ask for rotational assignments early, particularly in roles with which you have little or no familiarity. Often, if one becomes locked into a given track and accepts several promotions, it becomes impossible to go back to an earlier level, as in the case of the person who discovers that his advance along a technical track prevents his advance managerially because he's too far along to start at an entry-level managerial role. In most organizations, it is important to have managerial experience to be considered for upward mobility in an organization. Companies are reluctant to move into managerial roles people who are already well along in their careers in technical roles.

Getting the Feedback Needed for Shaping Your Career

Too many people hear only their boss's assessment of their performance. Of course, that's an important perspective, but if your boss suffers from guilt about hurting people, limited cognitive capacity, or intense rivalry problems with subordinates, you may not be getting the diagnostic information you need to shape a career.

Feedback does more than provide information. People sometimes ask the boss for feedback because they need reassurance to counteract their wavering self-esteem, or because they want to appear conscientious, or because they want to call attention to a performance that's going very well. But if information and growth are your main goals, be sure not to overlook these sources of feedback:

Mentors. Everyone needs a senior person (or senior people), not necessarily the boss, to help with his or her career. In a good mentor relationship, the senior person is honest without being devastating, but nevertheless may have limited opportunities to observe your work firsthand. Try to expand the opportunities for a mentor to observe you, perhaps by volunteering for a project on which you both can serve.

Subordinates. The people you manage can provide an interesting perspective, but it's not fair to try to force them to criticize you honestly if they don't want to. Additionally, if by asking for feedback you appear to need reassurance, they may perceive you as weak and lacking in confidence. That can undermine your position. Also, since your subordinates are presumably at a lower cognitive level (lower level of ability to think abstractly or with complexity), their judgment of you may be flawed. So feedback from subordinates needs to be sought judiciously and weighed against what others have to say. And don't ask subordinates for feedback if you're not willing to change. One advertising executive, when asked for her opinion, wrote a critical memo to her boss, who routinely stole her ideas and undercut her. The criticism was valid—the boss admitted that—but he stole two more ideas the following month. Soon afterward, the subordinate, more frustrated than ever, left, taking her good ideas to a competitor.

Upward appraisal. If you want subordinate input without so many drawbacks, consider an upward appraisal conducted by a third party who is trusted to be impartial and who is psychologically sophisticated. Upward appraisal is the most reliable way to get subordinates' input, but it requires formal organizational support.

Peers. Peers can contribute to your accurate self-assessment. But the risks are similar to those presented by subordinates. You don't want peers to perceive you as lacking in self-confidence, and there's no reason to assume a peer is on a higher cognitive level than you are and therefore able to judge your work accurately. Bearing the pitfalls in mind, there's a lot you can learn from an honest coworker.

Enemies. For an eye-opening assessment of your performance, try asking for feedback from someone who dislikes you. You know that this person has seen some fault in you, and he or she may not be overly concerned about sparing your feelings. This high-risk strategy is most successful when the other person is not excessively manipulative or a direct competitor who might use the opportunity to hurt you, either by a vicious critical attack or by misrepresenting your conversation later. If you're lucky, your asking could have the added benefit of reducing the enmity between you, partly through the compliment you pay by asking his or her opinion and partly because you may open the door to talking through your differences.

Senior people. If you can ask higher-ups for an assessment without your boss feeling threatened, do so. You need all the input you can get from people with higher cognitive capacity.

Monitoring systems. Sometimes managers, eager to avoid the hassles involved in asking others for feedback, monitor their own performance by watching for indirect cues. This method of gathering feedback avoids the potential social costs, but because many of the messages are so subtle, the information may be less accurate. As Susan Ashford and Anne Tsui point out, people may not return phone calls for many reasons. To infer that an unreturned phone call means negative feedback could be highly misleading.[2]

People outside your organization. If you do volunteer work or if you work with representatives of other companies, these people have seen how you get things done and can be comparatively low-risk sources of help.

Sources of feedback, including your enemies, may have difficulty being honest because of unconscious guilt and fear of hurting you. So start by telling your source that you're aware it's hard for him. Explain that you're interested in professional growth and that you'll be grateful, not hurt or angry, for what he has to say.

To improve the usefulness of the feedback you receive, ask about specific incidents. "You're not a good speaker" doesn't help much. Assist your source with probing questions: What did you think of my presentation to the management committee? Which was better, Jane's or mine? What could I have done differently? How? In what ways?

These can be difficult conversations, so you'll need to be prepared to persevere despite some discomfort. If, however, your source looks very uncomfortable, or if you've caught him off guard, don't pressure him for a quick answer. One incorrect assumption many managers make is that they'll get a more honest answer from someone who's responding "off the top of his head." Actually, the reverse is true. People's first reaction to a tough question is usually their most defensive one. Instinctively they try to protect their psychological equilibrium and to avoid feeling and causing discomfort. It's upon reflection and a more accurate assessment of the threat that they become more willing to speak openly. So if you ask a tough question, don't be afraid to say, "Would you rather talk about this later?"

To make the process work, you need to be sure that you're asking for feedback to learn how you can improve rather than seeking reassurance or trying to improve your image. Whom to ask, what to ask, and how to ask it will be more apparent if your goal is clear.

When you find people who give you honest, helpful feedback, don't forget to thank them and find ways to support their efforts. Your straightforward explanation of what information you found helpful and why will strengthen the affection and dependency bonds between you. Thanking them will alleviate much of the guilt they might feel about hurting you and will encourage them to help again.

Cultivating Mutually Beneficial Relations with Your Boss

Too often people think of a boss as someone who has to be endured or manipulated or obeyed. Too few people take the trouble to understand the psychological significance of being a follower or a subordinate. One has only to observe the accompanist of a soloist at a concert or recital to grasp how important a secondary role can be to the person in the lead position. Ideally, a good subordinate, like the accompanist, is a solid supporter of his or her boss. At the same time, the good boss is supportive of the subordinate. Just as the concert performance is a product of the joint efforts of two performers, performance at work results from working together.

Identifying with Your Boss

Are you supporting your boss? Think of it as your job to get your boss promoted. I'm not suggesting you become a teacher's pet or let yourself be exploited. But if your boss is working to achieve the organization's goals, you have a lot to gain by identifying with him or her. That means seeing the boss as someone whose goals you share and whose abilities and standards you want to emulate, and as someone who helps you become more competent, promotable, and self-confident.

When you identify with your boss, you learn more, and she is more likely to give you other chances to show what you can do and to help you succeed. When your boss is promoted, you'll have a supporter higher up.

You need to understand what your boss is accountable to his boss for and what he wants to accomplish. That's not always obvious. You may know that your boss has to expand his sales area, but not that he also hopes to improve communications so they won't be a weak link when his group expands. Pay attention to the steps he takes and ask about the bigger picture.

Sometimes a boss may not know where to begin to fulfill an aspiration or wish. It is important not only to support what he wants to do, but also to spell out how he might go about doing it. I think, for example, of the head of a savings and loan organization who wanted to better his community, but had no idea how to go about organizing the community to improve itself. A subordinate who could have successfully spelled out the steps would have been helpful to this boss.

Pay attention also to your boss's behavioral goals. If your boss is trying to listen more, can you present information in ways that make him least uncomfortable? What pressure is your boss under from his boss? Can you help?

The acid test comes when helping your boss requires criticizing him or keeping him from making a mistake. You may be in the doghouse temporarily. But if your boss is reasonable, he'll come around.

In some organizations, a boss takes credit for the work of his subordinates. This can be offensive if the subordinate is not clear about how credit is achieved in the organization. Before getting insulted about something like this, look for the usual practice and custom in a particular organization. Your basic task as a subordinate is always to make the boss look good. That doesn't necessarily mean that you should be contented with having the boss take credit for what you do. Yet, often it is more important for ideas to be accepted and implemented than to fight over who gets the credit. That's especially important if you don't want to exacerbate rivalrous feelings with debate over who gets the credit.

Receiving Support from Your Boss

It's nice if your boss says you have a great future. But what is he doing about it? Is your boss fostering your development?

"Sure, he helps me a lot," you might say. "I can always go to him with a problem." But help alone isn't development. Help is for now. Development is for the future.

By fostering your development, I mean that your boss guides and supervises you in such a way that you acquire not only new skills but new maturity—new ways of understanding people and solving problems. He or she is taking an active role in your growth, not just applauding from the stands. Here are some ways to tell if that's happening:

☐ Does your boss criticize you and confront you with poor performance and inappropriate behavior? If he likes you too much to do so or thinks it's not right to do so, as I noted in the previous chapter, he cannot help develop you. The confrontations should result in discussion of how you can improve and then in feedback about your subsequent performance.

☐ Does she have high standards and hold you to them, even when the organization doesn't require her to? If it's done constructively, then your boss is developing you in one of the best ways possible: by making herself a role model for you.

☐ Does he show you how he does things, including the touches that make for his personal style of management? Apprenticeship can be a powerful developmental tool. Education researchers Ann Brown and Annemarie Palincsar dramatically improved a group of seventh graders' reading skills by teaching the children to "approach a text the way a teacher does."[3]

☐ Does she ever hand you a task that's a little over your head, forcing you to stretch and learn? You gain the self-confidence that comes from doing something you didn't realize you could do. I'm not talking about a boss who dumps too much on you because she's overworked, but one who knows you are ready to take your next step, even if you don't know it.

☐ Does he nurture your ability to work independently? Is he willing to deny you help at times, in order to make you try harder? Does he back off once you've shown you can handle a problem? Most important, can he stand back and let you make mistakes (nonfatal ones) without jumping in the minute he spots trouble?

☐ Does he make your work visible to others in the company?

Does he give you credit for your work in public? Has he ever set you up to work on a task outside his own unit?

☐ Does he talk with you about your career, asking you where you want to go and explaining what potential he sees in you, what you need to learn, and how he expects various responsibilities to develop you? He may even have more in mind for you than you have in mind for yourself.

☐ Does he give you varied tasks, including some that test your weak points? Human resources directors Anthony Fairhead and John Hudson pointed out the importance of knowing your own "derailment factors."[4] These often involve overreliance on your best strengths. Kerry Bunker, Center for Creative Leadership, reported: "Learning from mistakes is easier and morecommon than learning from accomplishments. . . . Failure means a rude shock, a striking contrast. The lessons of success are not so obvious."[5] It's tempting to give a subordinate tasks he or she is best at; in the short run, more work gets done that way. But that doesn't develop the subordinate.

If your boss is not fostering your development, ask him for more active development. Tell him you feel you aren't learning how to be a more valuable employee next year than you are this year.

Think things through beforehand so you can be specific about what you'd like to learn; for example, how your boss decides when he's got enough information to make a decision. Fairhead and Hudson's research resulted in a list of five key experiences that executives felt had taught them the most: "starting an operation from scratch, turning a unit or business around, a leap in scope of assignment, a transfer from a line to a staff role, or heading a project or task force."[6] Don't expect your boss to just hand you a task force or a start-up, but you can put yourself in the running if you've shown an interest and some qualifications.

Ideally, all bosses should help develop their subordinates. But not all people who are bosses can do it. Your boss may lack the interactive skills, or may be too insecure or too competitive to develop subordinates. For that matter, he may feel too overwhelmed by pressure from above.

If you see that you aren't going to get the development you need from your boss, you have three other sources to try:

Other managers in your company. I discuss finding a mentor other than your boss in Chapter 14, "Mentoring for Growth."

Yourself. Develop yourself by observing others and by reading and study. Keep watching above for the subtle differences between work and management at one level and another.

The big, wide world out there. Attend conferences in your field and take advantage of meeting persons in other companies to get a wider knowledge of how people get things done. Seek out training opportunities that address your weaknesses or ambitions. (These are also opportunities to meet other managers.)

If your boss is helping you develop, don't just accept it passively. Become an active shaper of your own career. Ask your boss questions about the tasks he assigns and what you can learn from them. Tell him what you do learn. You might even offer to write up your experiences for him, to record what worked and what didn't. You'd be doing yourself a favor, too, since someday you will be in your boss's shoes.

Be aware of the psychological pitfalls of a relationship like this: First, overdependence—expecting your boss to be your fairy godmother and to guarantee you a safe passage to success; and second, the inevitable separation when you outgrow your need for this much guidance. It can be much like the way adolescents break away from their parents, and that's because at the unconscious level it is much the same thing.

Be sure to thank your boss from time to time for helping you develop. Remember, though, that your boss can only contribute to your development by providing guidance and opportunity. He or she can't really develop you. You have to develop yourself.

Should You Follow Your Boss?

You and your boss have worked well together. Now she's been promoted into another division and wants to bring you along. But do you want to go? Ask yourself some hard questions before grabbing her coattails.

☐ Will your boss have more power? Is her new role in the mainstream of company operations or in a peripheral specialty? Don't follow her down a dead end.

☐ Who is your boss's benefactor in the hierarchy? Is his future clear enough to indicate a bright future for your boss? If he is retiring soon or is a protagonist in an organizational conflict, your boss's advancement could be stymied.

☐ Do you fear being on your own? Are you wondering how you'll survive without your boss's protection and influence? If so, you've become too dependent on your boss. You probably need to make the break now. In the long run, it's far more risky to identify so intensely with your boss that you never establish your own place in the company.

Following your boss is a good move when it's part of *your* career path, not just the path of least resistance.

CHAPTER **12**

Mapping Your Managerial Education

Think of your efforts to move up in the organization. You may have taken courses in supervisory techniques, communication, or finance. Perhaps you've earned your MBA. But even if you aren't moving up in your organization, technological developments and changes in the marketplace will overtake your current level of skill. As you move up, the nature of educational requirements changes, as does the educational background of your subordinates. The need for training in specific skills gives way to a need to develop your higher-level intellectual capabilities, a broader perspective, and a deeper understanding of human behavior.

How should you prepare yourself for managerial and executive roles? One important clue lies in the new directions educational programs in large organizations are taking. More and more organizations are setting up comprehensive education programs—their own schools, in effect. Some, like AT&T's in-house master's program and GE's advanced management development program, are long established. Some companies, like Digital Equipment Corporation, develop specific programs for their managers in universities or business schools that encompass a cadre from all over the world. The Digital program is at INSEAD in Fontainebleau, France.

Education in the business world is already big business, and getting bigger. If organizations are allocating resources to these programs, that's clearly what they find their people need.

Management has become a profession in its own right. It is no longer simply a matter of a few supervisory duties tacked on to a technical role. Even nonbusiness institutions such as museums, libraries, and churches are beginning to recognize the need for the expertise a professional manager brings. The time has passed when companies could simply promote people into management roles because they had seniority or were the most capable workers in their group. The MBA or equivalent knowledge is becoming the minimum requirement for managerial roles in sizable organizations, just as a professional degree is required for teachers, engineers, and other professionals.

Some companies send promising managers to degree programs at universities, while others reimburse tuition for courses and programs undertaken independently. More and more organizations are conducting such programs under their own roofs with a faculty they have selected. Employees who seriously aspire to higher-level positions would do well to look into the programs their companies offer. And those whose companies do not provide or support such programs would do well to consider how they will acquire this essential level of knowledge. Without it, they may be able to advance in their specialty, but could be at a disadvantage when it comes to moving into general management. For example, it's important to keep in touch with university executive education programs. Each year *Business Week* does an evaluation of these programs, noting which specialize in given areas and which have particular competences. These programs should be reviewed to select those that fit your needs best.

This is not to say that you cannot manage well without an MBA. Certainly there are many good managers who never went to business school. But there is a core body of knowledge that good managers either learn academically or pick up along the way from other managers and their own experience. Increasing professionalism means that this core body of knowledge is becoming more technical and more sophisticated, and is therefore progressively harder to learn independently.

Many companies are also going beyond the MBA level in their educational programs. They recognize that organizations are not only growing but also diversifying, decentralizing, and shifting their modes of functioning to meet new kinds of competition; and they recognize that this increasing complexity will require executives to operate at higher levels of abstraction. Executives will need to conceive of what they are doing in a historical context, and they will need to recognize the effects of their business decisions on the community. High-level executives now need a whole range of competences and skills that simply were not required to the same degree just a few years ago. They must interact with the public and with government, articulate a business point of view both inside and outside the organization, and work interdependently with a wide variety of people. This means managers moving into higher-level roles must be more flexible, more sophisticated, and more knowledgeable than ever before.

Much of the education executives need in order to develop these competences is not available through existing programs, including advanced management programs of major universities. James Baughman, GE's manager of management education, says, "There is vast illiteracy on business school faculties" in both the mechanics of advanced technology and its management implications. His views are echoed by an executive from Texas Instruments: "As technology changes, universities tend to lag one to three years behind what's happening in the workplace."[1] Without special arrangements, as in the case of Digital, universities simply are not prepared to meet the particular needs of a given organization. Their programs do not focus on subjects as they relate to particular industries, as in-house programs can. For example, the AT&T program can emphasize the economics of public utilities instead of being limited to discussions of economic principles in general.

A Psychological Foundation

Another problem with typical business school programs is that they do not offer the kind of psychological background needed to manage people successfully. There are assumptions about human motivation behind everything we do. Managers need a solid psychological understanding to help them recognize and evaluate their own assumptions. They also need to evaluate the underlying psychological assumptions in areas as factual as statistics and finance. Otherwise they will act on tacit assumptions that may be untenable or conflicting, totally unaware that they may be undermining the very objectives they pursue.

Unfortunately, the only psychological background offered by most business schools is a set of generalized conceptions of motivation, such as Maslow's hierarchy of needs, Herzberg's two-factor theory, McGregor's Theory X and Theory Y, behavior modeling and modification, exchange theory, self-efficiency theory, and goal-setting theory. Students tend to view these offerings as gut courses, and executives find these generalizations insufficient for handling specific situations.

What would be sufficient? Managers need a comprehensive theory of personality. By this I do not mean adding together the generalized theories mentioned above. Careful examination reveals that these theories are based on questionable assumptions about what makes people tick. To paste them together and call that a comprehensive theory is nonsense. Such a conglomeration still would not apply to specific problems under specific circumstances. Managers need a theory that is sophisticated enough to do justice to the complexity of human beings—in short, psychoanalytic theory.

People sometimes say psychoanalytic theory is too complex. Yet these same people have no complaint about the complexities of accounting, econometric models, and marketing analyses. Executives simply can't afford to be any less sophisticated about people than they are about computers.

Managers must work with a wide range of people and understand the differences between them. They need to understand unconscious as well as conscious processes. This will help them recognize and cope with the unconscious guilt that cripples their managerial activity and impairs all performance appraisal. It will help them understand the sources of stress, so they can anticipate and alleviate or ameliorate it. It will also help them understand the changes in direction as younger people come into the organization. And it will help them understand the irrational reactions of people outside the organization when the organization's rational decisions affect their lives. The same psychological understanding will give them a better grasp of what goes on in their own families.

Probably the hardest part of managerial practice is dealing with the feelings of fear, self-doubt, and anger, both in yourself and in your associates. These feelings are repeatedly aroused by typical managerial situations—responsibility for and to others, competition and rivalry, change, ambiguous role definitions—yet they often operate on an unconscious level. And it is these feelings, unknown to most managers, that keep people in conflict with themselves and others, tearing them apart.

There is no longer any excuse for managers being simplistic about people. The psychological knowledge they need is available in a wide range of books.[2] There are courses taught by clinical psychologists and psychiatrists. These people, having been involved in the therapy of individuals, including very sick individuals, have a depth of understanding that provides insight into managerial situations. They can pass some of this understanding on to managers, and help them learn to apply it to specific situations. And there are seminars, like those at The Levinson Institute, where managers come together for lectures and practice in applying the theory.

Beyond the Fundamentals

Once you have your MBA or the equivalent and a grounding in human psychology, it's important to remember that you don't stop there. Those are the fundamentals on which to build. They are tools that need to be applied. The next step is learning to apply them appropriately. Applying the right technique in the wrong place is no better than having no technique to apply.

How can you judge applicability? You must learn to diagnose your organization. That is, you must learn to determine (1) where the organization stands and what its problems are and (2) what changes need to be made. This means learning to gather information from people by interviewing and observing—learning to listen. You cannot rely solely on survey techniques to find out what goes on in your organization because survey results are often misleading. Nor can you continue to be an effective manager without hearing the concerns of your own people.

Once you have gathered the information, it must be organized and interpreted. On the basis of that interpretation, you can formulate a plan of action and analyze the possible consequences of implementing that plan. Failure to diagnose situations and anticipate consequences has led to many costly mistakes. One organization had a system that worked well in an existing plant, so they designed their new plant to fit that system. They neglected to consider the different character of the work force in their new location—and now they own a plant designed for an inappropriate system.

Since change is such an emotionally disruptive process, the people who will be affected must be involved in the planning and problem solving as much as possible. This requires, in addition to understanding the psychology of individuals, understanding group process. Many managers fail because they don't know how to manage the conflicts and dynamics of the group they are supposed to be leading.

Many managers fail because they are inarticulate. You need to be able to explain your findings, opinions, plans, and projections to both superiors and subordinates, and perhaps to peers and the public as well. If you cannot write or speak clearly and simply, you can hardly expect to be successful. Even the most brilliant ideas are worthless if you can't communicate them. A less competent manager might easily be promoted over one who has better ideas but can't express them clearly. Company courses in writing and public speaking are well worth the time and effort for managers who want to keep moving up.

Another much-neglected managerial skill is that of aiding younger managers in their development. There is growing recognition in organizations of the need to begin developing future executives now. Company educational programs are one part of that effort, but much of what future leaders need to know comes from the experience of managing, and from modeling themselves after their superiors. Organizations will be looking for executives with a demonstrated ability to provide younger managers with supervised experience, help them recognize and remedy their weaknesses, and guide them in their education. Managers who wish to move up must learn to teach and coach others.

Combating Obsolescence

Obsolescence results from changes in the knowledge base, changes in technology, and loss of touch with events beyond the immediate task. There is a tendency, especially in the early part of your career, to invest all your energy in accomplishing the task at hand—usually at the expense of keeping your psychological periscope up. It's easy to work yourself deeper and deeper into a rut, and to pay no attention to the rest of the world. Since this happens gradually, you're unlikely to notice, so it's wise to plan formally in advance to combat obsolescence.

In-house management development programs are useful for bringing your basic skills up to speed and catching up on new developments in your organization, industry, or field. However, in-house programs do little to counteract the tendency to lose perspective on your own work and on developments outside the business world. Professional meetings have the same drawback. My recommendation is to take some kind of comprehensive refresher experience about every five years. Outside programs, such as advanced management programs at universities, can provide the perspective you need. As you come into contact with managers from a variety of backgrounds and industries, and see them struggling with the same issues in different forms, you begin to see the universality of your problems. This kind of perspective, along with the opportunity to share one anothers' ways of dealing with common issues, can make the difficulties of adapting to higher-level roles less overwhelming and more worthwhile.

Keeping up in this way may be more difficult for managers who have family obligations. Anticipating this problem, they may be able to make special arrangements. On many campuses there are established child care centers for members of staff and faculty. For older children there may well be summer programs in special areas such as language, drama, computer literacy, and so on.

Many organizations use advanced management programs as rewards for achievement, to keep people on the shelf for 6–13 weeks until a place can be found for them, or, worse yet, just to get them out of their boss's hair for a while. This means many managers end up at these programs with no idea what their companies are trying to accomplish, or what might be expected of them when they return. With their attention so unfocused, or even distracted, they get much less out of the experience than they could. But managers who want to maintain their vitality must recognize the value of such refreshers, and take the initiative in making effective use of them.

In addition to upgrading general managerial skills, managers in specialized areas such as finance, engineering, human resources, and so on, must keep up to date in their specialties. They need to refocus their activities, become acquainted with related research or innovative practices, and sharpen their competences. They need contact with others in the same discipline, as well as with university-level people who are involved in the latest research and thinking in their field. And their efforts should be systematic and analytic, avoiding the catch-as-catch-can approach of contemporary continuing education in medicine, teaching, and psychology.

The frequency with which refreshers are needed varies considerably. It depends on how fast things are changing. It's possible that what you're doing is the frontier because the pioneering work is being done in industry, as with genetic engineering and matrix management. In those cases, university programs have little to offer. Refresher experiences instead might consist of visits to other organizations where innovations are being introduced, to discuss how new procedures work. Conferences and special seminars might be important refreshers as well.

In all these explorations, it is important to keep the matter of psychological assumptions in mind, so you don't end up applying techniques inappropriately. You must realize that the people who develop new techniques often don't see their own assumptions, don't really know what makes the techniques work, and neglect the Hawthorne effect (that is, paying any kind of attention to a situation usually improves it—temporarily). You must always maintain a critical stance.

Business in the World

Managers often take pride in being practical and play down the importance of cultural and intellectual pursuits. Certainly there is nothing like being practical. But there is also nothing like learning the lessons of history and understanding contemporary events.

Contemporary events are best understood as the expression in our own time of themes that have appeared in art, music, and literature throughout the ages. Human nature and the human condition don't change much on the basic level represented in great works of art. The kind of perspective on contemporary events that is made possible by a broad liberal arts background can be a highly stabilizing influence in a rapidly changing world. Some new problems aren't as new as their "discoverers" would like you to think. After all, Euripides was writing about the generation gap in the fifth century B.C.

Many managers started out as undergraduates in technical fields such as engineering and accounting; they have plenty of training but little education. If they never fill in that liberal arts background, either with course work or through their own reading, they are likely to plateau. A broad background is more than a means to wiser business decisions. As people move up the ladder, they are asked to serve on the boards of operas, ballets, colleges, and other institutions. They can't afford to be ignorant of those activities. In addition, they meet a higher plane of people. Those who travel internationally must be able to converse with sophisticated, highly educated people at their own level.

Executives also need to be familiar with the history and culture of their organizations, as I noted in Chapter 5. To adapt effectively to changing circumstances, they must know how people adapted in the past to a wide range of conditions. Where this information is available in the form of written history or organized teaching, managers do well to take advantage of it. Otherwise, it's worth seeking out individuals who have been with the organization long enough to know what the organization has been through, and why and how it survived. With such assistance, the lessons, values, and conflicts of the past can be brought into the present for understanding and guidance.

As society becomes more fractionated and business more consolidated, the relative power and influence of business grows. People fear that power. Unless businessmen study political science and understand the conflicting forces within the body politic of both the United States and foreign countries, they and their organizations will be less able to understand and cope with the buffeting of political winds. It is not enough to complain about government regulations or the appropriation of assets by a revolutionary government; it is necessary to understand why these things came about. Those who aspire to high-level positions must undertake systematic study of such issues.

Limits to Growth

There is always pressure to learn specific skills in order to perform certain tasks better. But businesses are having to compensate for the narrowness of specialization—some by paying a premium price for those executives who have prepared themselves well, others by paying for the broader education of their specialists or suffering with the gaps in their knowledge. Company education departments are beginning to catch on to these needs and fill in these areas of their programs.

The need for specialists is real and growing, but managerial growth is stunted by specialization. Some people move so high in their specialty, in terms of salary or grade level, that they can't move laterally into general management. They lack the elementary managerial skills they would have picked up long ago as a general manager, and would have to step down considerably to get them now. There is an optimum time for moving over into general management, and if that's where you want to go, you must prepare yourself to move before it's too late. Of course, there is also a need for managers in specialty areas, and specialists will always do better in their dealings with managers of other departments if they have some understanding of the manager's world.

Wishful thinking won't get you where you want to go. Despite company efforts in career planning, you can't expect anyone else to guide your preparation for advancement. You may not stay in the same organization your whole working life, so you can't just plan to follow the company's program. You have to take charge of your own life and manage your own career. That means more than deciding where you want to be 5 years from now, and 10 years, and 20. It means looking at what you will need to know in 5 or 10 or 20 years, and how you are going to learn it.

No one can do everything suggested, develop every competence and skill, study every subject, understand everything about personality and motivation, and always act "correctly" on the basis of that knowledge, skill, and understanding. Think of a topographic map, showing you the lay of the land. These are the obstacles to be negotiated, the hills to be climbed or circumvented, and the rivers to be crossed or followed to their source. This map is drawn from the evidence of organizations' education programs, from the experience of some managers who have succeeded and others who have failed, and from a view of the projected future. Every detail may not be meant for you, because it is intended to be applicable to diverse managers who have one thing in common: the desire to be excellent.

CHAPTER 13

Advancing Without Mishap

A vice president, taking over a new worldwide unit, and confronted with several quarters of declining sales and profitability in her company, exhorted her new team to achieve great sales heights. She pressured each of her assembled subordinates to commit himself or herself to sales goals that far outdistanced their previous achievement. When one laggard failed to raise his hand, she bore in on him. What would he commit to? He said he didn't know what he could commit to because the economy in his country was even more sluggish than that in most other countries. Its slide had not yet stopped. The vice president would not accept his answers.

This scene occurred in a context of organizational decay. The company had not had any new products for several years. Nobody quite knew what to do with the prospective innovations that the company research and development unit had put forth. The corporate leader characteristically did not sanction innovation from below. Another quarterly loss would probably lead to his demise.

Failing to understand that, preoccupied with declining sales, and confident that exhortation would cause them to rise, the vice president had bungled her way into her new role. It would not take great foresight to predict that she would fail.

Many managers fail in this way. They do not give credence to psychological factors, to diagnosis, and to the forces operating in the specific situation in which they find themselves. They fall back on whatever managerial behavior had served them before.

This problem is not limited to managers taking on new situations. It can also mar the records of established managers who are unable to shift quickly enough from an established managerial stance to respond to changing circumstances. In short, they are psychologically imprisoned. They cannot adapt quickly enough.

Those who would advance their careers, therefore, should give careful attention to the psychological subtleties of moving into a new managerial role. Stumbling and fumbling are not conducive to advancing.

The great actor Alec Guinness recalled that his acting instructor, Martita Hunt, taught her students to emphasize verbs as the driving force of a sentence, the nouns being secondary.[1] In the same way, I have told people that they cannot count on their accomplishments when they are promoted, only their ability to do things. Their verbs, their capacity to act—not their nouns, their history—are what make them successful after they have been promoted. Incidentally, that's why performance appraisals should include descriptions of a person's characteristic (or uncharacteristic) behaviors, not just records of quotas met, deals made, and so on.

Starting Off on the Right Foot

Becoming Acquainted with Traditions

C . William Carey, CEO of Town & Country Jewelry, spent $15,000 on fortune-tellers to reassure workers in his Hong Kong factory that all was well.[2] That may sound like a waste, but it showed employees that Carey accepted their traditions and wanted them to feel secure.

Every department has traditions that bring people together, open up communications, or reassure people that the boss takes them seriously. But new bosses are often too busy to bother with such foolishness. For example, one department had always had a monthly complaints day for the whole group. The new boss had subordinates bring complaints directly to him. Some man-hours were saved, but something worthwhile was lost: subordinates missed the sense of helping each other.

When you're a new boss, ask your predecessor what rituals people enjoyed. Ask if he or she stopped any traditions and how subordinates reacted. When you learn what the traditions are, think about the needs they meet. The complaints day met subordinates' needs for affection (they saw themselves as a team) and for dependency (they relied on each other for sympathy and solutions).

If you have to do away with a tradition, tell subordinates in advance what you are doing and why. Acknowledge what psychological needs were met by that tradition and what you'll do to meet those needs in other ways. For example, subordinates who miss the complaints day could meet in smaller groups to discuss common problems.

Assessing New Subordinates

You're the new boss and new to the organization; you need someone to show you the ropes. Subordinates are willing, but you don't know who's dependable, who's showing off, and who's a manipulator. Unconsciously, you may trust subordinates who seem similar to you and ignore subordinates who are too shy, too informal, or too methodical.

How can you keep yourself from prejudging subordinates? You can't, but there are ways to keep yourself from acting on your gut reactions.

- ☐ Accept the fact that you will have a gut reaction.
- ☐ Test it. For example, if a subordinate seems like a great person, don't assume she shares your dedication and standards. Give her small projects and see whether she meets deadlines or takes advantage of your trust.
- ☐ Give subordinates time to get past their initial responses to you. A subordinate who is on her best behavior may be a manipulator. Someone who is initially hostile may return to her cooperative self.
- ☐ Take up your predecessor's offer to fill you in on subordinates' idiosyncrasies, but treat those opinions as just opinions. Otherwise, you could inherit his or her prejudices.

Essentially, you are giving subordinates permission to start over. Some may not have gotten along with your predecessor or may have gotten a bad rap.

Avoiding Misunderstandings

When you're new, you have to watch out for yourself, no matter how competent you may be. For example, a new manager had some good ideas and wanted her subordinates to know what was going on, so she told them her plans. But she neglected to find out what had happened before she came or what the subordinates themselves expected. To them, her new directives clearly implied that she thought they hadn't done well before, though they had been doing what the old boss asked. Some good people felt so unappreciated that they left. When her peers saw that she was losing good people, they took her to be an incompetent boss.

When you are new, here's how to make sure you and your people don't misunderstand each other:

☐ Ask your boss for background and have her make clear her expectations of you and of the group.
☐ Ask subordinates individually what they want to achieve in their roles and where they would like to see the department go. What would they like to change?
☐ Summarize what subordinates said and present your findings to the group, so they know you heard them. You may be tempted to make some promises to show them that you are on their side, but it's too soon for commitments.

Dealing with Survivors of Downsizing

Downsizing is becoming an increasingly common event, and you may find yourself directly involved. As a new manager, you can walk into some vicious booby traps in a downsized company. Psychotherapist Erwin Parson described how Vietnam veterans are often paralyzed with guilt for the things they had to do to survive. "Many . . . remain intensely identified with the dead—their buddies and their victims."[3] The same happens to managers who have seen friends laid off and may themselves have had to lay people off. They feel awful about what they did and betrayed by the superiors who forced them to do it.

When you take charge of your new group, you need to meet that anger head on. Get your people together and ask them what happened and how they feel about it. Of course, you may get a one-sided version, so you should ask your boss to tell you his or her version as well.

You are likely to hear things that will make you uncomfortable: tales of your predecessor's brilliance or of the brutal way your boss fired people. Don't cut people off; you'll exacerbate their anger and they may direct it at you. Besides, such stories let you know how your people feel.

Summarize for your group what you've heard. Chances are you can't do anything about their losses, but acknowledging the losses is important. If you don't acknowledge those feelings, your people will nurse them and you'll be fighting the effects of them for a long time to come.

Even when the group as a whole lets go of its grief, certain people will not. They may have had special attachments to a departed boss or to a way of life that is over. The downsizing may have come on top of a family disaster. Offer them special attention. If you find you can't help a person at all, recommend that he or she talk to a therapist for some grief therapy or crisis intervention.

Dealing with Your Predecessor's Legacy

When you take over a new managerial role, you inherit your subordinates' attitudes toward your predecessor. A striking example of this was recounted by Lorin Maazel, who succeeded the legendary George Szell as music director of the Cleveland Orchestra.[4] Szell had used "the Toscanini method—you scream, insult, throw tantrums, put down, browbeat," Maazel said, quickly adding that this doesn't mean Szell was inhuman. As a result, "there was this enormous resentment and love for the maestro." Maazel himself was less authoritarian, so players were able to express more of their feelings with him. But at first, they were releasing the pent-up feelings from their years with Szell—and directing them at Maazel. "There was this sort of backwash of resentment," said Maazel, "and I think it took three or four years for this situation to cleanse itself in the collective psyche," as the players gradually realized that he was a different type of leader. They became "relaxed and cheerful," said Maazel, and the orchestra sounded "looser and less fearful."

Succeeding an Authoritarian Boss

Some people respond to an authoritarian boss like Szell by cringing in fear. Such people will be inclined to project hostility onto their new boss and continue to assume the same posture. Others like working for an authoritarian leader, because they wish to be as strong as they imagine the leader to be. They identify strongly with that leader, and will allow the leader to abuse them in many ways—beat them, castigate them, drive them to impossible feats—in the belief that the leader will, by such actions, make them as strong as he or she. This is what happened with Vince Lombardi and Harold Geneen. Players and subordinates admired and respected those leaders because they sensed their own inadequacies, which the leaders seemed not to share. They assumed that the leader would beat or train those inadequacies out of them, making them as powerful as he. Out of their overidentification with such a leader, people become even more vicious to their subordinates than the leader is to them.

When the powerful leader is gone, the organization begins to lose its momentum—as both the Green Bay Packers and ITT demonstrated. The manager who follows an authoritarian leader will be reviled by the followers if he or she is not equally authoritarian. They will perceive the new leader as weak, and will challenge, test, and object to him or her every step of the way. They will demand the kind of rigid overcontrol to which they are accustomed. Again, this is a reflection of their own inadequacies. They fear they will be overwhelmed by events without their strong leader. Only when they discover that the new leader is indeed a strong person, one who is not frightened by them or the realities, as was the case with Lorin Maazel, will they buckle down and respond to his or her leadership. However, given their underlying sense of inadequacy, such people will always be prone to making decisions before all the facts are in, to impulsive controlling action, and to contempt for their own subordinates that justifies their authoritarian action.

If you are a more democratic manager following an authoritarian manager, you should expect the behavior described above. You should anticipate being tested, and prepare to be firm in response. You need not be authoritarian, but must be strong enough to put boundaries around the testing behavior. You must indicate very clearly that you are the boss, you are in charge, and you will not brook the open hostility that will characterize the testing behavior of such people. Ideally, they gradually will come to recognize the strength of their new leader, as Maazel's orchestra did, and will tend to project less onto you and react less on the basis of those projections.

You will have to present yourself in a firmly consistent way that will differentiate you from your predecessor, yet reflect strength and clarity of image. (Women in particular need to pay attention to this, since they may be inclined to a low-key, less aggressive style, and some people may expect them to be weak.) Vacillation out of fear, guilt, anger, or disappointment will only undermine one's role in such circumstances.

Succeeding a Charismatic Boss

When you succeed a charismatic leader, the problems are different. You live in the shadow of charisma. The charismatic leader may have founded the organization or served it for many years. He or she built the organization, developed its constituencies and reputation, engaged its staff, and gave it leadership. Or, like Lee Iacocca, he or she may have rescued it. Such a leader leaves a legacy: an established organization and a leadership tradition. Charismatic leaders also tend to be highly paternalistic. They often give loving attention to their peo-ple, and in turn people obey—for the leader, after all, developed the legend of which they are now a part. The leader is highly respected, even beloved. Like all pioneers, he or she is revered for having broken new ground.

When anyone is loved this way, people repress their underlying negative feelings or ambivalence. How can they be angry at such a good person? And yet the person leaves, which is unconsciously experienced as desertion. Stuck with their unexpressed anger, they cannot let go. They are left with their loss, and perhaps the wish that the charismatic leader will return. In most instances, they feel lost and helpless without the master builder.

Arthur Fiedler, the late famous conductor of the Boston Pops, was a charismatic leader. He was a musical legend; he fought great opposition to make the Boston Pops a famous institution. He also was to be seen riding fire trucks and engaging in public antics of many kinds. In private he was an irritable, self-centered man. In pub-lic he was a lovable cherub. Another charismatic leader was Fiorello

La Guardia. As mayor of New York, he was to be found at the scenes of big fires and catastrophes, and he read the funny papers to children over the city radio when the newspapers were on strike. He was known as "the little flower."

Who can succeed such a myth? Any successor, by contrast, must be next to nothing. Who is he or she to take the place of the demigod? No one can give love and affection as valuable as what the hero-on-a-pedestal gave. How could anyone deserve to be revered the way the charismatic leader was revered? The successor cannot help but be a shadow.

Joe Henson, president of Prime Computer, found himself in this situation, following Ken Fischer, who headed the company during its phenomenal growth in the late seventies. Henson was seen as responsible for Prime's slower growth in the mid 1980s, although the decline was industrywide and Prime still did better than its competitors. "It's no longer Fischer's company, but these are no longer Fischer's times," pointed out Jane Adams in *New England Business*. Unfortunately, it took a while for employees, as well as shareholders and financial analysts, to reach that conclusion.

A manager who follows a charismatic leader must walk a very fine line. If you remain in the shadows, people will continue to live with the memory of the charismatic leader, and your tenure will be short. If you try to undo what the charismatic leader did, you will encounter hostility and resistance. Any deviation from the previous course will be viewed as destroying what the charismatic leader so carefully built. Yet deviation is inevitable, because you have your own style, which, in at least some ways, differs from your predecessor's. Furthermore, as the environment changes, you must redirect the organization's activities to adapt to those changes if you are to help lead the organization to success. But for the followers, any change is disloyal to the predecessor. The new manager is like a stepfather who is hated by the children for usurping the father's role.

What's the best way to handle such a situation?

☐ Follow the steps I outlined earlier in this chapter under "Avoiding Misunderstandings" and "Dealing with the Survivors of Downsizing."

☐ Gather together all the people in the unit and tell them that, much as their previous leader was loved, respected, and revered, he or she is gone. That need not mean the organization will fall apart, however, or that its work will be diminished in some way. It does call for regrouping and refocusing, in keeping with the organization's new reality, namely its new leader and new tasks. It's appropriate to mourn the loss of the leader, and even to set up some kind of memorial, like naming a conference room for him or her. But the best memorial is to keep the organization alive and successful; and the best way to accomplish that is to recognize the new reality and change to meet it.

☐ Ask those who report to you what kind of help they need to fulfill their responsibilities. After asking them individually, summarize for them collectively what you have heard, without committing yourself to provide what they've requested. In a second round of individual visits, indicate what you expect from each of them, and then summarize for the group those responsibilities with which you are charged and with which you are charging them.

☐ Integrate the subordinates' expectations with your own in a statement of transcendent purpose or collected ego ideal related to the organization. Purpose is the basis of vision— your purview—and mission is your focus on that aspect of the scenario you intend to pursue. Goals and objectives then can be derived logically from this, to give thrust to the organization and to draw the boundaries of what it will and will not do. Purpose reflects the underlying value system of your unit of organization. Mission statements without vision, and vision without a basis in purpose, tend to be confused mishmashes.

These steps serve to define reality, to make clear the nature of the loss of the charismatic leader and legitimize mourning it, to demonstrate your caring interest in those who report to you, and to make appropriate demands on them in turn. You will have engaged with your people around contemporary problems, and defined your accountability to others above and what you must expect from those below.

You should expect those who were closest to the charismatic leader to steer you in the direction your predecessor established. They probably will want to take charge, sustain the momentum of the past. You must quickly establish yourself as your own person. That will be difficult to the extent that you feel guilty for taking a role that one or another of your subordinates expected to have; are too polite, and allow others to guide you; and have no support team as yet, and must depend on those who served your predecessor for information and even guidance. That's especially a problem if you've come into a situation where there is an organized and established social structure.

Succeeding a Failure

Lee Iacocca, taking over from John Riccardo at Chrysler, had another kind of problem. Riccardo, with his financial background, was seen as a "bean counter." While the decision to go with new designs in the Omni and Horizon had made him something of a hero to his engineers, that couldn't counteract years of losses and the prospect of the organization failing. Ian MacGregor encountered a similar situation at British Steel. A failing organization calls for a leader who is strong and clearly capable. A little charisma doesn't hurt, either.

A manager who follows an unsuccessful manager may inherit a failing organization in which people assume no responsibility for the failure. Perhaps they believe it's all their previous boss's fault, or the fault of higher management. Whatever the case, the fault certainly isn't theirs!

If you move in and try to rescue such an organization, you may encounter resistance. If you have to cut costs, rearrange work loads, and require people to live within their budgets and meet production or service goals, they will feel put upon. They will experience you as an attacker, whipping them as bad children. They will feel that you don't appreciate what they have done to date. Their passive resistance, resentment, and criticism will be a threat to your self-image. From your angle, they fail to recognize the dangers of their situation—the risk that heads will roll, or the unit will fold, or there will be even more stringent controls. They do not appreciate your efforts to save them and their unit.

In such situations, the resistance and psychological posture of subordinates can be a trap. The automatic response is to increase the pressures. They are like the delinquent child who becomes ever more delinquent to vex authority, even as the intensity of punishment increases. As the pressure grows, subordinates can see themselves as the unjustified victims of managerial aggression. From that martyred position they seek to undermine, limit, and even destroy the position of the now-authoritarian manager.

If you are that manager, your frenzied frustration will make your behavior more angry, impulsive, overcontrolling, rejecting, and generally inconsiderate. At the same time, feeling all alone, you might inflate yourself in your own eyes, and even reward yourself with the accoutrements of office as reassurance to yourself and proof to your subordinates of your position and power. No matter how well you protect your people, no matter how well you succeed in rescuing the unit, you become embroiled in this sadomasochistic relationship, from which it is difficult to escape.

Can this vicious downward spiral be avoided? Yes, by not letting it start. You could begin by pointing out, in stark and undebatable terms, what the organization is up against. Everybody in the unit must be able to understand that reality. Then invite people to consider what might be done to cope with the situation. With sufficient discussion of possible options, each person will come face-to-face with the size and shape of the problems to be surmounted and the degree of effort that will be required to solve them. At this point you would be in a position to present your own plan, incorporating as many of the useful ideas from your subordinates as possible. You should make each person in the organization assume responsibility for whatever part of the problem is in his or her domain. Then hold regular meetings to keep everybody informed of the unit's progress and whatever new problems are being encountered.

Essentially, your task is to make it clear that reality, and not you alone, demands certain behavior if the organization is to survive. And what reality demands is that people engage in mutually supportive efforts to accomplish certain tasks for survival. Your job is to lead the attack on problems that threaten the organization's existence, and to deflect your and your subordinates' resentment, anger, and hostility away from each other and into problem-solving efforts.

You may also find it necessary to deal with an entirely different consequence of succeeding someone who has failed: guilt. Moving ahead because someone else failed can make you feel guilty, which can distort your judgment. And if you convey to subordinates that you don't deserve the role, they'll treat you as if you don't. One manager succeeded a friend and covered up her mistakes. Subordinates resented this. And when the mistakes came to light later, the manager had a lot of explaining to do to his boss.

Establishing your own leadership role is essential. But that will make you feel even more guilty at first. So it's good to have a plan to help you act in spite of your feelings:

- ☐ Review the former manager's mistakes to clarify for yourself that she brought about her own downfall.
- ☐ Introduce yourself to your new subordinates and say you'll be speaking with each of them individually. Don't soften the blow by assuring them that nothing will change. You may have to eat your words.
- ☐ Speak with each subordinate and find out what obstacles he or she struggles with and what he or she expects or hopes you will change or maintain.
- ☐ Address a second general meeting, synthesizing what you've heard so people know that you listened to them. Then explain what you see as your goals and responsibilities. When your plans are counter to their wishes, don't try to make it sound otherwise.
- ☐ Speak again with individuals about what you expect of them, what they can expect of you, and by what criteria you'll judge performance. Write the criteria into behavioral job descriptions (see Chapter 5) so your guilt can't sway your appraisals.
- ☐ Keep in touch with a confidant or mentor who will encourage you to take difficult but productive steps and warn you frankly when you're being swayed by guilt.

When you've made it clear you're in charge, even subordinates who resist you will be resisting a real boss, not a substitute.

Succeeding a Bad Manager

If you succeed a bad manager and expect your new subordinates to be relieved and ready to get to work, you may be in for a surprise. More than likely they feel guilty about the manager's downfall. Consciously, they know he didn't do his job. But they know that their complaints about him caused him to be fired or transferred. Underneath that is the unconscious fear that they have destroyed him.

That fear is a product of magical thinking. I noted in Chapter 3 that young children often can't distinguish between wishing something and actually doing it. Magical thinking often resurfaces in adults when they feel threatened or threatening. Those feelings can inhibit your subordinates' ability to adapt to you.

Tell them why you were brought in, what skills you have, and how you'll use those skills to improve the department. This reminds them that the decision to replace their boss wasn't made by you or them, but by higher management. Don't knock your predecessor; that exacerbates their guilt.

As you talk individually with people, let them talk about their old boss, as long as they don't get nasty. If he was bad, they need to vent their anger. Some may even miss him. That's because all change, even for the better, is loss. Awareness of that should keep you from pushing subordinates too far too soon.

Sometimes one will have to restore a floundering or even dishonest organization. Sometimes one has to completely reverse the rules. When Kathy Birk became the manager of the Dean Witter branch in Indianapolis, she encountered the hostility of many small investors. After the 1987 crash, thousands of them filed complaints against their brokers. She had to reverse the style of management in that office, a goal she had not sought in the first place. She established a new climate of playing by the rules, emphasizing fairness and honesty with the customer and attention to the client's individual needs. Although the number of complaints against brokers in Indiana continued to grow, no formal complaints have been filed against her office. Her managerial style stresses conciliation and support over confrontation and authority.[5]

When the Old Boss Won't Leave

Suppose the manager you've succeeded still hangs around volunteering information and confusing your subordinates as to who is the boss. Why not just tell him to stay away? That cuts you off from information you might need, especially if you haven't had sufficient preparation. Subordinates may also resent your abusing their former boss.

Explain to the former boss that his frequent presence confuses the chain of command. Ask him to meet with you in his part of the building, not yours. If he continues to interfere, ask your boss for help, unless that will make you appear unable to handle difficult situations, or unless the old boss has unbreakable ties with higher management.

If you can't get rid of the pest, all you can do is forge ties with your subordinates that offer them more than he does. You're the one who can help them gain new competencies, manage new responsibilities, and make new connections. Find out where each subordinate would like to be in a year, what he or she needs to learn (or perhaps to unlearn), and what opportunities are available.

At the same time, let them know that ignoring your requirements in order to carry out the former boss's wishes will become significant incidents in their performance appraisal files. These will be taken as evidence of a failure to grasp reality—the reality of a new boss. But if you're offering a palpable future, most subordinates will choose that over a prolonged attachment to the past.

Succeeding Where Others Have Failed

Don't get too comfortable; you may not be there long. If your last several predecessors all failed on the job, you may wonder if you are doomed, too. How can you make the best of the situation?

- ☐ Find out why the others failed. If it's appropriate, ask your boss. The grapevine can also provide information, but it must be assessed carefully.
- ☐ Ask your boss for a behavioral job description. You shouldn't have to ask, but your predecessors may have failed for lack of clear direction or enough feedback about behavior. If your boss can't give you direction, devise a plan as best you can and ask your boss to approve it.
- ☐ Ask subordinates what they need from you. This is important in any case, but they may also tell you about your predecessors and the ways of the department. At a second meeting, tell them what you can do for them. Since their previous bosses weren't around for long, they may assume that you'll be gone soon and can do little for them. When the department has a

history of failure, building their support is a crucial part of your success.

☐ Observe your peers and your boss together. Your boss may be the reason others failed. New managers naturally concentrate on their own relationship with the boss, but observing peers can teach you more about how to approach the boss for a favor or how to give the boss criticism.

Succeeding where everyone else failed would be quite a feather in your cap. But don't become too set on collecting that feather. Overconfidence can keep you from seeing warning signs.

Leaving a Position

With all the problems a new manager faces, you would do well to anticipate what you can do for your successor when you depart for a new role. It will be important to thank each subordinate individually and the group as a whole. And it will be important to say good-bye—a task that is often avoided by people who find it uncomfortable or distressing or who really don't want to leave. Saying good-bye allows people to express their regrets, to mourn, and to close off the relationship, thus freeing themselves to establish a new relationship with the new manager. Not saying good-bye means there is no opportunity to mourn. Residual feelings will remain to plague the work group's adaptation to the successor. Entering an organization or unit and leaving it are not easy psychological tasks. Managers do well to think carefully about both processes.

CHAPTER **14**

Mentoring for Growth

A classical mentor relationship was that between Thomas Jefferson and James Madison, a relationship that was highly significant for the development of the Bill of Rights. Jefferson, the elder, was the mentor. Out of their work together, they became friends "because each needed an intellectual compatriot in the political arena."[1] Their only serious break came when Jefferson pushed for a Bill of Rights in the Constitution and Madison pushed for a stronger centralized authority. After their break, they were friends of equal stature. Each needed the other to enrich his thinking.

A mentor is a friend, a guide, a teacher. In Greek legend, Mentor was the wise old friend who helped the young son of Odysseus find his father. Mentor advised Telemachus when to fight and when to lie low; he taught cleverness and counseled patience. And under his guidance, Telemachus proved himself a worthy son of a heroic father.

In a similar way, organizational mentors develop the abilities and guide the careers of young managers who show promise. Mentoring is an active, creative process that demands energy and commitment invested in another person's career. Bosses aren't necessarily mentors—though it's ideal when they are. Bosses aren't mentors when they exert downward pressure without giving support, when they

---

Note: Portions of this chapter are adapted from "Up Through the Ranks: Mentoring for Leadership,"[2] which Katherine Davidson Kush coauthored.

criticize mistakes without teaching skills, and when they maintain rigidly formal boss-subordinate relationships. Nor are sponsors necessarily mentors. They push younger people along, or sometimes take them along as they rise, but sponsors don't necessarily teach subordinates anything or enhance their abilities. And models aren't necessarily mentors, because managers frequently model themselves after people who take no active part in their development.

A Mutually Rewarding Relationship

Mentoring is the young employee's best hope for success. It is also the way middle-aged managers can achieve a renewed sense of purpose and contribution.

Future Shock

"I know where I want to go, but I'm not sure how to get there,"many young employees realize when they enter organizations. Though they're bright and ambitious and have always succeeded in school, they suddenly realize how raw and inexperienced they are. They're full of ideas but they don't know how to implement them. And they're surrounded by rivals but don't know how to spot potential allies and helpers. Despite all their eagerness to compete and make a mark, young employees are often intensely self-critical. When promotions and other marks of success don't come as quickly as they want, they brood about their shortcomings, wondering, "Do I need more skills? More experience? More political pull?"

Young professionals discover that work is harder than they expected, even when they learn fast. That's because they're juggling so many balls—mastering skills and building reputations, making contacts and competing on several fronts. When they find mentors who teach them the political ropes and guide them through the troubled waters of their early careers, young managers are spared a lot of grief and anxiety. All young managers need frank advice and friendly support; they need older mentors to develop their talents and broaden their perspectives about what goes on in their organizations. For young managers worried that they won't get a chance to fulfill their potential, finding a mentor provides the best opportunity for achieving success.

Hindsight Can Be Visionary

"If I only knew then what I know now," people often say as they look back over their careers, "I could have avoided so much trouble and grief." From the vantage point of middle age, much that was once confusing or difficult is now clear and easy to execute. When people have developed their skills and mastered their jobs, they regret the time they once wasted in fumbling and error. "If only someone had told me these things, I could have accomplished so much more," they think. They feel unhappy and frustrated because the wisdom of hindsight has come late in their careers.

Other middle-aged managers who reach this point realize with a start that they've surpassed their heroes. They suddenly find themselves disillusioned with people they had admired, even idealized— and yet, at the same time, they're painfully aware of their own inadequacies. When they're not sure what to do, they no longer have authorities to turn to. "If I'm the expert that others turn to," such people think, "then the world must be in sorry shape."

These midcareer experiences are common, yet they take people by surprise and arouse strongly ambivalent feelings. Middle-aged managers feel more competent and respected than ever. But they also feel more constricted—by time, by psychological and intellectual limitations, by organizational pressures. They sometimes undervalue their abilities and accomplishments and regret what they haven't achieved; they sometimes try to compensate for such feelings with overintense competition or defensiveness.

Middle-aged managers have reached the period of generativity, when their skills are at their peak, but their occupational opportunities may have reached a plateau or even started to wane. They must face up to the limited time remaining for them to meet their goals; they must acknowledge that a new generation will soon be taking over. But this isn't a time only of hard facts and painful regrets. For when middle-aged managers share their hindsight with younger people, they develop the next generation of leaders and invest in the future of their organizations. They may no longer be the strivers and producers, but they may find deep gratification in adapting their goal- and task-oriented functions to the rich and creative work of developing young managers. The older manager's shared hindsight need no longer be cause for regret as it becomes the stuff of innovation in the young manager's hands. Mentoring, in other words, is the way out of the middle-aged manager's dilemma.

Any manager who has been around for a while and has learned from experience can usefully mentor younger people. Mentors don't have to be especially successful, assured, or dynamic. They do need to be interested in and concerned about younger people; they need to enjoy interacting with people and investing "psychological time" in others. Mentors enjoy the gratifications of their new role as respected "elders" even though they may not be very old. They find long-mastered work roles less stale as their focus turns from competition to teaching. They're stimulated by the challenge of finding the best ways to teach different people with different skills and personality needs. And they find new meaning in work, because in passing on their organizations' history and traditions to the next generation, mentors help their organizations adapt to the future without breaking with the past. And that process is the essence of survival.

Starting a Mentoring Relationship

Mentoring relationships usually start when an older employee takes a younger person under his or her wing. After years of competing to get and maintain a toehold, the older employee enjoys the relative ease and gratification of taking the symbolic teacher's or parent's role.

The relationship may start, for instance, when an older manager takes a young manager aside and says, "You raised some good points at that meeting, but the boss is furious about being upstaged. Let's talk soon about how to work on these plans." In this kind of interaction, mentors clarify their organizations' psychological contracts—those unconscious expectations that people and organizations have of each other. They help mentees understand the values, standards, norms, and typical modes of action that have long been established in their organizations. They pass on the organizations' histories and let younger people know how current policies are shaped by past actions. They point out the traditional paths to success and traditional stumbling blocks. They share the secrets of their success— and warnings about the pitfalls they didn't see in time. They help mentees develop the skills they need and the visibility to show them off. They make sure mentees meet the right people—at opportune times. In short, mentors develop younger people by stepping outside formal roles and frankly sharing their experience about how people in their organizations behave and feel.

Anyone who has ever felt grateful to a parent or other relative, teacher or coach, older sibling or friend, can become a mentor. That can mean establishing a close, long-term relationship with a subordinate. But it can also mean giving a friendly warning, a bit of advice, or a timely introduction, or entrusting someone with a special measure of responsibility. Any time a manager steps out of his or her formal role as boss and says, for instance, "Did you know that Martha's the one to see about that?" or "I wouldn't go for that promotion—wait until something opens up in Mike's department," he or she is being a mentor. In these ways, mentors reveal the underlying realities to younger people who can't assess the political climate until they get the inside word from people who know.

Young people who know they need mentors because they feel disoriented and uncertain about how to play the game don't have to wait passively for a mentor to appear. They can often initiate such relationships by letting the older employees around them know that they're willing—and even eager—to accept guidance and nurturing. Often young people bend over backward to show that they're not dependent on anyone, that they don't need advice, that they know all the answers and procedures. Inside they know they need help, but they're afraid of seeming stupid or opening themselves to attack if they show any ignorance or ask for any advice. These fears are almost always unrealistic. And when young people carefully look around and assess whom they can turn to for advice on which problems, they can usually find mentors for themselves. Some seasoned employees wait for the younger person to indicate that he or she wants guidance—and then take that as a sign of the young person's seriousness and ambition. Other older people, feeling intimidated by brash young rivals, won't speak up until they're asked to directly—and then they often have valuable insights they're willing to share. And even highly competitive people will brag about their exploits to young managers who can learn a great deal from such revelations.

Young employees, in other words, can usually find mentors simply by being more attuned to the people around them. A hard-driving boss, for instance, may not actually be disappointed in a subordinate's performance, but instead be testing the person he or she especially wants to groom for leadership. Others find a kindred spirit somewhere in the organization, with whom they talk now and then over lunch about those informal attitudes and practices that ultimately shape a career. Young people can also find potential mentors in other organizations. Informal relationships through professional organizations, community activities, or religious groups, for instance, can blossom into mentoring relationships. They can also form a network of alliances within the business community.

Managers from business-oriented families often have a rich source of mentors. When they run into problems and don't know what they're up against, parents or grandparents who've already been there can help them grasp what they're up against and how to deal with it. Teachers are often mentors, especially when they give people new insights about their particular abilities and strengths. Anyone who's taken an active interest in you or has stopped to introduce you to a new experience, way of thinking, or method of doing something has been a mentor. When people understand how they've been helped and from whom they've learned, they know where to look for mentors when they need them. And they also know how to mentor those younger people around them who need guidance and support.

Finally, even managers in difficult or hostile environments can find mentors. A woman manager who was determined to succeed in the face of considerable hostility states, "My boss was my mentor, whether he knew it or not. I learned all I know from him, whether he taught me or not." This boss wasn't the nurturing type and didn't go out on a limb for his only woman subordinate when others gave her a rough time. But she knew that he had hired her and that he agreed with her on certain issues. She recognized the support he did give and was able to unite with him in common purpose for a number of years. She saw that he had the power to get things done, and he would sometimes share his secrets. This mentor wasn't ideal—he didn't offer support or comfort in a kindly way. But this woman had a mentor where others in her position would not, because she fostered the best of the relationship and didn't allow herself to be defeated by the worst. She urged her boss into sharing more with her than he would have done on his own. This woman was right in saying that her boss was a mentor despite himself.

If you haven't yet established a mentor relationship, here are some suggestions for how to get started:

☐ Figure out what you want to learn and who in the company knows it.

☐ Observe and imitate. Why is the person you admire so successful? What are his priorities? His problem-solving techniques? His interpersonal skills?

☐ Participate in an activity, be it a marketing campaign or a United Way campaign, that will bring you into closer contact with your potential mentor or that will make your work visible to her.

☐ Ask her directly for advice. People tend to respond well to a concrete request in their area of competence.

It's not disloyal to have several mentors; in fact, it's advisable. You'll learn more, and if one mentor's rising star starts to fall, you won't be left adrift in outer space.

Understanding the Mentoring Relationship

A Winning Combination

In mentoring, the old adage is often true: opposites attract. A creative but erratic mentee may come to rely on a methodical, highly organized mentor; a gregarious, energetic mentor may bring out the best in an introverted, self-effacing mentee. Why? Because close mentoring relationships fulfill deep and often unconscious emotional needs for both the mentor and the mentee.

A close bond between people with very different personalities allows them to share characteristics that each lacks individually. Just as a reticent, shy man may need an outgoing, exuberant wife to bring emotion and color to his life—while that wife needs the calm and stability her husband brings to the relationship—mentors and mentees often develop rich relationships with people who behave in ways they don't permit themselves to, or who have developed skills they lack. A creative mentor may need a managerial mentee who can translate ideas into action. This was precisely the experience of two Jewel Companies executives, Franklin Lunding and George Clements. As Clements tells it, Lunding "would read things, then telephone, make suggestions, ask questions, or go to conventions and make speeches. Me, I had to be involved in the organization, be involved with the people, involved in the problems. I'm the type of guy that some-body always had to put something in my head and heart for me to really go."[3]

Lunding and Clements developed a good mentoring relation-ship because they knew they needed each other—and that the com-pany needed them both. They supported each other and didn't step on each other's toes. And when Clements came in turn to mentor Donald Perkins, the pattern held. "I've been wrong many times," Clements says, "and young people absolutely have to have the free-dom to make mistakes. . . . What was more important, me being right or Don learning?"[4]

Women who seek out male mentors of course will have to give careful attention to maintaining a professional relationship. And if they seek the help of a more powerful person in the organization, they run the risk of envious and jealous comments. Men with fe-male mentors also face the problem of having the mentoring rela-tionship turn into one of stronger emotional ties.

A Process of Transformation

Both mentors and mentees often feel almost magically transformed by the process. "He invented me," an executive told one of my former mentees, Agnes Missirian of Babson College, describing her relationship with her mentor.[5] Mentees change and grow through positive iden-tification with their mentors. They internalize and integrate facets of the mentor's ways of thinking and behaving and make them part of their own personality structures. This positive identification makes the firmest foundation for a young professional's career. It gives mentees a solid standard of measure and a feeling of worth and competence; it gives them valuable raw materials out of which they construct their managerial selves. Managers are initiated into organizations through their relationships with their bosses, and their attachment is ultimately more solid when their bosses are mentors. Mentees feel more confident of being accepted and becoming successful. They don't have to indulge in overly defensive competition for each step they make, because they're nurtured and guided. The path is psy-chologically easier for them. They enjoy their work more and are more likely to share that enthusiasm with others when they finally become senior employees who in turn mentor younger people.

Mentors, too, are changed by their new role. Some are like former athletes who find new life in becoming successful coaches. They enjoy building winning teams, sharing strategies, inspiring others to run plays they can't handle themselves. They are gratified to see the raw material of the young manager's potential take shape under their skilled guidance. Many people, in fact, think of mentors as Pygmalions, after the legendary sculptor whose statue of a beautiful woman miraculously came to life after he fell in love with her. In a similar way, mentors bring their mentees to life by forming an emotional attachment to them.

Ending a Mentoring Relationship

All relationships have elements of love and hate; mentoring relationships are always ambivalent and often volatile. Mentors and mentees have positive and supportive feelings for each other, but some of their unconscious feelings are also negative and rivalrous. And as the mentee becomes more experienced and catches up with the mentor, those negative feelings become harder to cope with. Suddenly the mentee is not so awed by the mentor's abilities; suddenly the mentor worries about being overtaken by the mentee. As mentors' usefulness to their raw young protégés wanes, they can feel their old regrets rise to the surface again in new forms: "She doesn't need the likes of me anymore" or "He's already accomplished more than I ever will." Even worse, the mentors sense their mentees' changed attitudes toward them, as the mentees wonder, "Why did I ever think he was so important?" or "What on earth did she have to teach me?"

These negative feelings are powerful and painful. And though people often try to deny them, they're very real. But that's only half the story. As they become stronger, the negative feelings allow mentors and mentees to ease up on relationships that have blossomed and borne fruit. These feelings allow people to let go when letting go becomes less painful than holding on. That's not to say that former mentors and mentees don't maintain ties and keep in touch—of course they do. But as mentees move on in their careers, they seek new mentors and eventually become mentors themselves. And their old mentors usually cope with their feelings of jealousy and inadequacy by again mentoring others who look up to them and need their help.

Mentees can help themselves and their mentors to make parting a sweeter sorrow by:

☐ Being prepared to deal directly when the time comes. Unconscious guilt about hurting your mentor may push you in the wrong direction, toward keeping your feelings in until you become explosively angry.

☐ Expressing your appreciation for what your mentor has given you, rather than devastating his self-esteem by just dropping him.

☐ Establishing a basis for a future relationship. If you've confronted the issue with respect for his self-esteem, you should be able to continue on a new basis as friends, and perhaps allies, as was the case with Jefferson and Madison.

As a mentor, you can reduce your sense of loss by doing the following:

☐ Don't put all your dependency eggs in one basket. Even if one protégé or subordinate or client is your favorite, help more than that one person.

☐ Pat yourself on the back. You deserve some credit for what you've taught others.

☐ Find someone with whom it's safe to discuss your feelings of loss. You can sound pretty cranky talking about these feelings, even though they're universal. So, look for a peer, friend, or mentor who has some psychological or intuitive understanding of the issues involved.

The Growing Importance of Mentoring

As technological change intensifies, and employee expectations rise, mentoring will increasingly become the heart of every manager's job. And with repeated reorganization, people will come to depend more on their boss than on the organization as a whole. Organizations will therefore increasingly rely on leaders who have been seasoned and experienced through mentoring. And at a time when more people are seeking greater satisfaction from work, mentoring is the ultimate job enrichment. Doing a job is fine, and doing several jobs may be better, yet all tasks become boring. But it's not boring to think about how you do your job and how you learned to do it—and then communicate that knowledge to someone who hasn't reached your level yet. It's gratifying to think about what your job means to you and to your organization, and then to share your enthusiasm and sense of purpose with someone else. In conceptualizing their work and building close, dynamic relationships with young employees, mentors add tremendous richness and complexity to their jobs.

And in the process of mentoring, older employees often find that they've enriched their lives in general. As they teach and guide others, they become more conscious of their own values, ideas, and concerns. They renew their ties with the past and forge new ties with the future. In the course of helping a mentee with a new assignment, for instance, a mentor may suddenly recall the long-forgotten pleasures of learning carpentry from a skilled uncle or learning baking from a creative grandmother. Mentors remember the pleasure of watching the skilled work of people who love their tasks and teach them well because they enjoy them. And as mentors see themselves as part of this process—teaching the next generation by sharing skills and enthusiasms—they escape the sameness of daily routines and participate in a future taking shape through their efforts.

CHAPTER **15**

Making Rewarding Job Changes

No matter who you are or what role you may have, it's highly likely that at one or more points in your career you will be changing your job. Roles that once used to be stable are now tenuous. Academic tenure doesn't mean much for college professors when universities excise whole departments. Optometrists are moving into chain-store operations where pharmacists have long since been present. The need for dentists is declining and they, too, are more often found in malls. Many physicians are now on salary and more will be. Some among them are having to become executives, often to their dismay. Deregulation of public utilities has compelled their executives to become aggressive marketers, and similarly, those industries that were protected by tariffs and now are about to lose that protection also will have to become aggressive competitors. Wal-Mart has put a lot of small-town merchants out of business, while at the same time major department stores have had to shift to boutique-style operation to adapt to rapidly changing tastes. Musicians in symphony orchestras experience lowered attendance and loss of interest. Researchers in one field or another lose their roles when financial support wanes in response to scientific vogues.

Such events have impact throughout the life cycle. The physicians I teach who are becoming executives, and some who are already executives, are largely in their forties and some in their fifties. Those proprietors in their fifties who have had to give up their businesses are too young to retire. They wonder what to do with themselves and how to make a new beginning. Young people who may have prepared themselves for academic appointments easily become superfluous at an early age.

Such changes necessarily constitute career upheaval.

Adapting to an Era of Career Upheaval

Measured in psychological distress, the recession of the early 1990s may have beaten the Great Depression. In New York State alone, 500,000 jobs were lost between 1989 and 1992.[1]

People's self-esteem was certainly battered in the 1930s. But today, because more people have more education, they've had correspondingly higher aspirations and expectations dashed. Professionals, who used to feel pretty safe, are much more vulnerable this time around.

Trust—people's willingness to depend on companies and each other—has been badly shaken. During the Great Depression, people kept alive their underlying wish to attach to and depend on a company. They believed that when the economy recovered, those dependency relationships would be resumed. And indeed that did happen.

But the recession of the 1990s has proven that companies and employees won't depend on each other as they once did. Employment is no longer for life. At the same time, many people have lost the strong interdependence of families that helped some weather the depression. The result is a shambles, a shell-shocked group.[2]

To protect yourself against future disruptions, let your expectations fit the times. Too many people I see expect an occupational cafeteria of choices and opportunities. They don't understand global management with its varying and evolving kinds of dependency relationships—and the opportunities it presents for those who train for it. Sometimes learning one new thing, such as Japanese or a particular operating system, opens a whole range of new managerial opportunities.

Coping with Uncertainty

"What would I do if I lost my job?" That is the question more people than ever before must ask themselves. One important step in answering that question is to review the modes of coping discussed in Chapter 2.

It's not just that economic realities have made employment so uncertain. Rather, the worry comes from an evolving change in the psychological contract between employers and employees, in the unwritten set of assumptions and expectations of each other that both sides bring to the employment relationship. Unfortunately, very few people have had any direct say in this change. As a result, they feel betrayed by their employers and by society because, suddenly, employment isn't for life anymore.

Also unsettled are those baby-boom professionals who are wondering if they want to stay in their careers. These psychological career crises often accompany what my colleague Elliott Jaques dubbed "midlife crisis" back in 1965. We know that in their late thirties, many people feel a last surge of independence, a need to assert themselves and to become who they feel they really are. For some, this precipitates a period of intense dissatisfaction with their chosen career. Still others are frustrated and dissatisfied because of the lack of opportunities for advancement that has followed downsizing and the flattening of organizational pyramids.

Recognizing When It's Time for a Job Change

"I started having fantasies about dyeing my hair, sneaking off to the airport, and just disappearing," said one careworn executive. He'd been laboring for two years to make a losing division profitable. What he really needed was a new job.

Many people get stuck in assignments that are destructive to their mental health, move them further from their ego ideals, and wear them down. They're asked to do the impossible and to do it fast. Sometimes their woes are compounded by a boss who's abrasive or manipulative.

What keeps these people from making a change?

Lack of self-confidence. Some people have an unconscious critical self-assessment, so that even if they are high achievers, they worry about failing in a new assignment.

The devil you know. Many people are reluctant to move because they know their current situations, however difficult and painful those situations may be. They fear that if they leave their current roles, they may get into greater difficulty in other organizations. That prospective threat is the devil they don't know. Usually also such people value certain aspects of their work as well as long-standing personal relationships. Often the company is meeting their financial and security needs admirably.

Burnout. People who've expended much effort with few satisfying results can become too emotionally exhausted to take charge of their situation.

Unconscious guilt. Some people stay because, unconsciously, they don't feel they deserve better. It's the same guilt that keeps battered wives with their husbands.

Families. Some women stay in their roles because they fear the impact on their spouses if they should take on a more responsible role. Several female executives in my experience have turned down opportunities to become chief executive officers of companies and public bodies, ostensibly for fear of the extra time demands such roles would make on them, but more worried about how their husbands would feel about becoming the equivalent of "Mr. Margaret Thatcher." Others may be reluctant to make a change because they subordinate their organizational role to their wish to give appropriate attention to their children.

For those who need a change but feel temporarily short on initiative, here is what to do:

- ☐ If you are burned out, you need to rest. If you say to yourself, "I can't afford time off," remember that unless you renew your energy, you'll never solve your problem.
- ☐ You need your friends now. Talk about what's happening to you. Begin organizing options.
- ☐ If possible, talk to your boss about a change of assignment. Your performance is bound to have been affected by your dislike of your job, and she may want to help you bounce back. Or she may be able to restructure your present assignment for some short-term relief.
- ☐ Consider therapy to guide you through the crisis if friends, rest, and your boss can't get you moving.

Exploring Whether to Change Your Job

Opportunities for growth are highly desirable. Without them, people would stagnate; even with competition, people could remain undeveloped. Yet, promotion within one's own organization, or a seemingly advantageous opening in another, may not be opportunity; instead, it may be a big step toward failure.

As with every other major decision about your life, you should do some serious thinking when faced with the opportunity for promotion or a new position. It is elementary that you don't want to fail, or have your company fail by choosing you. Moreover, you have only a limited number of years during which such opportunity is available. Failure to make the right choice at the right time can severely limit your subsequent opportunities.

Important Psychological Questions to Ask

The commonsense questions that determine acceptance or rejection of a promotion or new position are usually fairly easy to answer: Will the increased pay be worth the move? Is this move upward, or will it lead to a dead end? Will I have greater opportunities to move ahead or laterally? Will this change bring me closer to the power center of the organization? Will it give me a better chance to show what I can do? Will I learn anything new?

The more important questions, those that have the most to do with success and failure, are much harder to deal with. These call for what Karl Menninger often described as *uncommon sense*.[3] Much of the time they are not even formulated as questions because the defense mechanisms we use to maintain our own idealistic pictures of ourselves hide from our awareness those aspects of personality we are unwilling to face. We go to great lengths to hide from both ourselves and others what we feel are our most painful deficiencies and weaknesses. Sometimes we simply deny what we think are our limitations; sometimes we try to cover our deficiencies by making extra efforts with the talents we have.

What, then, are the important psychological questions to ask yourself as you consider accepting a promotion or a new position? These will have to do with how you handle the need to love and be loved, the aggressive drive, feelings about your wishes to be dependent, your conscience, and your modes of self-control. The triangulating points that confirm your decisions are your experiences in the past and the psychological specifics of the new position being offered.

Our actions and experiences in the past will indicate future possibilities because the dominant features of our personalities are relatively enduring. This is because we doggedly maintain those kinds of behavior that early in life proved to be most successful. Such patterns become our personal trademark—we and others recognize who we are because of the continuity of our behavior. In a sense, we are how we behave, and what we mean by personality is the totality of our needs (or wishes), feelings, thoughts, and behavior.

A fundamental axiom in considering new job opportunities, therefore, is that you should not accept a promotion or position that requires you to behave in ways that are quite different from the manner in which you customarily prefer to act. What factors should you take into account in making a decision? Four in particular are especially important:

A new position should permit you to maintain your preferred emotional distance from others. Consider, for example, how a person handles the need to love and be loved. If one characteristically prefers to be somewhat aloof from others, one will have difficulty when in a new role that requires working closely with others. Quite another problem exists for the person who needs so much the warm affection of many people close to him or her that it is difficult for that person to exercise power appropriately.

There are many variations between these two extremes. In moving up (or out) will you be cutting ties to friends and associates? Are such ties important? If you deny the need for such ties or assume they will continue to be available in the new position, you should carefully double-check, lest the brilliant attraction of this opportunity obscure the realities of your own personality.

A new position should allow you your characteristic ways of expressing aggression. A second major issue, how a person handles his or her aggressive drive, the push to mastery, tends to be grossly ignored in business. All of us must deal with our aggressive impulses. Executives and managers must be able to invest considerable energy in their tasks to capitalize on opportunity, to overcome obstacles, and to lead their organizations. People who compete for advancement know that they must demonstrate their abilities in their own achievements. There is considerable validity to the belief that a good executive must be aggressive.

Frequently, however, though some people can direct their aggressive impulses into the accomplishment of excellent, even brilliant jobs on their own, they fail miserably when they are promoted and must work through others. The same drive that stood them in such good stead as individual performers is not easily transformed into indirect support and guidance of other people who carry on the direct efforts.

To avoid deceiving yourself and inviting failure, you should ask yourself in considerable detail how you handle aggressive impulses most comfortably. Do you do best when you can organize and carry out a project firsthand? Do you have trouble when you have to let other people do the task? Do you complain about the need to pay attention to the details of relationships with other people in the organization before plunging ahead?

Some people, such as many accountants and engineers, handle their aggressive impulses by tightly structured control of their work. Others, such as some salesmen, do so by vanquishing customers. Still others, such as advertising and public relations persons, do so by persuasive efforts. A man or woman considering a new position will therefore have to ask what new demands the prospective position will make in terms of handling aggression. Will it be more constricting and therefore cause restless chafing? Will it demand more frequent open confrontation of others, and thereby be somewhat frightening to someone who needs to be more friendly?

The focus of aggression is an important consideration. Does a person direct his aggression toward himself and consequently make himself fail? This happens more often than most people realize.

All of us have our unique ways of figuratively putting our feet in our mouths or of spoiling our own efforts. Some people do so by talking too much, some by being sloppy in dress or appearance, some by putting their worst selves forward, and some by "stupid" mistakes. The reasons we do so are complex. You must examine the ways in which your self-directed aggression can result in self-defeat. What have you done before when your responsibility was increased? Did you run away from it? Did you fumble it to prove to yourself you couldn't handle it? Did you become ill and have to be reassigned? Did you start drinking too much? Fail to deliver what you are capable of delivering? Try to cover over your insecurity with bravado? Making a mistake once or twice is not necessarily an indication of self-defeat. Continuing blindly to make the same mistake is.

The difficulties inherent in dealing with both affection and aggression in assignments are reflected in classical managerial failures: the supersalesperson who becomes a terrible sales manager, the shop superintendent who cannot keep away from the shop floor when he or she becomes plant manager, the plant manager who is miserable as a vice president.

The salesperson in her continual contacts and interchange with others draws on those relationships for much of her gratification and channels her aggression directly into the sales task. As sales manager, her contacts are limited to supervising salespeople, and her aggressive energy finds inadequate outlet in shuffling papers.

The new plant manager who formerly was directly involved in production not only had worked closely with his staff, but also had solved problems on the floor. As plant manager, he is necessarily further removed from his old colleagues, and can no longer directly solve a production problem. When he tries to do so, he avoids the broader responsibility that is now his.

In each of these instances, sources of affection, regard, esteem, and personal ties are diminished sharply. Avenues for the more direct discharge of aggressions also are narrowed. Taken together, such changes can constitute psychological losses and, if they are experienced as losses, the person who suffers them may well wish he or she had never accepted the proffered position.

A new position should be congenial with your ways of handling dependency needs. Every move upward in an organization's structure requires increasing independence of thought and action. Most people would say, if asked, that they welcome the opportunity for greater independence. A person can rarely admit that he or she really wants to remain in a subordinate position, for that would be to admit failure and damage one's self-image. Yet many people neither want nor can handle independent responsibility, because their own needs to be dependent on someone else are paramount. In pursuing the satisfaction of these needs they become too preoccupied with pleasing their superiors, are reluctant to make decisions or act by themselves, and are unable to accept the dependency needs of subordinates.

When considering promotion, you should take a close look at how you have dealt with dependency needs. How much independent action have you really sought in the past? Have you become more independent with each step up the ladder or, despite increasing responsibility, have you subtly continued to lean just as heavily on your superiors or selected subordinates? Have you become increasingly anxious with each promotion? Despite having obvious talents that seem to send you forward, might you be far happier being a good contributor than an unhappy, unsuccessful leader?

Needs for dependency require extremely careful consideration because a significant number of people fail when they are moved from a number two position to a number one job. Dependency needs can become more acute if the new job is not adequately structured so that a person can continue to have ready access to superiors, if the job is not clearly defined, or if the person has not had enough experience to cope with the job.

Dependency needs are not bad, though the word dependency has acquired negative connotations. Everyone has dependency needs. The very fact that children have such a long period of dependency and go through a long process of separating themselves from their parents makes these needs a problem for everyone. We each work out our own way of dealing with them. Some people seek out highly structured organizations that are well routinized; others go to great extremes to stand on their own feet and never lean on anyone else. No one has to apologize for his or her particular mode of dealing with these needs. Rather, if you are to make rational decisions about promotion, in your own self-interest you must be brutally honest with yourself about what degree and kind of support you need to function well. Included in that necessary support is what you need from various members of your family and what a promotion will mean to those relationships.

A new position should increase your positive feelings about yourself. The fourth major psychological issue you need to confront is your ego ideal, or the image you hold of yourself at your future best. People often have conflicting images of what they would like to be, some of which are unconscious images. As a result, they are not certain who they are or what they really want to be. The consequence is that they tend unwittingly to pretend they want to do a certain kind of work when basically they would much rather do something else.

Sometimes people follow a given occupation for many years before deciding it is not for them. Sometimes the conflict has to do with a person's values: a number, for example, have gone from business into the ministry or into professional training of one kind or another. Whatever the reason, if a person is not certain in her own mind that she is following her own basic wishes, she will have great difficulty with her work. She may not be able to invest herself fully in her job; she may vacillate between one activity and another; she may find no real satisfaction in what she does. She will drain her energy fighting both herself and the demands of the job. If she accepts promotion in a field about which she has considerable question, she is asking for trouble. Promotion demands increased commitment to her task and to the organization, and thereby is likely to increase her conflict.

It is a commonplace that some people do what their parents want them to do, rather than what they want to do, as was the case with Philip in Chapter 1. Such a conflict is relatively obvious, and therefore fairly easy to deal with. When the conflict is more obscure, it is more difficult to resolve. One way of taking a look at the opportunity is to raise this question: "Do I want this promotion because of what I want to *be* or because of what I want to *do?*" If your motivation is to be something, you are likely to be pursuing a will-o'-the-wisp, for usually nothing you do really gratifies you. If, however, your motivation is to do—to sell, to manage, to invent, to cure illness—then the gratifications lie in the doing and, if you do something well, achievement is a consequence.

Here a caution is required. Conscientious people often feel less capable than they really are. They are all too aware of some of their shortcomings and expect themselves to perform extremely well. The distance between their ego ideal and their daily performance tends to be astronomical, and therefore the gap between their assessment of themselves and what they really are is too large and therefore false. To avoid depreciating your abilities, you should review what you have done. Usually, your past performance will realistically reflect your ability.

A second caution: just as a promotion or a prospective new opportunity is not necessarily the high road to happiness, it is not necessarily a threat to happiness. Increased responsibility doesn't mean increased stress for everyone. Some will fail with it, some will thrive on it. Whether you will succeed or fail depends on yourself, the structure in which you will have to work, and the kind of supervision you will have. If you consider a new position in these terms, and begin your consideration with an intensive, frank look at yourself, you will considerably improve your chances for doing what is best for yourself and the organization.

Basically, you have to ask, "Will I continue to be me in this new position, or will I have to be someone or something different?" Such a question is not intended to reinforce a rigid position (once a salesperson, always a salesperson) or to prevent growth and change. But it does recognize that, although we grow older, wiser, more capable, and more responsible, we cannot and do not change our personalities drastically.

There are two final considerations: First, it is not easy to look at yourself. If you want to take a good look at yourself, you would do well to talk to someone in whom you can confide, and whom you can trust to help you find honest answers—a spouse, a superior, a minister, or a professional consultant. Second, in the last analysis, you must trust your judgment of yourself. Usually, if a person decides a prospective new role is not for him or her, then that is the wisest decision. Most people know more about how they feel and their assets and limitations than those who seek to persuade them. Even if a person underestimates himself, he must live with his judgment of himself, and how one feels about oneself is more critical in success or failure than what one is objectively.

Resisting the "Grass Is Greener" Syndrome

A major issue you must face as you seek to move from one organization to another is that of idealization. There is a great tendency to assume that the grass is greener in a prospective organization that is flattering you by inviting you into its arms. However, you must recognize that all organizations are crazy. By that I mean, every organization is made up of many different people, each of whom has a distinct personality and an idiosyncratic range of needs. You who would try to be rational must recognize the multiple crosscurrents that abound in organizations. These arise as people try to adapt to each other, try to establish power relationships and structures, and try to provide leadership and counter opposition. No matter how much organizations try to be rational in the economic and organizational sense, the fact of the matter is that, as a result of all of these conflicting issues, organizations and the decisions that are made in them are significantly irrational.

Inevitably, the preferences of chief executives are going to dominate. Their interests will automatically and unconsciously be served first. They will prefer to do that which is familiar to them and that which they know best. Sometimes that orientation and the needs of the organization coincide. Sometimes the leadership can't keep up with the realities the organization faces, and there's a growing gap.

The pressures to develop mutually supportive colleagues often make new ideas unwelcome: most organizations have enough trouble trying to get people to work together on old ideas, let alone deal with new ones. Despite whatever it says, any organization or any group of people wants newcomers to go along and get along rather than to disrupt already tenuous arrangements. One has to cope with established organizational norms and organizational history, with the heritage of the founding fathers and the reverberations of those founding efforts into contemporary work. A newcomer usually will find it extremely difficult to get timely and accurate feedback on his or her performance and, often, even clarity of direction.

You can either be frustrated by these conflicting currents, events, policies, practices, and modes of behavior; or you can recognize them as you would recognize the winds and currents if you were sailing a sloop. Taking the latter perspective, you would then steer among these many crosscurrents to achieve your own goals, as well as to help the organization achieve its goals.

Dealing with a Counteroffer

If you receive a counteroffer from your boss, should you take it? According to a press release from the executive search firm Boyden International, "the majority of executives who accept a counteroffer . . . are fired or quit within 18 months."

Boyden was surprised by these results, but they shouldn't have been. Counteroffers fail because money usually isn't the chief reason for job dissatisfaction. Before accepting one, think over the following issues:

First, if you sought other offers because you enjoy your work but could earn more doing it elsewhere, a counteroffer makes sense.

But if you felt, "They aren't paying me enough to put up with these hassles," ask about changing the conditions that bother you, which may include the recognition you get. If your boss feels you should take the raise and stop complaining, the solution won't last.

Second, some counteroffers are made in order to meet EEOC requirements. If you're an unqualified token, the company often has little reason to develop you. You will eventually be left high and dry, lacking the training to advance but already too high up and too highly paid to start over. Ask your boss what vision he or she has for your future and what the specific plans are for bringing it about.

These are embarrassing questions to ask your boss, not least because the answers may be very unflattering. But the worse the news, the more important it is to hear it as soon as possible. I see too many careers wasted because people preferred no news to the bad news.

Returning to Your Old Organization

When you are the new kid on your own block, what do you do? Some organizations are asking managers who left to start their own companies, or who moved up and out, to come back to the fold. Other managers must reintegrate themselves after overseas assignments. These managers know the organization and its people. . . . Or do they? If you come back expecting things to be the way you left them, you may insult former peers by overlooking their progress and miss the chance to learn from them and the organization.

Treat this job as if it were a new job—which it is. Ask your boss or old friends for a summary of the time you were away. What political changes occurred? For example, if technical people now run the department, will you need to change the way you present ideas? If new people are in power, be careful about bringing up old battles or stories.

Don't expect too much of a welcome home. People may want to see how you have changed or what you intend to do before they get enthusiastic about your return.

Becoming a Consultant

We love to see the cowboy save the day and ride into the sunset. But how many of us would really enjoy moving from job to job? Contract work is growing, but it isn't for everyone. As one banker discovered, "I miss the interaction with peers and the professional recognition. . . . I'd like to be living with my decisions and not just taking my pound of flesh and moving on."[4]

Some managers switch to contract work after being laid off or fired. Some reach retirement age and still want or need to work. Others can't tolerate the structure or closeness of organizations. If you are interested in contract work, there are things to consider before hitting the trail:

☐ Will you be comfortable always being the new kid on the block? You will need the self-confidence to do your job without knowing the lay of the land.

☐ Will you be able to let go? Trying to hang around after you've finished will earn you a reputation as a meddler.

☐ Are you interested in problem solving for its own sake? You won't be around to watch your ideas in action.

☐ How much do you need an organization as a source of affection? You need to think about the things you will miss.

☐ Will you be able to sell yourself? You may have to make cold calls, write articles, or give lectures.

If contract work isn't what you expected, you may find returning to organizational life uncomfortable. You will have developed a wider perspective and may be more self-reliant. You will have to redefine your needs, expectations, and place in the organization.

CHAPTER **16**

Handling Job Loss Constructively

Unemployment has reached painful proportions. That means, of course, that a lot of people have been fired. Despite the euphemism "laid off," most are highly unlikely to return to their previous jobs. There will continue to be widespread unemployment all over the world because of the vast changes that are taking place in social and political institutions, not to speak of the competitive positions of businesses.

That means that it is just as important to know how to handle yourself when you're fired, since that eventuality is likely for many people, as it is to work toward getting hired. In fact, it's probably more important to know how to handle job loss because the residual feeling can so easily result in dissipation of energy, chronic anger that interferes with job interviews, impatient anxiety, and a weak bargaining posture. Inadequate outplacement activities used by some corporations often leave the displaced manager feeling deserted and unsupported, especially if he is getting no reply to the many resumes he has mailed.

Finding a new job has become more complicated and slower. A major reason is that in their reorganizations, companies often don't know what new or different talent they will need. Laid-off executives report that interviews that leave them feeling optimistic often turn out to be an exercise in futility when higher-level management reverses its plan of action, edicts a hiring freeze, or simply delays approving a hiring decision. Managers in such a position, especially

191

after the flurry of initial contacts and the busyness of pursuing multiple leads, often find themselves in a soundless void: the telephone no longer rings. In that vacuum, they often don't know which way to turn or how to sustain their inner momentum in the absence of external cues to guide their direction. In a sense, experiencing such a void is something like being lost in a desert. To cope effectively requires fending off the impulse to react without thinking and instead thinking coolly and carefully.

Anticipating Job Loss

When the axe is swinging off in the distance, it's already time to duck. Families are often taken by surprise when a manager is laid off. They may have known it was possible, but haven't thought about what to do. Now they have to revise their whole way of life under stress conditions that cloud judgment.

I advise people who foresee any possibility of losing their jobs to have a family meeting and discuss:

- ☐ What would the family's income be and what budget would it have to follow?
- ☐ How long would it take to find a new job? That is unpredictable, but many people grossly underestimate. It takes at least six months to a year to find an executive position.
- ☐ Which luxuries would be sacrificed? Perfect fairness can be too rigid. Music lessons the year before a child applies to music school can't be equated with a younger child's skating lessons.
- ☐ Which family traditions are most worth preserving? Choose those that promote family unity and loyalty, although a less expensive version may have to do.
- ☐ What effort would be asked of the children? They might have to do more chores or work in a new family business.

Families can manage calamities pretty well if their cohesion is maintained. There is a dramatic example of this in *My Father, My Son*, by Admiral Elmo Zumwalt, Jr., and his son Lieutenant Elmo Zumwalt III.[1] Young Zumwalt was exposed to Agent Orange in Vietnam; he subsequently developed cancer and had a child with serious birth defects. His father had given the orders to use Agent Orange.

Nevertheless, the family members chose to support each other through this tragedy rather than blame each other for it.

After Getting Fired

One of the first things you learn in karate is how to fall without hurting yourself. One job skill every employee should have nowadays is knowing how to be fired without too much psychological damage. Psychological factors can make the difference between a successful transition and one in which you never get over the blow.

Identifying What You Have Lost

What do you lose when you lose your job? The losses fall into all four categories of psychological need. You lose income, benefits, and security (dependency needs); relationships (affection needs); the satisfaction of getting things done (mastery and aggression needs); and your sense of self-esteem and progress (ego ideal striving).

Thinking of your losses in these terms helps you to understand some of your unexpected reactions and helps you to plan better. Job-seeking managers who interview too soon can come off as overly angry or needy. They haven't recognized their psychological losses and don't realize how betrayed and helpless they feel.

Some needs will be met by finding another job. One dollar bill is as good as another. But even finding new friends and new satisfactions doesn't mean you don't feel the loss of old friends and satisfactions. That's why it's so important to separate from your company as cleanly as you can. You want former bosses and peers to be references. More important, psychologically, is to maintain the affection of people you like. Be sure to say good-bye to your coworkers. Spend a little time with each, telling him or her what you gained from the acquaintance and what you'll miss. However low you feel, don't just sneak away quietly. You'll regret it.

If you become openly hostile to the boss or the company, friends who are staying may withdraw from you. That withdrawal cuts you off from an important source of support and "contact comfort," to use my colleague Ralph Hirschowitz's phrase. You may also sacrifice a valuable network by leaving on a bad note. And sometimes employees are invited back when times improve, so you don't want to burn your bridges.

Making the Problem Part of the Solution

Naturally, being fired creates a lot of anger. It's psychologically healthy to channel that anger into useful action such as job hunting or further education. Otherwise, it can turn into rigid bitterness, depression, substance abuse, or impulsive actions. You don't have to start job hunting the day after you're fired, but I don't advise a six-month breather either, even if you can afford it.

Try to see being fired as a chance to do something you haven't done yet. Many people report that they never would have gotten out of their ruts had they not been fired. Others began to grow only after they got out from under previous bosses. Talk to confidants, to your family and friends, to sympathetic former coworkers, and perhaps to a professional counselor or outplacement advisor, to help you think through what you would like to do with your future now that it's wide open again.

All managers should think about what they'll do if they lose their jobs, anyway. And not only think, but prepare—by getting education (formal or otherwise), making contacts, or saving money. These days, anyone can lose his or her job. Moreover, ego ideals evolve and the career you loved in your thirties may no longer be what you need in your fifties.

When one has to move into a new job, it is important to assess one's own strengths. What do you really know? What, in your own occupational history, is a solid base of information or skill or combination of both such that you know how to do something "with your eyes shut"? What specifically are the needs that your competence and skills can meet? For example, in a community where restaurant business is decreasing, a man who knows the food service business and has marketing skills might more readily focus on how to help a given restaurant get an increasing market share than seek business opportunities in an area with which he is less familiar. Rather than seek "greener grass" opportunities in areas about which you are less knowledgeable, how can you capitalize on what you already know? And if what you know is not in itself strong enough, who can you pair with to create combined skills that are more effective?

In such a situation also, you should look at where you are in the life cycle. For example, people in midlife and midcareer might well give serious thought to starting their own businesses because that's a time of life when many people think of striking out on their own. When they get older, they may feel they are too old to start from scratch, they may not have the energy to do so, or they may have become too dependent on an organization.

Managing the Blow

Being fired—even if you're glad to get out of a place you hated—is a loss, and humans go through predictable stages when they lose something significant. Unfortunately, many people are able to conceal that pain, even from themselves. That only means they suffer the effects—often including physical illness—without knowing why.

Here is Hirschowitz's advice on managing the blow:[2]

☐ Recognize the known stages of reaction. At first, you feel dazed and shocked. You may deny it's really happening. Next come several days or weeks of rage and, finally, gradual adjustment and looking forward.

☐ Don't try to skip stages that seem useless or childish to you. Especially don't avoid the emotional pain by using tranquilizers, alcohol, or drugs. Feel the pain, express it, tell others, and get comfort from them. If you suppress your rage, you put off your transition to the next stage. And the rage may erupt later, or simply weigh you down when you're trying to move ahead.

☐ Expect to be mad and find ways to cool off harmlessly: athletic activity, swearing to yourself, or whatever helps. This is important so that you don't take it out on your family, or on yourself through impulsive actions.

☐ Do your grief work. Mainly, that means talking with people who are good listeners. Tell them not only what happened, but how you feel, what you've lost, and what it means to you. As much as you feel like crawling into a hole, be sure to spend time with people. The comfort of human contact is the most important element in recovery from trauma.

☐ Pace yourself. Take your body's messages seriously; don't push yourself when you're tired.

☐ Take the long view. You will recover.

For a successful professional, getting fired may be more of a blow than he or she has ever suffered before. Normal people occasionally find themselves doing crazy things, such as pretending to go to work for weeks after being fired, just to avoid telling their families they've lost their jobs. You may find yourself slipping into behavior that you know is asking for trouble; unable to take the actions you know are necessary; or frightened by your suspicion of others, your impulses to become violent, or an urge simply to give up. If so, find a psychologist or psychologically trained counselor with whom to talk. Chances are you're not crazy and you don't need psychotherapy, but you're under intense stress and a professional can help you over the hump.

Too many managers aren't used to the idea of taking care of themselves when they're hurt. True, a boxer keeps boxing even when he's in agony. But that's only a few rounds, not week after week. If you want to make sure you come back strong and show what you're made of, it makes sense to come back with your wounds tended.

Be certain to avoid doubling your losses by withdrawing from friends. Unfortunately, some people feel they can't afford to return invitations or to go out in the style to which they and their friends are accustomed, so they stay home.

But financial worries are only part of the reason unemployed people isolate themselves. They also worry that their friends will look down on them or feel sorry for them. Worse, they fear they won't belong anymore because status and self-image are so tied to work in our culture. Essentially, they have lost their sense of who they are because they are no longer chemists or financiers or bosses.

If you are fired, you need to be aware of such psychological realities so you don't let them cut you off from friends. Socializing provides a relaxing and needed break from the job hunt or from feeling like a failure. You'll see that you can still make your friends laugh, still talk over current events, still enjoy some gossip. When your self-esteem has been battered, such reassurance and pleasure will help you regain your sense of self.

Be careful not to confuse networking with socializing. Calling people for contacts is important. But such calls are business and are no substitute for friendships.

CHAPTER **17**

Choosing a Second Career

As the years pass, most people—regardless of their professions or skills—find their careers less interesting, stimulating, or rewarding. By midlife, many feel the need for new and greener occupational fields. They yearn for opportunities to reassert their independence and maturity and to express the needs and use the talents of a different stage of life.

Some people feel they are no longer in the running for advancement, some that their talents and skills are not being fully used, and some that they have outgrown their jobs, companies, or disciplines. Others, feeling blocked by being in the wrong company, industry, or position, are bored. Some are in over their heads, while others have merely drifted into their jobs or have chosen directions prematurely. One or a combination of these feelings can make a person hate to go to work in the morning and can trigger thoughts of a way out.

The realities of contemporary life also stimulate people to think about a second career: the competition is stiffer every year, and job loss is an increasingly common occurrence. Even to the young manager, the accelerating pace of change makes obsolescence a threat. Rapid technological changes (which demand higher levels of education and training), more differentiated markets, and unpredictable economic circumstances, as I noted in Chapter 15, make it improbable that you will have a lifelong career in one field or one organization.

Many women, returning to the organizational world after having taken time to rear their families, decide to take a different path than the one they began. It's not surprising these days to find many such women in professional schools. These women have often developed a greater sense of self-confidence and direction, even while temporarily they were not pursuing their careers.

Other factors behind the wish for second careers are the effects aging and growth have on people. Although an intense period of skills training, job rotation, long hours of overtime, and much travel may have satisfied them when they were younger and just beginning their careers, as people get older they probably find the pace exhausting and the rewards insufficiently attractive to compensate for the loss of other gratifications.

But the reasons for thinking about a second career are not always positive. Some people want to change because they are always dissatisfied with themselves, some are depressed and angry, some have anxiety about death that induces restlessness, and some have overvalued themselves and believe they are more talented or capable than they really are. Some managers can't tolerate bosses. Others think they should have been CEO a long time ago. Some are unwilling to acquire experience, while others are competing with old classmates. Some are just competing—and not as well as they'd like.

Seeking a new career for these reasons is an exercise in futility. If a manager blames the job, the boss, or the company when the source of his discontent is really himself, his second career is likely to be as disappointing as his first. Therefore a person, before embarking on choosing a second career, must have an honest self-image and understand the changes he or she probably will go through.

Finding a New Direction

The most critical factor to consider in choosing a gratifying second career is your ego ideal. It can serve as a road map. Central to a person's aspirations, the ego ideal is an idealized image of oneself in the future. It includes the goals you would like to achieve and how you would like to see yourself. When a career helps satisfy the ego ideal, life and work are rewarding and enjoyable. When a career does not help meet these self-demands, work is a curse.

Because people begin to form their ego ideals in earliest childhood, developing an accurate understanding of them is difficult.

A careful review of family history and school and work experiences can go a long way in outlining the needs that are important to the ego ideal. You can help the process along by discussing with a listener or friend answers to the questions I raised in Chapter 1. If you still have some doubts about direction after you've talked these questions through, you might take a battery of psychological tests and interest inventories to complement the definition of your ego ideal. These, together with the guidance of a career counselor, are usually helpful in identifying career directions and boundaries.

Included in these considerations is the necessity for you to determine whether you are temperamentally fit for the job to which you are thinking of moving. The areas to explore are much the same as I described in Chapter 15, in the section on "Exploring Whether to Change Your Job."

Weighing Options

Second careers are usually evolutionary. They stem from some interest that has lain dormant or has been abandoned in favor of another occupation. Asked if he had had any idea of what he wanted to do when he left the chairmanship of Dain, Kalman & Quail, an investment banking firm in Minneapolis, for a new vocation, Wheelock Whitney answered, "Yes, really. I thought I'd like to pursue some other things that I cared about." Among these interests was the Johnson Institute, a center studying and treating the chemically dependent. Whitney had become deeply involved in the institute eight years earlier when his wife was undergoing treatment for alcoholism.[1]

Many turn to second careers that extend a previous occupational thrust; they may go into business for themselves in fields they already know. By searching the past for those budding interests that had no chance to flower, a person can draw a long list of career options. At the same time, one can eliminate those that are no longer interesting or pleasurable. In choosing his second career, William Damroth said he switched from the chairmanship of Lexington Corporation because "to me the main thing was that I couldn't continue doing what I enjoy the most, which is the creative role, the intense bringing together of all factors, saying, 'It ought to look like this.' For instance, what I'm doing today is much more satisfying than the long-range planning you have to do for a company. Today's satisfaction is immediate."[2]

After eliminating undesirable options, you should investigate what additional training is required for each of the remaining possibilities and how much you can afford to invest. To pick up some careers, people need to spend years in full-time professional or academic training; others they can approach through a course of reading, night school, or correspondence study. By seeing how the remaining options fit with how you prefer to behave and by understanding your ego ideal, you can usually narrow the field to one or two general directions. At this point, you should again ask a friend or counselor to act as a sounding board.

Finally, before you make a choice, you should consider a number of other critical issues:

Family. Whom do you have responsibility for—a mother-in-law, an uncle, a grandfather, a handicapped sister or brother? Do these responsibilities limit your options? Do your responsibilities to your spouse and children impose geographical or financial constraints?

Current job. If someone comes to a premature judgment or acts impulsively, he risks leaving his current job thinking that the company left much to be desired. Will your peers and boss see the move as a rejection of the company and of your work together? Feeling abandoned, they might attack you. The possibility of anger and disappointment is especially high when you and your superior have worked closely together and when you respect and admire each other. Furthermore, some people, disappointed that they failed to act when the time was right, will be jealous. They may unload on you their anger with themselves. Are you prepared for these conflicts?

It will help you to think about what it means to lose these peers and mentors. They have been significant elements in your support system. Perhaps also they have been close friends or social companions. Rather than thinking that you are being disloyal, recognize that people who prepare themselves for a second career are doing the organization as well as themselves a favor by making space for younger managers looking forward to promotion. In almost all organizations, incumbents are usually under continual pressure from those who would succeed them to vacate their roles so their successors will have opportunities to demonstrate what they can contribute.

Status. One's status in the community is directly related to one's status at work. Choosing another career may well result in changing one's status. How important is that to you? How important is it that you associate with the same people you have associated with before, that you play golf at the same clubs or take part in the same social activities? Because your spouse and children will also be affected, the family must discuss this issue together. The sacrifices may well be severe.

Rebuilding. If you're thinking of starting a new business or launching a new career, chances are that you will have to build a clientele. Rarely does a person move from one organization to another and take with him all of his accounts. For example, a lawyer told me that when he and his colleagues left a large firm to start their own, they expected their clients to follow them. Only a small fraction did, and the new firm had to build its clientele from scratch. Anyone starting his own business should expect to take from two to five years to build a stable of customers.

Freedom versus constraints. For a mature person, the pressure to be autonomous is very high. Therefore, in choosing an activity or direction, it is important to choose, insofar as you can, something that allows you maximum freedom to come and go, to do as you wish, while meeting the formal obligations of the role.

Year-long depression. I have never seen a person make a significant career shift without experiencing a year-long depression. I don't mean that people are down in the dumps for a year but that they feel loss, ambivalence, and fear that things may not work out. Caught in an ambiguous situation in which they are not yet rooted, they feel detached from their stable routines.

The longer a person has been with an organization, the more likely she has come to depend on it; the closer her relationships have been with her colleagues, the greater will be the sense of loss. The more her family has been tied to the organization, the more profound these feelings are likely to be.

Opportunity to talk. All change is loss, and all loss requires mourning (see Chapter 2). Even when promoted, one loses the support of colleagues, friends, and known ways of doing things. To dissipate the inevitable sorrow, you have to turn it into words. To detach from old ties and give up old habits, you have to talk about the experience.

Open options. Even if you have exercised great care in choosing a second career, the change won't necessarily work out. Economic vagaries as well as factors that you couldn't foresee may cut your second career short. If you left your old job on a positive note, however, it may be possible to get it back. Many organizations recognize that a person who has tested himself elsewhere and wants to return is likely to be an even better and more highly motivated employee.

Succeeding in a Major Career Change

"I'm in over my head and having a great time," said the former associate editor of *The Levinson Letter*, John Elder. In the course of a few months, he made a dramatic career move into computer programming. When he started his new job, he still had to learn almost everything, and he was plenty nervous.

There are times when being thrown into the deep end—or jumping in yourself—can be productive and even exhilarating. What are the elements that make it work?

A mentor. Elder was recruited by someone who had faith in his ability to learn and who stated clearly what gave him this confidence. A mentor is also a lifeguard, who ensures that your inevitable mistakes aren't fatal.

Mastery. As soon as Elder knew just enough, he wrote a small program that worked. He knew he'd scrap it once he learned better techniques, but in the meantime, it proved that he was becoming competent.

Career goal. Elder knew what he was aiming for. When he floundered, at least he was floundering toward something. That made it easier to ask for appropriate help.

Tolerance for ambiguity. Some people just can't stand the anxiety caused by too many unknowns, Elder observed. When they're thrown in to sink or swim, they sink, which is a waste of the abilities they do have.

Appreciation of superior knowledge. If you enjoy the presence of knowledge and skills greater than your own, you can tolerate being in over your head if you feel you're going to gain that knowledge or those skills.

CHAPTER **18**

Committing to Continual Change

I began this book by talking about old realities: life stages and the need to become an expert on yourself; the process of change and the importance of recognizing the underlying personal theme that constitutes continuity in the face of change—namely, pursuit of your ego ideal; carrot and stick modes of coping with successes and failures, particularly the propensity for harsh self-criticism; and retrospective appraisal of your career path. From that I turned to how you might take a proactive stance, attacking the multiform problems of career advancement and achievement, both propelling and steering yourself to maintain a coherent trajectory of increasing mastery. Becoming more proactive necessarily involves becoming more appropriately aggressive in dealing with bosses and organizational forces. It also involves broadening your competence and avoiding stumbling blocks. Crucially, it involves the making and breaking of relationships.

All of this necessarily occurs in a broader social context. I have touched on some of the elements of that context in these various chapters. Here I summarize them to reemphasize the need to give attention to those factors that make a significant difference in the careers of those who achieve in major organizations, as contrasted with those who are less likely to rise in organizational hierarchies.

Preoccupied with their own career efforts, most people pay too little attention to what's going on around them. They know about layoffs, about narrowing opportunities, about recession. They experience these things and read about them in the newspapers. But few stop to try to understand the implications of those events for strengthening themselves. It is to that issue this final chapter is addressed.

The New Reality

It seems likely that unpredictable economic circumstances and rapid technological advances will continue to hammer away at job security, forcing organizations into constant reevaluation and change. As public and private firms of all kinds contract and redirect their efforts, phase out old divisions that are no longer profitable, and open new operations that show promise, they will continue to "trim the fat," laying off superfluous employees at every level. Middle managers will bear the brunt of layoffs. Top-level executives' jobs may be safer, but even they, according to the business press, are being terminated more frequently and are having a more difficult time finding new jobs.

In addition, organizations are taking on new forms. IBM, long the model of the best and most profitable kind of organization, admired widely around the world as the leading American corporation, has divided itself into various components that can arrange mutually useful ties among each other and even with organizations outside of the corporate umbrella. Other organizations are evolving similar forms, frequently exemplified by a small corporate headquarters unit and highly flexible subunits that can change individually to meet the demands of their respective marketplaces. When the technology of one organization reaches its boundaries in that context but, combined with the technology of another, can develop new fields, joint ventures multiply. The same is true when those ventures have to be international or multinational for financial or political reasons.

Even in those organizations that maintain much of their historically stable structure, promotions are likely to be limited and large numbers of professionals, particularly those in their forties, are likely to find themselves on organizational plateaus. The reasons are simple. Not only is there contraction and constraint, but also no organization can promote all of the people who are within its structure. In fact, no organization can make use of all the talent it has because it must narrow its focus of activities to the thrust that promises greater return on investment or greater likelihood of perpetuation.

Some organizations have sold off their old businesses and converted themselves into new and different organizations. The great packinghouse firms that used to dominate Chicago have long since gone. Motorola no longer makes televisions. AT&T and the baby Bells are no longer merely in the telephone business; they are heavily involved in computers and other forms of communications technology that call for completely different kinds of people than those who once dominated the then-regulated utilities. In a certain sense, they are like colorful butterflies who, once emerged from their cocoons, can flit about opportunistically to take advantage of economic blossoms.

Finally, it is no longer enough for a person to know the discipline or profession or business in which he or she is engaged. Increasingly, people must know their customers' businesses. And in many organizations they must also know their suppliers' businesses. With increasing attention to serving the customer and the need to guarantee the quality of the product—even the components that come from suppliers—inevitably one has to broaden his or her purview, and therefore professional activities take on a new, more comprehensive perspective.

Maintaining Adaptability and Flexibility

People must continually reevaluate their careers, plan new goals and new directions that will give them greater flexibility and a measure of independence from the vagaries of organizational life. They must deal not only with the repetitive threat of unemployment, but also with the even greater threat of underemployment and obsolescence. That's why it is important to seek out organizations and roles in which you can enhance and increase your adaptive skills.

But better skills preparation by itself won't be enough if those skills are in the service of a narrow occupational path. What benefit is there in becoming more proficient in a career that may be nonexistent in five years? Furthermore, what use is increased skills preparation if one is unwilling to recognize the realities of his or her own personality and the degree to which those, unchanged, make career advancement impossible? Similarly, unrealistic fantasies about what

205

may be possible in any employing organization can only lead to disillusionment, if not outright failure.

Increasing Your Understanding of the Past and Contemporary World

It's an old story that less than half of college graduates use their college majors often in work and more than half are in careers they didn't plan on. In repeated surveys, graduates say they wish they had taken more of such courses as English, psychology, and business administration, and built broad skills such as communications, human relations, and administration, rather than specific occupational training. College doesn't seem to help in nurturing leadership ability, clear thinking, or in choosing goals in life.

In a study of 3,000 officers and directors of 200 large American companies, Michael Useem found that graduates of Harvard, Yale, and Princeton, where it is possible to pursue only liberal arts, who received no further professional schooling went on to careers at least as successful as graduates of the Harvard Business School.[1] They became vice presidents in large companies earlier than the business school graduates, received more invitations onto other company boards later in their careers, and were just as likely to become CEOs. Useem says the reason for the special success of the liberal arts graduate is the product of the kinds of problems senior executives solve. The more than 75 top executives of America's largest corporations he interviewed stressed repeatedly the need to think broadly and to understand how society works. To operate in a contemporary business, they need to be familiar with the processes of government and the complexities of political forces. They need to understand economics and the social and political environment in which firms operate.

According to a long-term career study of AT&T managers by Douglas Bray and associates, those who majored in the humanities and social sciences have better overall interpersonal and administrative skills than those who obtain baccalaureates in business and engineering.[2] Bray found that early in their careers with AT&T, only a quarter of the engineers and a third of the business majors were considered good prospects for rising high in management, but nearly half of the humanities and social sciences majors were identified as having such potential. After 20 years with the company, 43 percent of the humanities and social science majors had risen to middle and higher levels of management, as contrasted with 23 percent of engineers and 32 percent of the business majors. People with specialized training have an initial advantage at the entry level in the business world, but then the liberal arts majors get ahead of them and stay ahead.

Students trained in the liberal arts are better able to formulate valid concepts, analyze arguments, define themselves, and orient themselves truly to their world. David McClelland and his associates found that the liberal arts curriculum prepared students more effectively than career-oriented programs to adapt to new environments, think critically and conceptually, integrate broad ranges of experience, set goals and develop independence of thought, and seek leadership roles.[3]

"When aspiring young photographers ask me for counsel, I suggest that they first become students of the humanities, that they fill their lives with more than just technical information about the interworkings of the camera. To make enduring photographs, it is far more important to know about the interworkings of the human mind and soul—for the heart and mind are the true lens of the camera." So said the famed photographer Yousuf Karsch.[4]

Educating Yourself Beyond Narrow Skills

Most people who enter the business world specialize early on. They are intent on getting a reasonable start, earning a reasonable livelihood, becoming proficient in a given area or discipline. Usually, they have to be as practical as possible. That heavy concentration and narrow focus gets in the way of their flexible adaptation as they move up in the organization, as the McClelland study and AT&T experiences demonstrate. It also tends to keep them narrow when they do move up, and they are therefore less ready to assume civic, cultural, and other responsibilities in their communities.

When, sometimes in some desperation, professionals seek to broaden themselves in the limited programs of the Aspen Institute or Dartmouth College or brief reunion programs of their respective universities, their interest and curiosity are aroused. They begin to sense what they need to learn more broadly and to yearn for the opportunity to examine the issues and topics that arise in those liberal education programs. They express pleasure and gratification in these experiences and criticize themselves for not having undertaken them earlier.

The wise aspiring person will recognize this problem early. While he or she is developing additional skills, whether in extension programs or night courses or in-service training, he or she will also undertake parallel learning in the liberal arts. Every community college has such courses, which provide another perspective on the world, contact with a different range of people, and a psychological reawakening to the many pressing philosophical and moral issues that burden all human beings.

Most organizational problems involve more complex moral and psychological issues than are superficially apparent. Increasingly, the problems of conflicts of values have less to do with black and white, right and wrong, than the costs of alternative choices. Choosing between allocating research funds to one or another activity may have significant ramifications for the employment of thousands of people. Deciding to apply certain kinds of conservation efforts may result in the loss of many jobs and the destruction of whole communities. Closing a plant may be necessary if one's products aren't selling, but to do so may involve undermining the economy of a large geographical area.

Today's successful careerist must have maximum adaptability and the capacity to apply broad knowledge in many different areas to a great variety of potential problems. He or she must have a sense of the problems of the past and must be able to think critically, reason carefully, and take into account different cultures. Knowledge of the basic questions, ideas, and truths that have been the foundation stones of Western societies, and the ability to link them to current activities, are fundamental to a strong leadership role. You get trained to do something, but you have to be educated to understand the significance of what you're doing. Training tends to be transitory and quickly obsolete, while education endures. Training is related to being employed, education more broadly to living.

Although technical specialists get an early start, and may even earn more in the early part of their careers, they are most vulnerable because they become more readily obsolete. Also, after a few years of specialized work, they must move into managerial ranks or be supervised by younger people. Few like or are prepared for managerial careers, and they are then consigned to a lifetime of what they regard as hackwork, with little novelty, challenge, or recognition.

This happens even with more highly trained professionals. A cancer surgeon told me he was shifting to chemotherapy because surgery had become so automatic for him, and he could do no more good for his patients by surgery than he was already doing. Chemotherapy was a new and promising area for him. This was a significant career shift that combined the roles of internist and radiologist.

Furthermore, 15 years after the completion of any professional training, a person is usually satiated with that activity. She yearns for a new stimulation. The more intelligent she is, the greater the hunger. Unless a person is on the frontier of new knowledge, she either seeks career alternatives or pursues her work routinely and seeks stimulation elsewhere. Her work output thereupon becomes merely routine or barely satisfactory.

The best predictor of recurrent social trends is still a grasp of the past. Human motivation is still better understood through great literature than by taking the usual academic courses in psychology. Societies in transition today have problems that conceptually are little different than societies in transition in the Middle Ages. Radical social and religious movements clash again and again. A person who knows these phenomena will be less panic-stricken by changing circumstances and will choose his course more wisely.

The market value of the ability to read and research, to plan and deal with abstractions, and then to organize and articulate them, will survive any fluctuations or shifts in specialization. The engineer, no matter how technically competent, who doesn't see beyond the drawing board can't anticipate what he and his company are likely to be up against and its significance to him. The executive who cannot foresee, for example, what the consumer movement or growing federal regulations will demand of his organization in the form of new designs, new products, or new safeguards, is likely to cost his company thousands if not millions of dollars and much goodwill with expensive rearguard actions.

This point was given added emphasis when Mitsubishi chose Minoru Makihara to be its president. The Japanese had always promoted from within. It was unheard of to think of promoting a man who had not been educated in Japan to head the crown jewel of Japan's most powerful business group. Makihara graduated from

Harvard in 1954 and spent more than two decades in London, Seattle, and New York. "By his very presence, the polished cosmopolitan, Mr. Makihara reinforces the message that the biggest problem facing Japanese business today is not profits but politics."[5]

Those who can project the past into the future, who can think on their own in broader terms, who can conceptualize and analyze problems, and clearly articulate proposed solutions orally and in writing are likely to be always in heavy demand. If there is no room in your firm for such contributions, maybe that is an indication you might look elsewhere or start your own business, for you are vulnerable to obsolescence where you are.

Today, people should be developing parallel interests. Already we see combined academic efforts: law and management, administration and social work; counseling in the ministry. Many in middle age who have made midcareer shifts have turned hobbies into occupations. One of my psychologist colleagues is now a professional photographer, as is an executive friend.

Inasmuch as second careers invariably develop from previously dormant or less well developed interests, multiple career paths necessarily must follow from current interests, skills, and aspirations. In other words, you should start with what you have rather than cast about for some mythical ideal. Whatever career changes subsequently occur will be built step-by-step out of the present.

Of course, you may not be able to pursue two or three kinds of professional training simultaneously, but you can do so in tandem and can take courses that may serve several specialty interests. The study of archeology, for example, may well help the young executive in international business to understand better the cultures of the countries in which he serves. Simultaneously, it may provide stimulating vacations, a change of pace, and an option for a second career.

Protecting Your Independence

The adult, already established in a career, must continue to work hard at constantly upgrading his or her skills through reading professional and trade journals and attending seminars and training courses. The professional or technical skills, acquired painfully during the years of costly education, quickly become obsolete. Those skills and knowledge acquired in a professional school have a half-life of about 10 years. That is, within a decade, half of this knowledge becomes dated and the other half turns out to be wrong. For years teachers have been required to continue their education while working. Physicians, psychologists, social workers, nurses, and others are being required to take courses to keep their licenses active. And postdoctoral training programs for professionals from psychologists to astrophysicists are growing rapidly. Thus, planned respecialization is in tune with the contemporary ethos that demands continual learning.

Established professionals are already beginning to think of career alternatives, as the growing interest in franchising has suggested. Fewer are thinking of their careers as an end point. New college graduates are thinking of having two or three different careers. Many technical specialists are pursuing MBAs in night school or other special programs. In many instances, corporations and government organizations reimburse tuition for advanced learning. But, in addition to preparing for other roles in organizations, people should prepare to go out on their own, to market themselves, to become their own free enterprise. They must look to themselves, rather than to their organizations, as an employer and as the major force that determines the course of their lives. Only they can really manage their lives and determine their fates.

In the same way that craftsmen offer the products of their skills on the market, people in organizational roles should train themselves in some additional skill, profession, or service they can offer others as independent practitioners. Some professional training, of course, doesn't lend itself to this approach. Not many people mine coal independently. But each person can prepare to do something on his or her own.

You might well argue that if everyone is preparing to enter everyone else's field, why bother? Won't that be saturated too? Perhaps. But in moving from one field to another, you bring insights and skills from your previous field. You bring new insights from a different constellation of experiences. Engineers who become psychologists see psychology differently than do nurses who become psychologists. Their contributions are significantly different. Besides, if others are leaving those fields or additional multidisciplinary skills are required, new openings are created. The creation of new industries will require new kinds of specialists. There were few computer experts 30 years ago.

If you accept that fact, you can train yourself on the job or in school so that, if and when the time comes to change job or career, you will have suitable alternatives that you can exercise at your discretion, rather than remaining the prisoner of boredom, satiation, or organizational politics. Planning should begin early and last through retirement. Adaptability and flexibility are the key words in any individual's career planning.

By increasing your understanding of the past and of the contemporary world, you can maintain a constant scan of the environment, getting information not only from coworkers and professional colleagues, but also from other social and economic spheres. Only then can you make reasonable decisions about your own life. Each person must depend on himself or herself for job security by defining and redefining goals, by educating himself or herself beyond narrow professional or technical skills, by protecting his or her independence—in short, by innovating his or her own career. Each person should ask, "How can I use what I am learning in activities that I would do by myself that I would offer as a service?"

Finally, it's your career. You must plan it, manage it, guide it, refocus it, and fine-tune it in keeping with your experiences in the stage of development in which you find yourself. While many people can help, you necessarily are at the helm. Smooth sailing!

Notes

Chapter 1

1. Erik H. Erikson, *Childhood and Society*, 2d ed., New York: Norton, 1963.
2. Kenneth Keniston, *Young Radicals: Notes on Committed Youth*, New York: Harcourt, Brace & World, 1968.
3. Elliott Jaques, *Requisite Organization*, Arlington, Va.: Cason Hall & Co., 1989, and *Executive Leadership*, Arlington, Va.: Cason Hall & Co., 1991.

Chapter 2

1. Douglas W. Bray, Richard J. Campbell, and Donald L. Grant, *Formative Years in Business*, New York: Wiley, 1974.

Chapter 3

1. Edward Gross, "Embarrassment in Public Life," *Social Science and Modern Society*, July–August 1984, 53.
2. Barnaby J. Feder, "Carbide to Sell India Assets to Build Hospital for Bhopal," *New York Times*, April 15, 1992, D1.

Chapter 4

1. Robert Schrank, "Two Women, Three Men on a Raft," *Harvard Business Review*, May–June 1977, 100–108.
2. William McGurn, "Losing Well Is the Best Revenge," *National Review*, December 8, 1989, 16.
3. Judy B. Rosener, "Ways Women Lead," *Harvard Business Review*, November–December 1990, 119–125.

Chapter 5

1. Harry Levinson, *Organizational Diagnosis*, Cambridge, Mass.: Harvard University Press, 1972.

Chapter 6

1. *New York Times*, March 8, 1992, 5.

2. *New York Times,* March 4, 1992, 1.
3. *Fortune,* November 18, 1991, 202.
4. Daniel Pinkwater, *Fishwhistle,* Reading, Mass.: Addison-Wesley, 1989.
5. Elliott Jaques, *Executive Leadership,* Arlington, Va.: Cason Hall & Co., 1991.
6. John P. Kotter, *The General Managers,* New York: Free Press, 1982.
7. Edwin B. Lambeth, "Gene Roberts," *The Quill,* June 1991, 14–15.
8. Ibid., 20.
9. *Rolling Stone,* 20th Anniversary Special Issue, 1987.
10. Michael Matteson and John Ivancevich, *Controlling Work Stress,* San Francisco: Jossey-Bass, 1987.

Chapter 7

1. *The Levinson Letter,* June 2, 1986.
2. D. Manus Pinkwater, *Return of the Moose,* New York: Dodd, Mead, 1979.
3. Harry Levinson and Stuart Rosenthal, *CEO: Corporate Leadership in Action,* New York: Basic Books, 1984.
4. Elliott Jaques, *A General Theory of Bureaucracy,* New York: Halsted, 1976.
5. Brian O'Reilly, "A Body Builder Lifts Greyhound," *Fortune,* October 28, 1985, 130.

Chapter 8

1. Harry Levinson, *Organizational Diagnosis,* Cambridge, Mass.: Harvard University Press, 1972.
2. Jerry B. Harvey, "Some Thoughts About Organizational Backstabbing: Or, How Come Every Time I Get Stabbed in the Back, My Fingerprints Are on the Knife?" *Academy of Management Executive* 3, 1989, 271–277.

Chapter 10

1. Elliott Jaques, *Requisite Organization,* Arlington, Va.: Cason Hall & Co., 1989.
2. Harry Levinson, *Psychological Man,* Cambridge, Mass.: The Levinson Institute, 1976.
3. Margaret Davies, *Colette,* New York: Grove Press, 1961.

Chapter 11

1. Isaac Asimov, *The Hugo Winners,* Vol. 2, Garden City, N.Y.: Doubleday, 1971, 812.
2. Susan J. Ashford and Anne S. Tsui, "Self-Regulation for Managerial Effectiveness: The Role of Active Feedback Seeking," *Academy of Management Journal* 34, 1991, 251–280.
3. "An Old Idea Makes a Comeback," *Time,* June 12, 1989, 71.
4. Anthony Fairhead and John Hudson, "Leadership Template: Roadmap for Managers," *Issues and Observations* 9(3), 1989, 1.
5. Kerry Bunker, "Leaders in the Dark Chasm of Learning," *Issues and Observations* 9(3), 1989, 5.
6. Fairhead and Hudson, op. cit., 1.

Chapter 12

1. "School for Survival," *Time,* February 11, 1985, 74.
2. Larry Hirshhorn, *Beyond Mechanization,* Cambridge, Mass.: MIT Press, 1984, and *The Workplace Within: Psychodynamics of Organizational Life,* Cambridge,

Mass.: MIT Press, 1988. Manfred F. R. Kets de Vries, *Prisoners of Leadership,* New York: Wiley, 1989. Manfred F. R. Kets de Vries and Danny Miller, *The Neurotic Organization,* San Francisco: Jossey-Bass, 1984. Manfred F. R. Kets de Vries and Associates, *Organizations on the Couch,* San Francisco: Jossey-Bass, 1991. Harry Levinson, *Psychological Man,* Cambridge, Mass.: The Levinson Institute, 1976. Howard Schwartz, *Narcissistic Process and Corporate Decay,* New York: New York University Press, 1990. Abraham Zaleznik, *The Managerial Mystique,* New York: Harper & Row, 1989. Abraham Zaleznik and Manfred F. R. Kets de Vries, *Power and the Corporate Mind,* Chicago: Bonus Books, 1985.

Chapter 13

1. Alec Guinness, *Blessings in Disguise,* New York: Knopf, 1986, 55.
2. *New England Business.*
3. "The Unconscious History of Vietnam in the Group: An Innovative Multiphasic Model for Working Through Authority Transferences in Guilt-Driven Veterans," *International Journal of Group Psychotherapy* 38, 1988, 275–301.
4. *New York Times.*
5. Seth Faison, "Trying to Play by the Rules," *New York Times,* December 22, 1991, 3–1.

Chapter 14

1. Lee Wilkins, "Madison and Jefferson: The Making of a Friendship," *Political Psychology* 12, 1991, 593–608.
2. Harry Levinson and Katherine Davidson Kush, "Up Through the Ranks: Mentoring for Leadership," *Addendum, The Levinson Letter,* 1979.
3. Eliza G. C. Collins and Patricia Scott, "Everyone Who Makes It Has a Mentor," *Harvard Business Review,* July–August 1978.
4. Ibid.
5. Agnes K. Missirian, *The Corporate Connection,* Englewood Cliffs, N.J.: Prentice-Hall, 1982, 43.

Chapter 15

1. Sarah Bartlett, "New York Logs 500,000 Lost Since 1989, a Record High," *New York Times,* April 16, 1992, B1.
2. Jon Nordheimer, "From Middle-Class to Jobless, a Sense of Pride Is Shattered," *New York Times,* April 13, 1992, 1.
3. Karl A. Menninger, *The Human Mind,* 3d ed., New York: Knopf, 1948, 9–14.
4. "The Growing Ranks of Contract Workers (Freelancers Who Hire Themselves Out to Companies for Long-Term Projects)," *Dun's Business Month,* March 1986, 56–57.

Chapter 16

1. Elmo Zumwalt, Jr., and Elmo Zumwalt III, *My Father, My Son,* New York: Macmillan, 1986.
2. Ralph Hirschowitz, "Getting Fired," *The Levinson Letter,* May 16, 1988, 3.

Chapter 17

1. "Don't Call It 'Early Retirement,' An Interview with Wheelock Whitney and William G. Damroth," *Harvard Business Review,* September–October 1975, 103.
2. Ibid., 113.

Chapter 18

1. Michael Useem, "We Need the Humanities," *The Boston Globe,* August 2, 1983.
2. Douglas W. Bray, Richard J. Campbell, and Donald Grant, *Formative Years in Business,* New York: Wiley, 1974.
3. David G. Winter, Abigail J. Stewart, and David C. McClelland, "Grading the Effects of a Liberal Arts Education," *Psychology Today,* September 1978, 69–74ff.
4. "Notable and Quotable," *Wall Street Journal,* July 10, 1980, 12.
5. David E. Sanger, "Unusual Path to the Top at Mitsubishi," *New York Times,* April 13, 1992, D1.

Index

A

Ability: conceptual, 10–12; limited, 47. *See also* Skills
Accountability, by boss, 105–106
Achievement: aspects of ongoing, 127–137; background on, 127–128; and boss, 132–137; broadening experience and perspective for, 128–129; feedback sources for, 129–132; opportunities for, 127
Actions, control of, 72
Adams, Jane, 156
Adler, David, 94–95
Advancement. *See* Promotion
Affection: boss's handling of, 101; need for, and work load, 78; in teams, 92
Age of Worry, 15
Aggression: application of, 65–66; boss's handling of, 101; and coworkers, 88; inadequate management of, 44–45; and job change, 182–184; managerial skills in, 65–67; and need to be loved, 78; passive, 47; style of, 66–67
Ambiguity: by boss, 116–117; in second career, 204
Anger: and change, 14; and downsizing, 152–153; and guilt and shame, 26, 33; and job loss, 196; and old boss, 161; and slumps, 74; speaking up to boss on, 111
Anxiety, about job loss, 192
Apologies: for guilt, 30; for shame, 34
Ashford, Susan J., 131, 217
Asimov, Isaac, 128, 217
Aspen Institute, and broadened education, 209
AT&T: and change, 207; culture of, 53; education programs of, 139, 141; executives of, 23, 208–209
Attitudes, improving managerial, 61–74
Autonomy, and second career, 203

B

Backstabbing, by coworkers, 97
Bartlett, Sarah, 218
Baughman, James, 141
Behavior: erratic and discourteous, 45; problems of, in boss, 103–110
Behavioral job description: for learning the organization, 58–59; for success, 162; and work load, 81
Behavior skills, for managers, 69–71
Bell system, and change, 207
Bhopal, India, catastrophe in, 34, 35, 59
Birk, Kathy, 161
Blame, of self, 37

217

Boss: abrasive, 123, 124; abusive, 118–119; ambiguous, 116–117; aspects of speaking up to, 99–112; authoritarian, 154–155; background on, 99–100; as bad manager, 160–161; behavioral problems of, 103–110; charismatic, 155–158; charming, 125; as con artist, 125–126; defensive, 121–122; dependent narcissistic, 124; disapproving, 119–120; disdainful, 123–124; exploitative, 122; failed, 158–160; fawning, 125; following, 136–137; and friendship, 89–90; grandiose, 124; identifying with, 132–133; learning from, 114, 116, 122; manipulative, 125–126; meddling, 117–118; narcissistic, 123–126; nice, 118; problems with, 113–126; remaining by, 161–162; sadistic, 124–125; and senior people, 113–114; silent, 114–115; support from, 108, 133–136; unhelpful, 115–116; weak, 120–121; and work overload, 82–83, 84–85

Boston College, business majors at, 61

Boston Pops, charismatic leader of, 155

Bowditch, James, 61

Boyden International, and counteroffers, 188

Bray, Douglas W., 23, 208, 215, 219

British Steel, predecessor's legacy at, 158

Brown, Ann, 134

Bunker, Kerry, 135, 217

Burnout, and job change, 180

Business Week, 140

C

Camaraderie: concept of, 88; limits on, 89–90; in teams, 92

Campbell, Richard J., 215, 219

Career: alternatives for, 213–214; back tracking of, 14–15; change from upheaval of, 14–16, 178; choosing a second, 199–204; stages of, 3–7

Career guidance, by boss, 107–108

Career mastery: organizational dimensions of, 49–126; personal dimensions of, 1–48; transformational dimensions of, 127–214

Carey, C. William, 150

Celebrations, for successes, 26–27, 71

Change: adaptability and flexibility for, 207–214; aspects of committing to, 205–214; aspects of coping with, 13–23; background on, 13–14; broadened education for, 209–212; and independence, 212–214; and managerial education, 144, 209–212; as new reality, 206–207; in organization, 16–23; and psychological balance, 16–19; and rebuilding strength, 22–23, 203; and social context, 205–206; sources of, 13; stock taking for, 19–22; as transient, 23; and value stability, 21–22. *See also* Job changes

Charles River, observing, 64

Chicago, and change, 207

Chrysler: and competitiveness, 57; predecessor's legacy at, 158

Churchill, Winston, 119

Clements, George, 171–172

Cleveland Orchestra, predecessor's legacy at, 153

Colette, Sidonie-Gabrielle, 122

Communication: and managerial education, 144; organizational, 51–52

Compliments, and self-knowledge, 8

Conceptual abilities, self-knowledge on, 10–12

Conflicts, speaking up to boss on, 111

Conscience, superego distinct from, 25

Consolidation stage, in careers, 6–7

Consultancy, as job change, 189–190

Contract work, issues of, 189–190

Coping skills, for managers, 71–72

Coworkers: aspects of relations with, 87–97; background on, 87–88; backstabbing by, 97; dislike of, 94–96; ending feuds among, 96–97; friendships among, 88–90; and peer cooperation, 94; and promotion, 90; and sexual attraction, 90; teams of, 91–94

Crisp, Wendy Reid, 75

Criticism: public, 104, 125; and self-blame, 37; and self-knowledge, 8–9; and unconscious guilt, 32

Culture, organizational, 53–56

D

Dain, Kalman & Quail, leaving, 201

Damroth, William G., 201–202, 219

Dartmouth College, and broadened education, 209

Davies, Margaret, 217

Dean Witter, predecessor's legacy at, 161

Delegation, and work load, 80

Dependency needs: and assuming responsibility, 46–47; and boss, 101, 136, 137; in career stages, 4, 5, 6; and job change, 184–185; and self-blame, 37

Depression: and change, 17; and second career, 203

Development, fostering, 134–135

Digital Equipment Corporation, education programs of, 139, 141

Direction, by boss, 105

Distance, emotional, and job change, 182

Distorted thinking: about coworkers, 95–96; and unconscious guilt, 32

Downsizing, dealing with, 152–153

E

Ebert, Ronald, 93

Edison, Thomas, 80

Education, managerial: applicability of, 143–144; aspects of, 139–148; background on, 139–141; broadened, 209–212; in identity stage, 4; and liberal arts education, 146–147, 208–209; and limits to growth, 147–148; and obsolescence, 144–146; organizational programs for, 139–140, 148; outside refreshers for, 145–146; psychological foundation for, 141–143

Ego ideals: and affection, 92; concept of, 25; and coping with change, 14; and guilt, 30; and job change, 185–187; and organizational culture, 55;

and predecessor's legacy, 157; and second career, 200–201; and speaking up to boss, 100–101; and success, 26; and work load, 75, 78, 79, 84

Elder, John, 204

Embarrassment: coping with, 36–37; and shame, 34

Emotional distance, and job change, 182

Enemies, feedback from, 130–131

Environmental scanning, and career alternatives, 214

Equal Employment Opportunity Commission (EEOC), 189

Erikson, Erik H., 3, 215

Euripides, 146

Exercise, as relief from stress, 18, 192

Expectations: control of, 72–73; for work load, 75–76

Exxon, and shame, 35

F

Failure: aspects of, 39–48; background on, 39; by boss, 153–160; gaining from, 40–41; judgments about, 25–26; in organizations, 41–43; and reality, 40; reasons for, 44–48

Fairbanks, Philip, 1–2

Fairhead, Anthony, 135, 217

Fairness, by boss, 103–105

Faison, Seth, 218

Family: and job change, 180; and job loss, 193; and parents, 32, 37; and second careers, 202; and stress, 18–19; for women, 19, 72–73

Feder, Barnaby J., 215

Feedback: for narcissistic boss, 126; about promotion, 42; on self, 8; sources of, 129–132; on success, 27

Feelings, and speaking up to boss, 109, 112

Feuds, ending, 96–97

Fiedler, Arthur, 155

Fischer, Ken, 156

France, managerial education program in, 139

Friendship: with boss, 89–90; with coworkers, 88–90. *See also* Camaraderie; Peers

G

Geneen, Harold, 125, 154
General Electric (GE): education programs of, 139, 141; managerial style at, 61–62, 109
General Motors, organizational characteristics of, 51–52, 53
Generativity stage: in careers, 4–6; and mentoring, 167
Grant, Donald L., 215, 219
Great Depression, 178
Green Bay Packers, predecessor's legacy at, 154
Greyhound, tough boss at, 83
Grief: and change, 20–21; and job loss, 196. *See also* Loss
Gross, Edward, 34, 215
Group behavior, in teams, 92–94
Guilt: conscious, 30–31; coping with, 29–36; and problem boss, 116, 118; and promotions, 152, 159–160; recognizing unconscious, 32–33; and shame, 34; and success, 28. *See also* Unconscious guilt
Guinness, Alec, 150, 218

H

Harvard University, liberal arts at, 208, 212
Harvey, Jerry B., 97, 217
Hatred, and coworkers, 95
Hawthorne effect, 146
Henson, Joe, 156
Herzberg, Frederick, 142
Hirschowitz, Ralph, 194, 196, 219
Hirshhorn, Larry, 217
Hong Kong, tradition in, 150
Hudson, John, 135, 217
Hunt, Martita, 150

I

Iacocca, Lee, 57, 155, 158
IBM: and change, 206; and culture of, 53, 80
Ideals. *See* Ego ideals
Identity stage, in careers, 3–4
Idiosyncrasies, of boss, 108–110
Impostors, feeling like, 27
Impulsiveness, and failure, 46

Independence, protecting, 212–214
India, Bhopal disaster in, 34, 35, 59
Indiana, complaints against brokers in, 161
Inflexibility, and failure, 46
INSEAD, education program at, 139
ITT: predecessor's legacy at, 154; public criticism at, 125
Ivancevich, John, 72, 216

J

Japan: competition with, 57, 63; promotion in, 211–212
Jaques, Elliott, 11, 65, 81, 116, 179, 215, 216, 217
Jefferson, Thomas, 165, 174
Jewel Companies, mentoring in, 171–172
Job changes: aspects of, 177–190; background on, 177–178; and career upheaval, 14–16, 178; consultancy as, 189–190; and counteroffer, 188–189; exploring, 180–190; and idealization, 187–188; in old organization, 189; psychological issues of, 181–187; time for, 179–180; and uncertainty, 178, 179–180
Job description, behavioral, 58–59, 81, 162
Job loss: anticipating, 192–193; anxiety about, 192; aspects of, 191–197; background on, 191–192; and isolation, 197; managing, 195–197; opportunities from, 194–195; psychological issues of, 193–197
Joe's case, 10–12
Johnson Institute, work of, 201

K

Karsch, Yousuf, 209
Keniston, Kenneth, 215
Kets de Vries, Manfred F. R., 217–218
Kotter, John P., 216
Kush, Katherine Davidson, 165n

L

LaGuardia, Fiorello, 155–156
Lambeth, Edwin B., 216

Language skills, for managers, 63–64, 70–71
Laughter, as relief from stress, 19
Learning skills, for managers, 69–70
Levinson, Harry, 216, 217, 218
Lexington Corporation, leaving, 201
Liberal arts: and adaptability for change, 208–209; and managerial education, 146–147
Lombardi, Vince, 154
Long, Shelley, 88
Loss: and change, 20–21; and end of mentoring, 174; identifying, 193–194; of predecessors, 153, 157, 161; and second career, 202; after success, 27–29; and teams, 93. *See also* Job loss
Love. *See* Affection
Lunding, Franklin, 171–172

M

Maazel, Lorin, 153, 154, 155
McClelland, David C., 209, 219
McGregor, Douglas, 142
MacGregor, Ian, 158
McGurn, William, 216
Madison, James, 165, 174
Mahoney, Richard, 63
Makihara, Minoru, 211–212
Managerial styles: and failure, 47; of women and men, 47, 88, 155
Managers: adaptability and flexibility for, 207–214; attitude and skill improvement for, 61–74; coworker relations of, 87–97; kinds of knowledge for, 62–63; minority, 82, 99; parallel interests of, 212; and problem bosses, 113–126; professionalism of, 139–140; slumps by, 73–74; and speaking up to boss, 99–112; transformational dimensions for, 127–214; trends for, 61–63; work load of, 75–85. *See also* Education, managerial
Manipulative skills: of boss, 125–126; for managers, 68–69
Maslow, Abraham, 142
Massachusetts Institute of Technology (MIT), skill building at, 15
Matteson, Michael, 72, 216

Maxwell, Robert, 124
Menninger, Karl A., 181, 218
Mentor, 165
Mentoring: aspects of, 165–175; beginning, 168–171; in career stages, 4, 5, 167; combined characteristics in, 171–172; concept of, 165–166; ending, 173–174; feedback from, 130, 136; and future shock, 166; and hindsight, 167–168; importance of, 174–175; and managerial education, 144; from outside the organization, 170; and problem boss, 116, 118, 121; and promotions, 160; relationship of, 166–168; rewards of, 166–168, 175; in second career, 204; transformation in, 172–173
Midler, Bette, 88
Miller, Arthur, 79
Miller, Danny, 217–218
Missirian, Agnes K., 172, 218
Mistakes, coping with, 29
Misunderstandings, avoiding, 152
Mitsubishi, promotion at, 211–212
Monitoring systems, feedback from, 131
Monsanto, and reading skills, 63
Moonlighting, and coping with change, 15
Motorola, and change, 207
Mourning: and change, 20–21; and job loss, 196. *See also* Loss

N

Narcissism: forms of, 123–126; and work load, 80, 83
National Association for Female Executives, 75
New York City, charismatic mayor of, 156
New York State, jobs lost in, 178
Nixon, Richard M., 34
Noncompulsiveness, and work load, 78
Nordheimer, Jon, 218
Northern Telecom, employment guarantee by, 15
Nuclear Regulatory Commission, 82

O

Observation skills, for managers, 64–65
Odysseus, 165
Oedipal conflict, and unconscious guilt, 31–32
O'Reilly, Brian, 216
Organizations: aspects of, 49–126; behavioral job descriptions in, 58–59; change in, 16–23; charts of, 50–51; climate of, 100, 103; communication in, 51–52; in competitive environment, 52; coworker relations in, 87–97; culture of, 53–56; education programs of, 139–140, 148; employees in, 52, 54; failure in, 41–43; financial data on, 51; first impressions of, 49–50; handles on, 50–53; history of, 57; influential people in, 57–58; learning about, 49–59; mood of, 52–53; and problem bosses, 113–126; shame of behalf of, 35–36; skills and attitudes for managing, 61–74; and speaking up to boss, 99–112; values of, 65, 66; work load in, 75–85
Outsiders: feedback from, 131, 136; mentoring from, 170
Overcontrol, by boss, 109
Overstimulation, and work load, 80

P

Palincsar, Annemarie, 134
Parents: and self-blame, 37; and unconscious guilt, 32
Parson, Erwin, 152
Paul, 11
Peers: and coworker cooperation, 94; feedback from, 130; support among, 35; and work load, 75
Penance, for guilt, 30
Perfectionism, and work load, 78–79
Performance appraisal: and speaking up to boss, 106–107; and unconscious guilt, 32; and work load, 81
Perkins, Donald, 172
Perot, Ross, 53
Personality, need for comprehensive theory of, 142

Philadelphia Inquirer, 68–69
Pinkwater, Daniel, 64, 216
Pinkwater, D. Manus, 216
Political skills, for managers, 67–68
Positive traits: and guilt, 30–31; and job change, 185
Power, and work overload, 83
Predecessor, legacy of, 153–162
Prime Computer, predecessor's legacy at, 156
Princeton University, liberal arts at, 208
Promotion: aspects of, 149–163; background on, 149–150; and coworkers, 90; and differential diagnosis, 70; following boss in, 136–137; lack of, 41–43; and leaving a position, 163; losses with, 28–29; and organizational culture, 54; and predecessor's legacy, 153–162; speaking up to boss on, 107; starting well, 150–153; subordinates' impact on, 151, 152, 157–163; success in, 162–163; and work overload, 82
Psychological contracts: mentors for clarifying, 168; speaking up to boss on, 111–112
Psychological injuries, and failure, 45–46
Pygmalion, 173
Pynchon, Thomas, 79

R

Reaction formation, and work load, 79
Reading skills, for managers, 63
Reagan, Ronald, 40
Reality: change as, 206–207; coping with, 158–159, 162; and failure, 40; and work load, 85
Relationships: for coping with change, 15, 18–19, 22–23; of coworkers, 87–97; for stress management, 73
Responsibility, inability to assume, 46–47
Retirement: and consolidation stage, 6–7; as psychological injury, 45–46

Riccardo, John, 158
Rickover, Hyman, 123
Risk taking, and teams, 91
Roberts, Gene, 68–69
Rosener, Judy B., 216
Rosenthal, Stuart, 216

S

Salinger, J. D., 79
Sanger, David E., 219
Schrank, Robert, 215
Schwartz, Howard, 218
Second career: aspects of choosing, 199–204; background on, 199–200; in career stages, 5, 6; finding direction for, 201–204; and parallel interests, 212; success in, 204
Self: aspects of, for career mastery, 1–48; background on, 1–3; broadened perspective for, 2; career stages for, 3–7; change for, 13–23; development of, 131, 136; and failure, 39–48; feedback on, 8; gaining knowledge of, 7–10; negatives of, 42; personal work on, 9–10; plateaued, 41–42; registering potential of, 43–44; success and failure to, 25–37; understanding, 1–12; unneeded, 41
Self-blame, coping with, 37
Self-centeredness, and failure, 45
Self-confidence: and job changes, 179; lack of, and work load, 79
Self-esteem, formula for, 25
Self-image, and work load, 79
Self-knowledge, on conceptual abilities, 10–12
Senior people: appealing to, 113–114; feedback from, 131
Sexual attraction, between coworkers, 90
Sexual harassment, and speaking up to boss, 105
Shame: on another's behalf, 35–36; coping with, 33–35
Siegel, Bugsy, 124
Skills: in aggression, 65–67; behavioral, 69–71; coping, 15, 71–72; improving managerial, 61–74; language, 63–64, 70–71; learning, 69–70; ma-
nipulative, 68–69; observation, 64–65; political, 67–68; reading, 63
Speaking up to boss: appropriate circumstances for, 100–101; aspects of, 99–112; on boss's behavior, 103–110; on conflicts, 111; for new ideas, 101–103; on organizational problems, 110; on psychological contract, 111–112
Specialization: and continual change, 209–212; and managerial education, 148
Springsteen, Bruce, 70
Status, and second career, 203
Stewart, Abigail J., 219
Stress: combating, 72–73; from embarrassment, 36–37; from guilt, 29–36; from mistakes, 29; and psychological balance, 16–19; from self-blame, 37; from success, 26–29; temporary withdrawal from, 17–18
Subordinates: feedback from, 130; and promotion, 151, 152, 157–163
Success: acknowledging, 26–27; behavior with, 70–71; blues following, 27–28; celebrating, 26–27, 71; fear of, and work load, 77–78; judgments about, 25–26; in promotion, 162–163; in second career, 204
Superego: conscience distinct from, 25; and guilt, 30; and narcissism, 124; and political skills, 68; and shame, 33
Support, by boss, 108, 133–136
Szell, George, 153, 154

T

Teams, advantages of, 91–94
Teets, John, 83
Telemachus, 165
Texas Instruments, and managerial education, 141
Thatcher, Margaret, 180
Therapists: for coworker mediation, 97; for downsizing survivors, 153; for job change issues, 180; for job loss, 196–197; and loss from change, 21; and slumps, 74; for unconscious guilt, 33

Thinking: distorted, 32, 95–96; magical, 161
Time horizon, and conceptual ability, 11–12
Tolkien, J.R.R., 93
Toscanini, Arturo, 153
Town & Country Jewelry, tradition for, 150
Traditions: acquaintance with, 150–151; and organizational culture, 55
Transformational dimensions: and achievement, 127–137; aspects of, 127–214; and continual change, 205–214; and job changes, 177–190; and job loss, 191–197; managerial education for, 139–148; mentoring for, 165–175; and promotions, 149–163; and second career, 199–204
Tsui, Anne S., 131, 217
Tylenol scare, 59

U

Uncommon sense, use of, 181
Unconscious guilt: causes of, 31–32; and end of mentoring, 174; and feedback, 131; and job change, 180; recognizing, 32–33; and work load, 77, 80, 84. *See also* Guilt
Unemployment. *See* Job loss
Union Carbide Corporation: atonement by, 34; and shame, 35
Upward appraisal, feedback from, 130
Useem, M., 208, 219

V

Values: and boss's requests, 104–105; conflicts of, 210; and job change, 185–186; organizational, 65, 66; stability of, 21–22
Vietnam veterans: and Agent Orange effects, 193; guilt felt by, 152

W

Wal-Mart, 177
Watson, Thomas J., Jr., 80
Welch, John F., Jr., 61–62, 109
Whitney, Wheelock, 201, 219
Wilkins, Lee, 218
Winter, David G., 219
Women: balancing career and family by, 19, 72–73; failure for, 40, 47; and job change, 180; managerial style of, 47, 88, 155; and mentoring, 170, 172; refresher education for, 145; and second careers, 199–200; and speaking up to boss, 99, 105; stress of success for, 26, 28; and work load, 79, 82
Work: complexity of, 11–12; contract, 189–190; defined, 81
Work load: aspects of controlling, 75–85; avoiding being swamped by, 76–85; and boss, 82–83, 84–85; expectations for, 75–76; and organizational problems, 80–82; outside perspectives on, 83–85; reasons for overloading of, 77–80; and refusing assignments, 76

Y

Yale University, liberal arts at, 208

Z

Zaleznik, Abraham, 218
Zumwalt, Elmo, Jr., 193, 219
Zumwalt, Elmo, III, 193, 219